Most contemporary moral philosophy is concerned with issues of rationality, universality, impartiality, and principle. By contrast, Lawrence Blum is concerned with the psychology of moral agency. The essays in this collection examine the moral import of emotion, motivation, judgment, perception, and group identifications, and explore how all these psychic capacities contribute to a morally good life.

Blum takes up the challenge of Iris Murdoch to articulate a vision of moral excellence that provides a worthy aspiration for human beings. Drawing on accounts of non-Jewish rescuers of Jews during the Holocaust, Blum argues that impartial principle can mislead us about the variety of forms of moral excellence.

A specific feature of the book is its engagement with feminism. Blum defends the "care ethics" espoused by feminists, although he also criticizes it for overstating its case and for oversimplifying its complex relationships with justice and group identities.

Moral perception and particularity

Moral perception
and particularity

LAWRENCE A. BLUM
University of Massachusetts, Boston

CAMBRIDGE
UNIVERSITY PRESS

Published by the Press Syndicate of the University of Cambridge
The Pitt Building, Trumpington Street, Cambridge CB2 1RP
40 West 20th Street, New York, NY 10011-4211, USA
10 Stamford Road, Oakleigh, Melbourne 3166, Australia

First published 1994

Printed in the United States of America

Library of Congress Cataloging-in-Publication Data
Blum, Lawrence A.
Moral perception and particularity / Lawrence A. Blum.
p.   cm.
Includes bibliographical references.
ISBN 0-521-43028-3. – ISBN 0-521-43619-2 (pbk.)
1. Ethics.   2. Ethics – Psychological aspects.   I. Title.
BJ1031.B65   1994
170 – dc20   93-25284
                                                              CIP

A catalog record for this book is available from the British Library.

ISBN 0-521-43028-3 hardback
ISBN 0-521-43619-2 paperback

Contents

Acknowledgments

My greatest personal and intellectual debt in the writing of this series of essays is to my "moral psychology" group – David Wong, Owen Flanagan, Margaret Rhodes, Amelie Rorty, Jennifer Radden, Ruth Anna Putnam (and "when-in-town" members Vicky Spelman and Jorge Garcia, and former member Andreas Teuber) – which has met biweekly since 1984. Our discussions have helped to develop, and to show the importance of, a psychologically informed approach to moral theory. Without this unequaled setting for intellectual exploration, these essays would not exist.

For intellectual companionship and friendship over the years – and for assistance of many kinds – I am especially indebted to David Wong. Our friendship has been an incomparable source of philosophical conversation and personal support since I began the work in this volume. Marcia Homiak and Victor Seidler have been good friends and intellectual comrades since the beginning of my philosophical career and have deeply shaped the way I approach the subject of ethics. I am grateful also to Owen Flanagan and Michael Slote for suggesting that I collect my essays on moral theory, and to Owen for personal and intellectual support at crucial times.

I want to acknowledge some other important intellectual debts as well. Philip Hallie's book *Lest Innocent Blood Be Shed* prompted lines of reflection on moral goodness during the Holocaust that issued in three of these papers. His book, Pierre Sauvage's film on the same subject *Weapons of the Spirit*, and Samuel and Pearl Oliner's book *The Altruistic Personality: Rescuers of Jews in Nazi Europe* have all been inspirations for me regarding the possibilities of human goodness. They have helped me see that moral philosophy needs to take more serious account of moral excellence and how it should do so. Susan Wolf's marvelous and seminal article "Moral Saints" and Thomas Nagel's book *The View from Nowhere* provided the provocation for several of the essays here, and I continue to struggle to define my own views in relation to theirs.

My greatest intellectual debt is to Iris Murdoch, whose views are discussed in several of the essays and whose strikingly original essays in *The Sovereignty of Good* first pointed me toward taking seriously moral perception, moral excellence, and moral psychology more generally. Owen

ACKNOWLEDGMENTS

Flanagan's, Amelie Rorty's, and Martha Nussbaum's writings have helped show me how to carry out the project of moral psychology in the context of contemporary moral theory. Bernard Williams was a pioneer in espousing a more psychologically informed, nonimpartialist moral view, and his writings have been a constant source of inspiration and stimulation.

As mentioned in the first essay, my own work in the area of what has come to be called "care ethics" is grounded and sustained by the many feminist ethicists working this territory. I am especially indebted to Carol Gilligan and Nel Noddings both for their path-breaking work in this area and for intellectual exchange and support.

I wish to thank my wonderful colleagues and students at the University of Massachusetts at Boston for providing a nurturing and intellectually stimulating environment over the decade in which I worked on these essays. I hope that my students' reluctance to accept abstract moral theory before having been apprised of the connections with their own lives has helped keep my work somewhat better grounded in moral experience than it might otherwise have been. In any case, I am grateful to my students for all I've learned from them.

The final stages of preparing this manuscript were carried out under an Ethics and the Professions Fellowship at Harvard University; I am very grateful to the Ethics Program for this timely support. I especially wish to thank Jean McVeigh, Helen Hawkins, and Brenda Wicks for their immense assistance regarding my uncertain forays into a new word-processing system, and for help of many other kinds as well. I received support from the National Endowment for the Humanities for a year's leave during which several of these essays were written. Work on the book was also supported with a Faculty Research Fellowship from the University of Massachusetts, Boston. I am grateful for this institutional support.

I want to thank Virginia Suddath, a former student, for some vital last-minute editing.

Personal examples form the core of several of these essays, and I have learned much about the need for, and the way toward, moral perception from my children — Laura, Sarah, and Ben. My life partner, Judy Smith, is an exemplar too of many personal and moral virtues. On a deeper level, she remains an inspiration for the sense of moral excellence and caring I have tried to elucidate in these essays.

SOURCES

Two of the essays in this volume (Chapters 1 and 11) are being published for the first time. Nine are reprinted, with various degrees of revision, from prior publications. I gratefully acknowledge the following for permission to reprint my essays:

Chapter 2, "Iris Murdoch and the Domain of the Moral," originally appeared in *Philosophical Studies,* Vol. 50, No. 3 (1986), pp. 343–68, and is reprinted here in revised form by permission of D. Reidel Publishing Co.

Chapter 3, "Moral Perception and Particularity," originally appeared in *Ethics,* Vol. 101, No. 4 (1991): 701–25, and is reprinted here with minor revisions (and with a postcript) by permission of University of Chicago Press.

Chapter 4, "Moral Exemplars: Reflections on Schindler, the Trocmés, and Others," appeared in *Midwest Studies in Philosophy,* Volume 12: *Ethical Theory,* edited by French, Uehling, and Wettstein. © 1988 by the University of Notre Dame Press. Reprinted by permission.

Chapter 5, "Vocation, Friendship, and Community: Limitations of the Personal-Impersonal Framework," appeared in O. Flanagan, Jr., and A. Rorty (eds.), *Identity, Character, and Morality: Essays in Moral Psychology* (1990), and is reprinted with minor revisions by permission of MIT Press.

Chapter 6, "Altruism and the Moral Value of Rescue: Resisting Persecution, Racism, and Genocide," appeared in L. Baron, L. Blum, D. Krebs, P. Oliner, S. Oliner, and M. Z. Smolenska (eds.), *Embracing the Other: Philosophical, Psychological, and Historical Perspectives on Altruism* (1992), and is reprinted in revised and expanded form by permission of New York University Press.

Chapter 7, "Virtue and Community," is to appear in Roger Crisp (ed.), *How Should One Live: Essays on the Virtues* (1994), and is printed here in an expanded and revised version by permission of Clarendon Press.

Chapter 8, "Compassion," appeared in Amelie Rorty (ed.), *Explaining Emotions* (© 1980), and is reprinted with minor revisions by permission of the University of California Press.

Chapter 9, "Moral Development and Conceptions of Morality," appeared (under the title "Particularity and Responsiveness") in Jerome Kagan and Sharon Lamb (eds.), *The Emergence of Morality in Young Children,* and is reprinted in substantially revised form by permission of the University of Chicago Press. © 1987 The University of Chicago. All rights reserved.

Chapter 10, "Gilligan and Kohlberg: Implications for Moral Theory," appeared in *Ethics,* Vol. 98 (1988): 472–91, and is reprinted with minor revisions by permission of the University of Chicago Press.

PART I

Particularity

1

Introduction:
Iris Murdoch, moral psychology, feminism, communitarianism

These essays represent my continuing effort to help bring moral psychology into more direct contact with contemporary moral theory. By "moral psychology" I mean the philosophical study of the psychic capacities involved in moral agency and moral responsiveness – emotion, perception, imagination, motivation, judgment. Moral philosophers have been too focused on rational principle, on impartiality, on universality and generality, on rules and codes in ethics. The importance of the psychological dimension of the moral life – that is, on moral life and experience themselves – has been masked, implicitly denied, or at least neglected. In such a moral and psychological inquiry, one cannot remain content with a strict separation between the disciplines of philosophy and psychology (and the social sciences more generally). Philosophers and psychologists engaged in studies of morality are concerned about the same phenomena and need to learn from one another.

Iris Murdoch's 1970 collection *The Sovereignty of Good* first steered me in this direction. Murdoch laments philosophy's inability to "encounter" an expanding domain of psychology, and she says, "A working philosophical psychology is needed which can at least attempt to connect modern psychological terminology with a terminology concerned with virtue."[1] Clearly much progress has been made in this direction since these words were written. Virtue theory is close to being a mainstream concern in moral philosophy. (Yet at the same time, much of the virtue literature fails to explore adequately the psychologically rich territory that an understanding of the virtues actually requires.) A few philosophers have begun to mine social and cognitive psychology for its moral-theoretic insights.[2] Psychologists such as Lawrence Kohlberg have seen

---

I wish to thank David Wong for helpful comments on this chapter.

1. Iris Murdoch, *The Sovereignty of Good* (London: Routledge and Kegan Paul, 1970), p. 46. Numbers in parentheses in the text refer to pages in this volume.
2. Here the exemplary work of Owen Flanagan, Jr., must be mentioned: *Varieties of Moral Personality: Ethics and Psychological Realism* (Cambridge, Mass.: Harvard University Press, 1991).

the necessity of normative philosophy for a responsible approach to a psychological theory of moral development.

I intend these essays to contribute to this emerging tradition of moral psychology. Yet many of Murdoch's criticisms of the then-current practice of moral philosophy still have not, I think, been adequately heeded. She speaks on several occasions of the absence of the concept of *love* in moral theory, of its being "theorized away" (1). She brings out powerfully (in her novels as well as her philosophical essays)[3] the importance of *moral perception* for any full account of how people come to choose the actions they do. We make choices within the world we see, and what (and how) we see is itself an integral part of the quality of our moral consciousness.

Murdoch also laments the exclusive focus on *action* in moral theory (16), with consequent neglect of attitude, perception, emotion (although the last gets insufficient attention in Murdoch's own discussion). In a famous example of a mother and daughter-in-law, Murdoch brings out how our thoughts and attitudes even toward people with whom we come not to have any contact can be appropriate objects of moral assessment. Murdoch says unabashedly that moral philosophy should have something to tell us about how to make ourselves morally better. It should recommend a worthy ideal and have something to say, grounded in a well-informed view of human nature, about how to direct ourselves toward that ideal.

These challenges have been inadequately addressed in the two and half decades since Murdoch voiced them, and it is striking how little moral philosophers have written on Murdoch and her work. Yet I have the impression that many philosophers have read *The Sovereignty of Good* and found it intriguing, and possibly deep. The essays in this volume take up Murdoch's challenges, and I hope they will contribute to bringing her concerns into closer contact with moral theory as presently practiced.

One current tendency within moral theory that has taken up some of Murdoch's work in a deliberate (though still not very systematic) way is feminist ethics. Feminist ethics is a quite diverse and rich territory, but the element I refer to here is feminist interest in a "morality of care," with which the essays in Part III of my volume are concerned. Some feminists have seen in Murdoch's attempted resuscitation of a notion of love in ethics, and in her notion of "attention" (drawn originally from Simone Weil), elements of a consciousness with which many women approach

---

3. Unfortunately, Murdoch's *Metaphysics as a Guide to Morals* (New York: Allen Lane, 1992) appeared just as I was completing this collection and I was not able to make use of it in my remarks.

the moral life; and they have seen this moral consciousness as distinct from, and unexpressible within, familiar deontological and consequentialist moral theories.[4]

Feminist currents in ethical theory have undoubtedly been a prime factor in keeping alive concerns with the emotional and perceptual – and more generally, the psychological – dimension of moral life. Here the psychologist Carol Gilligan has had a noteworthy and salutary effect on moral philosophy. Feminism has sparked and has continued to press some of the dissatisfaction with traditional approaches that I have attempted to address in these essays. Whether or not one thinks that caring, empathy, compassion, emotional understanding, responsiveness to need, and the like have some link to femaleness (and feminists themselves are divided on this question), it is indisputable that an interest in feminism has helped sustain attention to these qualities of character and their place in an adequate conception of the moral life.

The essays in Part I concern *particularity,* a term meant to encapsulate some important lacunae in traditional Kantian and utilitarian, deontological and consequentialist, theories. Chapter 2, "Iris Murdoch and the Domain of the Moral," argues that a Murdochian attentive love or concern for a particular other person is a moral accomplishment not captured in "impartialist" moral theories – those emphasizing principles generated from a purely impartial point of view. Nor is it captured in the idea of the "personal point of view" (the point of view of our individual projects and commitments), a currently influential notion for expressing dissatisfaction with, or the limitations of, traditional impartialism.

Chapter 3, "Moral Perception and Particularity," explores the roles of moral judgment and perception of particulars in the moral life, especially in bridging general principle and particular situation. I argue that both perception and moral judgment are complexes of semidistinct moral capacities, rather than single unitary ones. Again, I argue that these mor-

4. Sara Ruddick's widely reprinted "Maternal Thinking," *Feminist Studies* 6, 1980: 342–67, has perhaps the best-known feminist use of Murdoch's notion of loving attention. Other sustained and interesting feminist uses of Murdoch in ethics are in Meredith Michaels, "Morality Without Distinction," *Philosophical Forum* 17, 1986: 175–87; Margaret Urban Walker, "Moral Understandings: Alternative 'Epistemology' for a Feminist Ethics," in E. B. Cole and S. Coultrap-McQuin (eds.), *Explorations in Feminist Ethics: Theory and Practice* (Bloomington: Indiana University Press, 1992) (originally published in *Hypatia: A Journal of Feminist Philosophy,* 4, 1989: 15–28); and Sheila Mullett, "Shifting Perspective: A New Approach to Ethics," in L. Code, S. Mullett, and C. Overall (eds.), *Feminist Perspectives: Philosophical Essays on Method and Morals* (Toronto: University of Toronto Press, 1988).

ally central phenomena concerning particularity are not accounted for in principle-based or impartialist theories.

Part II takes up Murdoch's challenge to explore moral excellence. Chapter 4, "Moral Exemplars: Reflections on Schindler, the Trocmés, and Others," uses various case studies of moral exemplars to argue that there are irreducibly different kinds of moral excellence, with distinct underlying psychologies. Chapter 5, "Vocation, Friendship, and Community: Limitations of the Personal-Impersonal Framework," extends the argument of Chapter 2. I argue that there are several morally significant kinds of action and motivation that fit neither the "personal point of view" nor the "pure impersonality" models prominent in recent moral theory. In particular, some familiar modes of moral excellence fail to get a hearing if portrayed (as Susan Wolf portrays them in her seminal essay "Moral Saints") as devotion to some impartially defined "good of everyone" or to a Kantian moral law.

Chapter 6, "Altruism and the Moral Value of Rescue: Resisting Persecution, Racism, and Genocide," explores how best to understand the morally exemplary actions of rescue of Jews by non-Jews during the Holocaust. I argue that the framework of "altruism," or even "extremely risky altruism," fails to capture fully the moral accomplishment involved. The nonaltruism-based values of resistance to racism, to persecution, and to genocide must also be included in order to accommodate our considered assessment of these heroic rescue actions.

Chapter 7, "Virtue and Community," explores Alasdair MacIntyre's claim that virtue and community are closely linked. I distinguish several plausible forms of this claim and argue that MacIntyre is in an important sense right. I further argue that standard ways of conceptualizing morally good actions as "supererogatory" or "going beyond the bounds of duty" falsify the consciousness of the exceptionally virtuous agent and mask the crucial role that community can play in supporting virtue.

Three of the chapters in Part II – 4, 6, and 7 – draw on accounts of rescue during the Holocaust. Philosophers have recently begun to turn their attention to the Holocaust as an event demanding philosophical reflection. I agree with Alan Rosenberg and Gerald Myers's[5] admonition that responding philosophically to the Holocaust is fraught with peril – that one's writing may be unequal to the task and may thereby insult or offend the memory of Holocaust victims. At the same time (Rosenberg and Myers say), *failing* to address the Holocaust has its own peril – that an event of such momentous moral significance *not* come to have a secure place in the

5. Preface to *Echoes from the Holocaust: Philosophical Reflections on a Dark Time* (Philadelphia: Temple University Press, 1988), esp. p. ix.

standard reference points of philosophical contributions to ethics. Iris Murdoch (herself fascinated with the Holocaust) rightly said that moral learning requires common objects of attention. The Holocaust needs to be such an object for moral philosophers.

In these essays, however, I have admittedly avoided facing up to the two most morally salient features of the Holocaust – the appalling evil of its perpetrators and the deafening indifference of millions of ordinary people who were neither perpetrators nor victims. Instead, I have focused on the glittering specimens of human goodness in the face of that evil and indifference. Two of the essays (Chapters 4 and 7) draw substantially on the remarkable example of the French village of Le Chambon, which sheltered refugees in numbers equal to its own population. Chapter 6 follows from Samuel and Pearl Oliner's comprehensive international study of rescuers of Jews.[6] No doubt, my own Jewishness is partly responsible for my fascination with these particular instances of moral goodness, but I think any serious study of moral excellence has much to learn from an encounter with the exemplary individuals discussed in these essays.

Part III contains various explorations of the "morality of care" – as was mentioned, an important strand in feminist ethics and, more generally, a central focal point in current dissatisfactions with traditional Kantian and utilitarian moral theories. Chapter 8, "Compassion" (the earliest piece in this collection), is an account of that virtue. In exploring that one virtue, I aim to suggest the complex and variegated terrain of those virtues connected with "caring," against a tradition (sometimes found in writings sympathetic to the morality of care, including some of my own) that flattens them out by portraying them all as simply species of "sympathy" or "benevolence."

Chapter 9, "Moral Development and Conceptions of Morality," is concerned with the moral development of children and aims to vindicate developmental precursors of the care virtues. I argue that underlying influential theories of moral development are assumptions about morality that "theorize away" responsiveness to the plight of others on the part of very young children. This essay contains a sustained criticism of the claims of principle-based and impartialist ethical theories to encompass the entire field of morality.

Chapter 10, "Gilligan and Kohlberg: Implications for Moral Theory," is a defense of Carol Gilligan's "morality of care" against Lawrence Kohlberg's criticisms. It contains further criticisms of principle-based and impartialist theories, complementing those of Chapter 9.

6. *The Altruistic Personality: Rescuers of Jews in Nazi Europe* (New York: The Free Press, 1988).

Chapter 11, "Gilligan's 'Two Voices' and the Moral Status of Group Identity," criticizes Gilligan for her tendency to portray moral consciousness in an overdichotomized fashion – care versus justice, responsibility versus rights. In particular, I argue that there can be a moral legitimacy to some of our group identities (professional, race, gender) that cannot be captured in either the language of care or that of justice.

As noted, several of these essays (especially Chapters 6, 9, 10, and 11) engage directly with, and take their cue from, theories and findings of the social sciences. They either presuppose or aim to show that philosophers should find illuminating the explorations of morality in which social scientists – such as the Oliners, Richard Schweder, Jerome Kagan, and (especially) Carol Gilligan and Lawrence Kohlberg – have been engaged. At the same time, I am hoping that social scientists will see that the criticisms and questions emerging from a moral philosopher's approach to their endeavors provide a fruitful and even essential perspective.

One other theme is prominent in several of the essays (especially Chapters 5, 7, and 11) yet not reflected in the organization of this collection – *communitarianism.* In these essays, I have in various ways aspired to link moral psychology with communitarianism. As argued in Chapter 5, the various strands of communitarianism would be strengthened were they to be more fully informed by a moral psychology.

"Communitarianism" is not really a single, unified doctrine but encompasses a family of tendencies within both moral and political philosophy. The opposition of all these tendencies to a familiar individualistic conception of the person and to a purely libertarian conception of society has masked the variety of concerns and doctrines under the rubric of "communitarianism."[7] I want to situate my several discussions of moral psychology and communitarianism in these three essays within a more general framework. Although there are various ways of dividing up this territory, one can distinguish, for my purposes here, three strands within contemporary communitarianism – *identity communitarianism, virtue communitarianism,* and *social (or political) communitarianism.*

Identity communitarianism explores the moral significance of the

---

7. A tendency to see communitarianism essentially as a unitary doctrine (deploying various arguments) can be found in many (usually anticommunitarian) writings, even good ones such as Will Kymlicka's *Contemporary Political Philosophy: An Introduction* (Oxford: Clarendon Press, 1990), Chapter 6, "Communitarianism." Failure to note the differences between distinct strands within communitarianism, however, mars not only anticommunitarian but also communitarian writings. (Charles Taylor's essay mentioned in footnote 10 is an important exception to this.)

particular group identities that make us who we are.[8] Identity communitarians claim that certain strands of liberalism contain a faulty notion of the person because they give insufficient place to these particularistic group identities. *Virtue communitarianism,* identified most prominently with Alasdair MacIntyre's work (especially *After Virtue*), claims that moral and other virtues must be understood primarily in the context of communities. Communities nourish, support, and partly define virtue. Virtue communitarianism is located primarily in moral rather than political theory. As mentioned earlier, virtue theory aims to correct an overemphasis in moral theory on rational, universal principles and impartiality; virtue communitarianism can be seen as a tendency within virtue theory to emphasize the communal rather than the purely individual character of virtue. (This issue is discussed further in Chapter 7.)

Social communitarianism advocates that a society or polity promote, embody, or encourage certain goods to be shared across that polity; these goods – solidarity, family stability, mutual commitment, civic participation, and the like – are seen specifically as "communitarian" goods. Social communitarianism has generally been viewed not as a moral view but as a political or social one. It is true that social communitarianism, like virtue communitarianism, is concerned with the promotion of moral goods, often understood as virtues; but the class of moral goods with which virtue communitarianism is concerned is much more extensive than that in social communitarianism and is not limited to social goods and virtues. Virtue communitarianism is concerned with the whole of virtue that could plausibly be seen as affected by the communities of which a person is a part (integrity, courage, compassion, as well as civic responsibility, solidarity, civic loyalty), whereas social communitarianism is concerned only with the latter three – virtues or goods that are distinctly communitarian in character.

Identity communitarianism differs from the other two in not specifically advocating the promotion of particular positive values or goods at all. Unlike social communitarianism it does *not* necessarily advocate the promotion of shared goods or virtues for a whole society. Rather, identity communitarianism concerns the moral meanings given by individuals to their various particular group identities. Those moral meanings can be negative or can require the individual to struggle to give a meaning to the identity different from the usual one. A white South African, for example, might fall into either of these categories. She might see her identity as shameful and unfortunate, or she might try to construct an antiracist,

---

8. Michael Sandel refers to these identity constituents as "encumbrances." Identity communitarianism also refers to the "embedded," "situated," or "implicated" self.

antiapartheid form of white South African identity, defined specifically against the reigning understanding of that identity.

Thus understood, identity communitarianism is essentially a moral rather than a political doctrine.[9] An identity communitarian (in contrast to the social communitarian) might think that the state or polity should be *neutral* with regard to the possible moral meanings of group identities, seeing these as appropriately functioning in domains outside state action and control. It is, however, entirely consistent to subscribe to both identity and social communitarianism.

Similarly, an identity communitarian need not believe in the links between community and virtue averred by the virtue communitarian. Although both identity and virtue communitarians are concerned with morality, they are so in somewhat different ways. The group identities – such as gender, institutional, professional, national, ethnic, and racial identities – with which the identity communitarian is concerned may or may not be "communities" in the sense in which a virtue communitarian like MacIntyre conceives of community as required for virtue. The latter types of communities are generally geographically located, encompass a substantial portion of their members' day-to-day lives, and are rooted in specific traditions. The difference between the two forms of community on this score lies partly in the fact that the identity communitarian need not claim, as the virtue communitarian does, that group identities *necessarily* give rise to specific virtues. As I argue in Chapter 11, there is much room for individual interpretation in determining how group identities provide moral meanings.

Identity communitarianism as a moral doctrine has been little pursued in moral philosophy. In Chapters 5 and 11, I attempt to explore how particular group identities can give moral meanings. What is the moral psychology involved, and how can we conceptualize it in a way that allows us to express the values embodied in these group identities?

In particular, Chapter 5 explores how our professional identities can be sources of moral meaning, moral action, and virtue and begins to delineate a philosophical framework more adequate than the influential "personal/impersonal" one for expressing the moral psychology of the "professionally excellent" person. Chapter 11 explores group identities more generally, extending the moral psychology of Chapter 5; but in particular, it

9. I thus want to distinguish my notion of identity communitarianism from a notion of "identity politics" claiming that certain specific identities (often racial, gender, sexual-preference, ethnic) should be an individual citizen's primary identification for political purposes within the polity. Although certain forms of identity communitarianism will have political implications (depending in part on which encumbrances are in question), I want to leave open for further exploration what these might be.

concerns *gender* as a morally significant group identity. I argue that for women their gender – their identification *as women* – can be an important source of positively valued and valuable moral orientation.

Despite these differences, there is one natural connection between identity communitarianism and virtue communitarianism. This connection holds when a key morally significant group identity (for a particular individual) corresponds to her identity as a member of a virtue-sustaining community. In that case the group identity can be integral to what allows that community to sustain that person's virtue.[10] This connection is precisely the concern of Chapter 7, "Virtue and Community," which argues, in a MacIntyrean spirit, that the Le Chambon villagers' identification as members of that community was decisive in their exemplifying exceptional virtue during the Nazi occupation. The essay attempts to work out the moral psychology of the villagers that made possible the link between community and virtue.

I have not been concerned in these essays with social communitarianism. As a largely political rather than moral doctrine, this form of communitarianism might seem to require less in the way of a moral psychology than do the other two. But although this is not the place to do so, I would nevertheless argue that social communitarianism too requires a moral psychology. Such a psychology would help the social communitarian avoid the familiar liberal criticism that any vision of the common good for a polity could be achieved only through coercion. An adequate moral psychology would help point the way to a middle ground between pure state neutrality and coercion – a middle ground of "structured encouragement and promotion" of certain communitarian goods and virtues. But this argument will have to be made on another occasion.

10. My discussion here draws on Charles Taylor's essay "Cross-Purposes: The Liberalism-Communitarianism Debate," in Nancy Rosenblum (ed.), *Liberalism and the Moral Life* (Cambridge, Mass.: Harvard University Press, 1989).

2

Iris Murdoch and the domain of the moral

In *The Sovereignty of Good*[1] Iris Murdoch suggests that the central task of the moral agent involves a true and loving perception of another individual, who is seen as a particular reality external to the agent. Writing in the 1960s she claimed that this dimension of morality had been "theorized away" in contemporary ethics. I will argue today that twenty years later, this charge still holds true of much contemporary ethical theory.

Murdoch's view is that morality has everything to do with our concerned responsiveness – what she also calls "loving attention" – to other particular individuals, where this responsiveness involves an element of particularity not reducible to any form of complex universality. In Murdoch's writing personal relationships are the principal setting in which this moral endeavor takes place. Thus loving attention to a friend or to one's child involves understanding his or her needs and caring that they are met. The moral task is not a matter of finding universalizable reasons or principles of action, but of getting oneself to attend to the reality of individual other persons. Such attention requires not allowing one's own needs, biases, fantasies (conscious and unconscious), and desires regarding the other person to get in the way of appreciating his or her own particular needs and situation.

Because one's love for the other person is inextricably bound up with the importance of that person to one's own life, seeing the other in herself – distinct and separate from oneself – is, Murdoch emphasizes, a difficult task. Yet one ought to help the friend simply because the friend needs help and not as a way of shoring up the friendship or guarding against the loss of a friend; only the former motivation will count as exemplifying morality in its Murdochian aspect.

An early draft of this essay was read to the "Rationality and Moral Values" symposium at the University of North Carolina at Greensboro in April 1985. I thank participants in that colloquium and especially my commentator, Laurence Thomas, for helpful comments. Portions were also read to a colloquium at the Department of Philosophy and History of Ideas of Brandeis University, whom I also thank for helpful comments. I thank Marcia Lind and Owen Flanagan for acute criticisms of a later draft and Thomas P. Scanlon for conversations about Nagel's views.

1. Iris Murdoch, *The Sovereignty of Good* (London: Routledge and Kegan Paul, 1970).

Although Murdoch is correct to emphasize the domain of personal relations as a moral domain, and as one which has been insufficiently attended to in contemporary ethics, neither she nor I wishes to confine particularity to personal relations. Rather, compassion toward a stranger, or, more broadly, toward someone with whom one has no preexisting relationship of substance, is to be encompassed as well. All that is necessary is that the agent understand or attempt to understand the other person's good, and that she act from a genuine and direct regard for the good of this particular other person (or persons). She must act out of regard for the other's good and act so as to promote that good.[2] The other need not be in a negative or undesirable state such as distress or suffering, in order for the Murdochian response to be appropriate; she may simply be able to be better off, for example, by introducing her to a new source of satisfaction or pleasure whose lack she may not have previously felt. Here too the moral task is not to generate action based on universal and impartial principles but to attend and respond to particular persons.

As in the case of personal relations, the agent has the task of avoiding confusing her own needs and situation with those of the other person. Obstacles can stand in the way of understanding a stranger's situation and what would benefit him in that situation. For example, while genuinely desiring to help the other, one can be so taken with the thought of one's power to help that one fails to see that what one could do best for him is to enable him to come to grips with the situation himself rather than relying on one's direct helping efforts. Compassion, concern, love, friendship, kindness are all sentiments or virtues which normally and in some cases necessarily manifest the Murdochian dimension of morality.[3]

2. The element of "regard for the other's good" is meant here to build in a concern to understand what the other's good is; so that it is not being claimed that it is good to act with a mere intention to benefit, independent of any genuine grasp of the need or good of the other. Laurence Thomas has rightly pointed out that this element is insufficiently emphasized in the account of moral value given in my *Friendship, Altruism, and Morality* (London: Routledge and Kegan Paul, 1980); see his review in *The Philosophical Review* 92 (1983), pp. 135–9. This defect is not present in Murdoch's account, which I follow in this essay.

3. These virtues can be construed as dispositions to respond in a Murdochian manner – with concerned attention to particular individuals – rather than as implicit expressions of an underlying universal and impartialistic, action-guiding principle. In this way I see kindness and compassion as different from "benevolence" understood as "love of humanity" or a concern for the overall good of humanity. The latter is a sentiment directed at others not in their particularity but in their generality, as members of the human species. Bishop Butler, in *Five Sermons*, ed. S. L. Darwall (Indianapolis: Hackett Publishing, 1983), first distinguished between a sentiment directed toward the good of a particular person, and one directed toward persons in general, though his account of this distinction is not always consistent. Murdoch's views differ from Butler's, however, in the greater depth involved in loving attention than Butler

I want to contrast Murdoch's view with two currently influential views in moral philosophy. The first, which can be called "impartialism,"[4] represents the common ground between Kantianism and utilitarianism. Attention has often been focused on the great differences between these two theories, but recently important convergences between them have been recognized.[5] Both views identify morality with a perspective of impartiality, impersonality, objectivity, and universality. Both views of morality imply the "ubiquity of impartiality" – that our commitments and projects derive their legitimacy only by reference to this impartial perspective. Both views imply that the impartially derived "right" takes moral precedence over personal "good."[6]

The second view with which Murdoch's is to be contrasted has emerged more recently in direct reaction to impartialism. Represented by some influential writings of Bernard Williams,[7] and by Thomas Nagel,[8] and Samuel Scheffler,[9] this view advances two claims: First, the domain in which impartiality and impersonality reign supreme has some limits; impartiality is not (legitimately) ubiquitous. Second, there is a domain of personal life and projects the nature and legitimacy of which as a source of reasons for action do not depend on its relation to the objective, impartial perspective. Williams, especially, emphasizes that individuals properly pursue some goals simply because they provide meaning to their own lives, or because they cohere with a set of concerns or values they regard as essential to their sense of their own integrity. Nagel's

implies in the affections toward particular other persons. I am concerned to argue in this essay that there is an element of morality – found in Murdoch's account – which does not fit into the impartial/universal mold. This argument will hold whether or not this element is also found in the virtues mentioned.

4. This term is that of Stephen L. Darwall, in *Impartial Reason* (Ithaca: Cornell University Press, 1983), though he applies it only to Kantianism, not utilitarianism.

5. See Bernard Williams, "Persons, character, and morality," and other essays in *Moral Luck* (Cambridge: Cambridge University Press, 1981); Alasdair MacIntyre, *After Virtue* (Notre Dame: University of Notre Dame Press, 1981); and Michael Sandel, *Liberalism and the Limits of Justice* (Cambridge: Cambridge University Press, 1982).

6. The priority of right over good mentioned here is moral, not definitional. On a definitional level, utilitarianism differs entirely from Kantianism in defining the right in terms of the good. Both, however, give *moral* priority to the right.

7. "A Critique of Utilitarianism," in B. Williams and J. Smart, *Utilitarianism: For and Against* (Cambridge University Press, 1973), and "Persons, character, and morality." It should be said that in other of Williams's writings, e.g., "Egoism and Altruism" and parts of "Morality and the emotions," he takes a view closer to Murdoch's. Williams's later *Ethics and the Limits of Philosophy* (Cambridge, Mass.: Harvard University Press, 1985) appeared while this essay was in its final stages, and it was impossible to give it adequate attention, though some remarks will be made about it below.

8. Thomas Nagel, *The View from Nowhere* (Oxford: Oxford University Press, 1986).

9. Samuel Scheffler, *The Rejection of Consequentialism* (Oxford: Oxford University Press, 1982).

conception of the legitimacy of reasons stemming from the personal domain does not require reasons so deeply grounded but can encompass mere personal desires and interests. In either case, the legitimacy of acting from such personal reasons is connected with our personal autonomy. We do not always need to be justified in thinking that the pursuit of our goal is, purely impersonally or objectively speaking, a good thing, something that everyone has reason to support or to affirm our pursuit of. Although the domain of the personal is of a character entirely different from that of the objective-impartial, it is no less legitimate as a source of reasons for action. So Williams, Nagel, and Scheffler argue.[10]

Nagel, Scheffler, and Williams do differ on some important points, which might obscure the similarities in their views of morality. Nagel and Scheffler unequivocally grant independent, reason-generating legitimacy to the impartial point of view, whereas Williams mounts a sustained attack on impartiality. So Williams is much more strongly critical of a Kantian perspective in ethics than are either of the others. By contrast Nagel calls for a stronger role for the objective perspective in our lives,[11] and criticizes Williams for a too-ready dismissal of the claims of impartiality.[12]

Within the commitment to impartiality, Scheffler sees the impersonal domain in purely consequentialist terms, and Nagel leans in the same direction,[13] but for Williams Kantianism, rather than consequentialism or utilitarianism, remains the paradigm "impartialist" philosophy. Both Nagel and Williams imply that on some occasions it is appropriate to act for purely personal reasons, paying no homage whatsoever to the impartial perspective. For Scheffler the impartial point of view must always be taken into account, but "the independence of the personal point of view" (from the impersonal/impartial one) is taken to mean that it is appropriate for the

---

10. There are some differences in the terminology used by these three philosophers to refer to the two domains and the attendant forms of reasons for action. Williams refers to the domain in question as "personal" and involving "integrity"; Nagel calls it "subjective," involving "reasons for autonomy," and Scheffler speaks of the "personal point of view." I will refer to it as the "personal," or "subjective," domain.

11. Nagel, *View from Nowhere,* p. 187.

12. See his review of Williams's *Moral Luck, Times Literary Supplement,* May 7, 1982.

13. (See, e.g., *View,* p. 162). Nagel notes some similarities and differences between his view and Scheffler's. For example, for Scheffler as for utilitarians *every* personal interest is reflected in the domain of impersonal value; whereas for Nagel only certain interests are (e.g., avoidance of pain, but not the desire to climb Mt. Kilimanjaro). Despite this, Nagel says he does not believe that Scheffler's "agent-centered prerogative" is strictly incompatible with his own view, although, given his own exemption of some subjective reasons from the need to be weighed at all against impersonal demands, he expresses some reservation about adding on to this moral latitude the further "moral indulgence" of an agent-centered prerogative (*View,* pp. 174–5.) These differences are not material to my argument.

15

agent to give the personal point of view more weight in determining one's action than it would have from the impartial point of view.

Despite these differences, all three philosophers share the view that morality itself is to be characterized in impartial or impersonal terms, and that there is a legitimate personal domain of reasons that lies outside morality altogether and the force of which lies at least partly outside morality.

I believe Murdoch's account of morality is significantly distinct from the Nagel-Williams-Scheffler view (the "NWS view") as well as from Kantianism and utilitarianism. None of these views leaves adequate room for the Murdochian virtues. It is especially important to distinguish Murdoch's view from the NWS view. Since both are critical of Kantianism and utilitarianism, they have sometimes been insufficiently distinguished from one another.

Murdoch's difference with Williams, Nagel, and Scheffler lies not in the two theses mentioned above. Defending Murdoch's view, I would agree that impartiality has no claim to ubiquity, and that not all personal reasons for action require vindication from the impartial point of view. My quarrel is that the NWS view leaves no room for Murdochian particularity as a dimension of *morality* and of a moral consciousness. I will argue that this particularity, as seen either in compassion for strangers or care for friend and family, is neither impersonal nor personal, neither objective nor subjective. It is a dimension of moral life that is "theorized away" by an exhaustive division of reasons for action into these two types. Thus Williams's, Nagel's, and Scheffler's views are marred by a too-narrow view of morality itself, a view shared with their utilitarian and Kantian opponents: All accept an identification of morality with an impartial, impersonal, and objective point of view. These writers all give the impression that the sole or major issues of personal conduct concern the clash between personal and impartial reasons for action, between an impersonal "right" and a merely personal "good." Nowhere in Nagel, Scheffler, and Williams is articulated the Murdochian moral task of caring for or attending to particular other individuals—a task that is (as I will argue) a matter of neither personal good nor detached objectivity.

Let me begin my argument with an example described in some detail, which will serve as a point of reference in the later discussion. Ann is a friend, though not a close friend, of Tony. One evening they run into each other by chance and talk. Although Tony does not state this directly, Ann perceives that he is in quite bad shape, and in need of some comfort and a sympathetic ear. Ann volunteers to spend the evening with Tony (thereby jettisoning her own plans)—an evening which, as it turns out, drags on well into the night. But Ann is correct in her assessment that she can offer

16

significant support and comfort to Tony during the evening; it is clear by the end that she has really helped him.

For Murdoch, Ann's action here can be described in moral terms. Ann has given "loving" attention to Tony, seeing a need not explicitly addressed to her, and discerning that this is a need she is able to meet. She has had to allow Tony's plight to weigh with her so that her offer to help comes across as sincere yet not implying that she is engaging in substantial self-sacrifice; for, were this to happen, the two of them might not be able to establish sufficient ease and trust with each other to allow Ann genuinely to comfort Tony during the evening.

By stipulating that Ann and Tony are not close friends I mean to describe a situation in which Ann need not have a *duty* of friendship to stay with Tony (although if she does, this would not necessarily preclude a Murdochian reading of Ann's action, in which she acts not from this duty, but rather from direct concern for Tony). By not setting it in the context of a richly textured and deep personal relationship, I mean the example to be, though closer to the "personal relations" end of Murdochian morality, still not too far from the "stranger" end either.

My first arguments will be addressed mainly to Nagel's views. More fully than Williams or Scheffler, Nagel attempts to distinguish the personal/subjective and the impersonal/impartial/objective points of view, and most explicitly accords independent reason-giving force to each. The implications of my argument for Williams and Scheffler will be indicated later.

For Nagel, the objective/impersonal point of view is characterized in terms of detaching from one's own point of view, accepting the way one lives "from the outside," seeing oneself as merely one among others, providing a standpoint of choice from which all choosers can agree on what should happen, seeing the world from nowhere within it. Thus an objective reason is one equally applicable to anyone. Anyone has reason to do something to relieve someone's pain, or at least has reason to want this to happen. The state of affairs to be promoted in action has objective value. It is good in itself, or it removes something bad in itself.

Counterposed to objective reasons are three types of personal or subjective ones, of which the one relevant here is a reason of "autonomy," grounded in an individual's own desires, projects, aims, concerns, commitments. A subjective reason does not require vindication from an objective point of view; it stands as a (legitimate) reason for the agent in question whether or not it is a reason for anyone else to care whether the agent acts for that reason. Nagel says that someone might have a subjective (but not likely an objective) reason to try to become a pianist, or to climb Mt. Kilimanjaro.

It is natural to think of reasons as reasons for which someone can act. So reasons can be seen either motivationally or justificationally; they can refer either to why someone does act, or to legitimate reasons for acting. To bring Nagel's view into relationship with Murdoch's as seen in the Ann-Tony example, the reasons in question must be both motivational and justificational. Clearly Nagel means reasons to be justifying action; "subjective" and "objective" refer to legitimate types of reasons for action, whether someone in fact acts from them on a particular occasion or not. But in addition, they can be construed psychologically or motivationally. To say that someone acts from (or according to) an objective reason is to say that he acts from a reason which he *takes to be* objective – that is, he takes it to be applicable to everyone equally, to be generated by a detachment from his own perspective, and the like. To say he acted (in the motivational sense) from a "subjective" reason would, then, be to say that he did not take his reason to be applicable to others, but to stem only from his own desires, projects, and the like. Since Nagel is, at least in part, speaking of what considerations we should use to guide our actions, we must assume that "reasons" are to be understood motivationally as well as justificationally. The agent must intentionally adopt the objective standpoint, not merely act from considerations which, unbeknownst to him, conform to that standpoint.[14]

I shall argue that Ann's reason for action in the example described above need be *neither* objective *nor* subjective, in either the motivational or the justificational sense. Let us consider objectiveness first. We have portrayed Ann as acting from concern for Tony, that is, as taking (what she perceives to be) Tony's difficulties as a reason to help. Concern is not necessarily generalizable in the way that principles are; in order for it to be intelligible that Ann act out of concern for Tony, we need not imagine that she have the same concern for all other persons, or even any other persons, whom she regards as in a situation similar to Tony's. She need not be regarding Tony's condition as an "objective" bad, a bad simply anyone would have reason to want Tony to be rid of.[15] She need not think of her reason as generalizable to others.

The intelligibility of Ann's action as stemming from a nonobjective

---

14. I am indebted to Marcia Lind for showing me the necessity to clarify the distinction between justificational and motivational perspectives regarding Nagel.

15. I am presenting Nagel's view without using all his machinery and terminology. Nagel employs the notion of "agent-neutrality" to refer to *impersonal* value – contrasting it with "agent-relative" value (value relative to a particular agent) – and says that *both* kinds of values are "objective." For reasons explained later, I think this terminology misleading, and will stick with "objective" as synonymous with "impersonal."

reason is in a sense provided for by Nagel's own view, and indeed by the NWS view in general. For these views recognize the existence of reasons – namely, ones directed toward what one conceives to be one's own good or the realization of one's projects – that are legitimate yet nonobjective. I am claiming the same legitimacy for Murdochian, nonobjective reasons. Just as I may want to be a first-rate pianist without thinking that others have a reason to promote by being so, so I may, out of friendship or care, endeavor to help a friend or acquaintance to achieve her goal of becoming a first-rate pianist, without thinking that others have a reason to do the same. Just as Ann may be concerned to rid herself of her own depression without thinking that anyone else has a reason to do so, or even to want this to happen, so she may, out of concern for Tony, want Tony to be rid of his depression, without thinking that others have a reason to want or to promote this either.

Murdochian, nonobjective reasons are as distinct from objective reasons as are reasons of autonomy interpreted as reasons stemming from concerns of the self. Essentially this point was made by Butler. He argued that just as I can have a desire, or "affection," for an object (e.g., food) which will serve my own good, so I can have a desire for another person's good. Neither desire is the same as an emanation of objective and detached conscience or reflection (though either desire can be affirmed by, and perhaps in that way somewhat changed by, conscience).[16] A desire for the good of a particular other person, then, is analogous to a desire for one's own good (or for an object which serves that good) in being a type of reason that is distinct from an objective reason.

Could an impartialist reply to this argument by suggesting that Murdochian reasons for action, say concerned responses to individual other persons' needs, can *themselves* be justified or generated from an objective point of view? It might be suggested that it is only from an objective point of view that Murdochian reasons can be seen to be legitimate reasons for action; so that the Murdochian agent, as well as the agent acting more directly from objective considerations, would be acting, ultimately, from objective considerations. Thus Murdochian reasons would, after all, be a species of "objective" reason.

Nagel appears to provide an analogous argument regarding "reasons of autonomy." On the one hand reasons of autonomy are personal or subjective reasons – reasons coming from within the perspective of a particular agent.[17] On the other hand, Nagel says, these reasons can be validated, as

16. See Butler, *Five Sermons*.
17. Sometimes Nagel uses "subjective" to mean "what appears to be (a reason)," leaving it open whether it actually *is* a reason or not. He is not consistent in this, however, and he

applicable to anyone who has them, from an objective point of view. Thus, it could be argued, both Murdochian reasons and reasons of autonomy are forms of objective reasons.

This argument fails, however, to ground Murdochian reasons in (by deriving them from) impartiality and impersonality. It is certainly correct that one can look at Murdochian reasons – and reasons for autonomy – both the point of view of the person who has them, in the sense of taking them as reasons for his action, and from a point of view outside that person from which one reflects on their legitimacy. From that reflective point of view (let us say) we can see both Murdochian reasons and reasons of autonomy to be valid ones.

This reflective point of view cannot, however, automatically be identified with that of impartiality and impersonality. Ironically, Nagel's view itself makes this clear. For Nagel argues against the impartialists that the objective point of view – the point of view characterized as detachment from the self, as being from nowhere in the world, and the like – is only part of the truth about who we, as moral agents, are. The whole truth is that we are both subjective and objective; our lives and agency can be viewed from both a personal and an impersonal point of view. This means that the reflective point of view from which this whole truth about us can be seen is not "objective" in the same sense in which "objective" characterizes only one of the two components of that truth.[18] Perhaps we can speak of two meanings of objectivity here – one (objectivity$_1$) in which objective means impartial and impersonal and is specifically counterposed to "subjective," and another (objectivity$_2$) in which it refers to a reflective standpoint from which both subjective and objective$_1$ perspectives and reasons can be seen as legitimate.[19]

If we confine "objectivity" to "impartiality," how might an attempted derivation of Murdochian reasons from objectivity go? The clearest case of an objective derivation of Murdochian reasons would regard those reasons as generators of agent-neutral good. For example, someone's

also uses "subjective" to mean something like "reasons that come from within the individual agent," though this leaves it open whether the reason in question might also be an impersonal or agent-neutral (and in that sense objective) reason. My own definition in the text is meant to exclude the latter possibility. (I am indebted to Christine Korsgaard for helping me to clarify Nagel's terminology and views in this area.)

18. I owe some version of this reading of Nagel to Warren Quinn, though he would not necessarily have approved of the use to which I am putting it.

19. In *Ethics and the Limits of Philosophy,* especially Chapters 5 and 6, Bernard Williams argues that ethical reflection does not always or necessarily take the form of, or go in the direction of, systematic ethical theory. Although his distinction between "reflection" and "theory" is not the same as mine between "reflection" and "impartiality or impersonality," the point the distinction is meant to serve is similar.

welfare can best be promoted by someone who knows that person and who is in a position to help. A friend knows the person best and is in a better position than others to help. Therefore, there is a special reason that applies only to friends (and others at a similar emotional distance) for a friend to help someone in need. But the grounds of that special relationship are derived from purely agent-neutral considerations (serving the individual good of persons).

This argument does not hold. It does not capture what we normally regard as the grounds of the responsibilities of, and values of, special relationships. For one thing, it does not account for why, of two persons, one a former friend, the other a stranger, equally knowledgeable about and in a position to aid a third, we regard the former friend as having a stronger responsibility to help. Nor, more generally, does it account for why, when two persons are equally knowledgeable about and in a position to benefit a third, we regard the friend as having a stronger responsibility or obligation.

More important, we feel that particular relationships are not simply generators of agent-neutral good, but are rather expressive of a good internal to those special relationships, and that the moral dimension of those relationships, as generators of reasons for action, is bound up with this particularity, at least the particularity of that type of relationship. Thus the care of a parent for a child is not the same kind of thing as the care of a friend for a friend, or a sister for a brother, and the special responsibilities bound up with each are inextricably linked with the particular form of that care.

Even if the derivation were successful, the overall argument would fail, for Murdochian reasons are not reasons of special obligation. This is partly because the latter do not necessarily or even typically cover the same moral territory as Murdochian reasons – partly because what we do for friends is often not demanded by any obligation, either because it is more than what is demanded (giving up one's vacation to help a friend move), or because it consists in doing something lying outside the obligation structure altogether (phoning one's friend to see how he is doing, simply because one has not spoken to him in a long time), and partly because the existence of obligations underdetermines the particular acts chosen to instantiate them.[20] Beyond this, I have intentionally chosen a

20. The nonreducibility of acts of friendship to obligation is discussed further in Chapter 9, "Moral Development and Conceptions of Morality." The underdetermination by the type of relationship of acts of friendship and other forms of caring for persons standing in close relationship is argued more extensively in Chapter 3, "Moral Perceptions and Particularity," and in Chapter 10, "Gilligan and Kohlberg."

form of relationship between Ann and Tony weaker than one that would generate strong obligations of friendship. And so it is not at all clear that Ann has the sort of friendship obligation to Tony that would require the helping act she performs. More generally, Murdochian reasons do not always take place in the context of personal relationships and for this reason alone cannot be part of Nagel's "reasons of obligation." In summary, even if Nagel is right to think that reasons of obligation are ultimately grounded in agent-relativity, Murdochian reasons comprise a further category of reason distinct from impersonal, agent-neutral, objective reasons.

Before proceeding, I want to clarify what I mean by "Murdochian reasons." For it might be thought that if Ann is acting genuinely *for a reason* in helping Tony, then that reason must be generalizable to others; and so Ann's reason, even though admittedly not an "objective," agent-neutral one, would still be of a general, and in that sense formally universal, form, even if the agent were not herself aware of this. She would thus be committed to some specification of the features of her situation such that anyone in a situation containing such features would have the same reason to act as she has.

This construal of generality holds only for a certain understanding of what it is to act "for a reason." When I judge my action to be right, I am committed to judging a comparable action right for others in situations relevantly similar to mine, and I am committed to some view of what "relevant similarity" constitutes. Stephen Darwall articulates this view when he claims that an agent's reason for acting must be regarded by the agent as, objectively speaking, justified.[21]

But Ann does not necessarily act for a reason in this sense. She is acting for a reason in the (Murdochian) sense that Tony's distress is the consideration for the sake of which she offers to help him. This requires her to have a certain cognitive relation to Tony's situation; she must understand – with an understanding grounded in her attention to Tony – that he is in distress. But she need not make the further move, required by Darwall's definition, of taking a stand on whether she is justified in acting on that consideration.

---

21. Darwall, *Impartial Reason*, pp. 28–34. Darwall is here contrasting "the reason why she acted" – an explanation of the agent's action with no implication that the agent is aware of the reason for which she is performing the action – with "the agent's reason," in which the agent knows the reason for which she is acting. Both are to be contrasted with "a reason for action," which refers only to justified reasons for performing the action, with no implication that someone is acting for that reason. A similar typology of reasons can be found in E. J. Bond, *Reason and Value* (Cambridge: Cambridge University Press, 1983), Chapter 1. I am claiming that a Murdochian reason is "the agent's reason," but disagreeing with Darwall about whether that notion requires that the agent regard her reason as justified.

She need not, nor (as I envision her) does she, take up a perspective – a perspective as it were "outside" her action – from which the issue of justifiability is raised. She need not think, or form the judgment that, her action is "right," or "the right thing to do," and so she need not be committed to generalizing such rightness to others. Although such an act lacks the form of moral reflection required by Darwall's sense of "reason," it need not be thoughtless, irrational, or impulsive.[22]

Ann's act can have value – specifically moral value – even though it lacks the commitment to formal universality of the Darwallian view of reasons for action. It is true that such an act can contravene other moral strictures; out of a Murdochian responsiveness one may act dishonestly, or against some obligation. (Note, however, that commitment to any specific principle of rightness fails to protect against a similar contravening of some *other* principle.) A commitment to universal rightness would protect against this eventuality. Nevertheless some protection is afforded by attaching the condition (that I am assuming operative in the Ann-Tony case) that the agent act on the Murdochian reason *only* when he *not* have the affirmative belief that what he is doing is wrong or immoral, and not even have any grounds for concern that this might be the case. This condition seems to be met by Ann and Tony; Ann may lack the belief that what she is doing is wrong, yet without reflecting on whether what she proposes to do for Tony is morally wrong – for nothing in the situation would constitute grounds for such concern.

I now want to argue that Ann's reasons for helping Tony, and Murdochian reasons in general, are not subjective or personal reasons – reasons of autonomy – either. Reasons of autonomy are understood as grounded in

22. Even if, in acting for what one takes to be a reason for action, an agent were, contrary to my argument, committed to thinking of her reason as applicable to others as well as to herself, this would not commit her to thinking that any other particular situation, including future situations that she may face, is one in which the agent in question has a reason to act. For it is quite possible, and by no means unusual, when actually faced with some particular situation, to fail to see it as exactly analogous to one's own (current) situation in the relevant respects. This fact is often masked in philosophy discussions where the descriptions of the examples are assumed to have already incorporated all the relevant features; but in life, situations do not come labeled in this way. A similar point is made by Thomas E. Hill, Jr., in "Self-respect reconsidered," in O. H. Green (ed.), *Respect for Persons: Tulane Studies in Philosophy* 31 (1982), p. 132, n. 5. This does not mean that the notion of relevance of considerations is an entirely arbitrary or subjective one. But it does mean that one can be committed to the formal principle of generality of reasons without thinking of one's current reason for action as being in a substantive sense agent – relatively generalizable to others. For further discussion of the role of reflectiveness in moral action, see Chapter 9, "Moral Development and Conceptions of Morality."

personal desires, projects, commitments, or interests. But on the most basic level Ann is not acting out of any of these. Helping Tony is not something Ann *wants* to be doing. Clearly, we can imagine she wants to be spending the evening as she had originally planned. Nor is Tony, or helping Tony, part of any project or prior commitment Ann has undertaken. Ann does not perform this action *because* she wants to or is involved in a project of which this action is an integral part. Rather, she comes to the action from her response to another person, a response which, while not independent of her relationship with that person, is independent of the desires and projects she brings to that situation. She acts as she does (in Murdochian fashion) because of a fact external to herself, not, as in Nagel's reasons for autonomy, from a desire or interest within herself.

This point is masked in Nagel's brief remarks at the one place where he comes close to articulating Murdochian reasons: "Anyone may of course make the end of another person his own, but that is a different matter: a matter of personal sympathy rather than of objective acknowledgment."[23] Ann's action is a matter of both sympathy for Tony and an acknowledgment of his situation as something outside herself, a reality to which she is responding. That acknowledgment is part of what it is for her to have that sympathy for Tony, not, as Nagel implies, merely a response to a desire-like inclination inside herself.

Can it not be replied to this that Ann's friendship with Tony is indeed a good to Ann, so that when she acts out of friendship for Tony she does act for the sake of a personal good, and in this way from a reason of autonomy? By implication Nagel includes friendships in his list of generators of reasons for autonomy. He says of "particular concerns for other people that reflect our relations with them" that "they acquire value only because of the interest we develop in them and the place this gives them in our lives, rather than evoking interest because of their value."[24]

This depiction of acting from friendship does not ring true. In caring for our friend's welfare do we think that we are responding to a value grounded in the interest which we take in her? As Murdoch emphasizes, an appropriate concern for a friend is a concern for something seen as having value in its own right, and not only in terms of its role in one's own relationship to that person. This is not to deny that many specific actions undertaken with regard to a friendship are done for the sake of the good of friendship. One may act so as to affirm a relationship with someone, or to shore up a faltering relationship. But if all of someone's

23. Nagel, *View from Nowhere,* p. 168.
24. Ibid., p. 168.

actions toward her friends were guided in their aim and motivation by the importance of the relationship to her own life, one would think that the one thing necessary for genuine friendship was absent, namely, a concern for the friend for her own sake.

It is certainly true that we may seek friendships as personal goods, and seek to hold on to friendships *because* we value them. But it is only a hollow shell of a friendship when one party sees the other's welfare as having value only because of the interest he develops in that person. Although the value (from the friend's standpoint) of a friend's welfare is not simply an agent-neutral value – a valuing of *anyone's* welfare, simply because the other is human – neither is it simply a personal value. It must be seen as having value in its own right, though that value is specifically the value of a friend's welfare. Thus we may seek friendships as personal goods, but many situations involving friendship present themselves as calling for actions one does not seek and might wish had not arisen, and which could very well not have arisen within that particular friendship. And yet one performs those actions willingly, and often gladly, out of friendship.[25]

A more general issue is at stake here. The language of "reasons of autonomy" suggests that action taken from such reasons involves consciously seeking or striving to realize a certain goal. But much (though not all) action of a Murdochian sort has much more to do with responding to an unsought reality external to one's explicit projects and endeavors. In this regard Murdochian reasons are akin to objective/impartial ones – they lie outside, and can act as a constraint on, individual personal goals. And yet the Murdochian consideration (the other's distress, say) does not appear to the individual in the form of a purely detached and external datum. It is much more bound up with the particular agent in her individuality, for, as we have seen, the Murdochian agent responds to the (particular) other in a way which does not (necessarily) involve the notion that this is the way in which *all* must respond. But although this responsiveness involves the agent's own individuality, it does not necessarily, as do reasons of autonomy, involve the pursuit of personal goods and goals.

The upshot of this argument is that the disjunction of subjective and objective, personal and impersonal reasons does not exhaust types of reasons for action. Murdochian reasons – acting from loving attention to particular persons – are neither personal nor impersonal. It is in this way

25. For further argument on the way that regarding a friendship as a personal project is distorting of the friendship, see Chapter 5, "Vocation, Friendship, and Community."

that Nagel's view, in Murdoch's words, "theorizes away" an entire dimension of moral consciousness and moral life. Personal conduct is not simply a struggle between impersonal rightness and a personal good, between impersonal principles and personal desires.

Essentially the same diagnosis applies to Scheffler's and Williams's views. Scheffler gives the impression that the task of the morally serious agent is to give an appropriate place to the demands of an impartial consequentialist good, while not having one's own life and concerns swamped by this acknowledgment. Scheffler's solution to this problem is to accord independent weight to the personal point of view; this has the moral effect of allowing an agent to pursue his own projects to a greater degree than a purely impartial consequentialist would allow, although not restraining him from pursuing a pure consequentialist project, should he wish to do so.

One finds no recognition in Scheffler, however, that a good deal of the moral life involves not being responsive to pure consequentialist demands but responding to particular other persons whose lives our lives are bound up with or touch in some way. This task is not nearly so unrealistically demanding as the pure consequentialist project; but at the same time it has a claim on us which the personal point of view fails to include. One can reply that Scheffler simply did not set out to discuss this area of life, or even of the moral life. Yet his book conveys a general sense of what the tasks and concerns of the morally responsible agent are. And, as in Nagel's work, the concerns of Murdochian morality are entirely omitted.

Williams is much more concerned than either Nagel or Scheffler to defend the legitimacy of personal pursuits and of the personal point of view and, therefore, throws into question the entire objective/impartial domain. But this concern omits an entire dimension of the moral life which would remain even if the impartial/impersonal were abandoned. And the writings of Williams with which we are concerned can leave an impression that one has been presented with a sophisticated defense of high-minded selfishness. Although this would not be a just interpretation, these writings fail to provide a coherent conception of morality which remains once the Kantian one is abandoned.[26]

26. This gap is to some extent remedied in Williams's *Ethics and the Limits of Philosophy*. In it, Williams introduces the domain of the "ethical," which is distinct from both the personal and the moral, the latter still understood in essentially Kantian and impartialist terms. This view has the virtue of recognizing nonimpartialist claims that arise from outside the individual and reside at least partly in the welfare of other persons; yet Williams never makes entirely clear how the "ethical" is to be characterized or how it relates to the moral. My own argument is that the category of the moral should be broadened to include at least some of what Williams puts in the domain of the ethical.

Murdoch's views of morality pose a challenge, then, to a view of morality shared in some ways by Kantianism, utilitarianism, and their critics such as Nagel, Williams, and Scheffler; and that is the identification of morality with an impersonal, impartial, objective point of view. But Murdoch should not be thought of as providing a complete conception of morality to replace the impartialist one. Murdoch's view is necessarily incomplete as an account of the whole of morality, for it fails to give sufficient attention to morality's less personal and individualized aspects, as Murdoch herself recognized.[27]

And yet there is one challenge to my argument from the impartialist camp which needs to be addressed, if only briefly: Could it not be said that while there is value in the phenomena of compassion, loving attention, friendship, and the like, to which Murdoch draws attention, nevertheless that value is not *moral* value? It is good, it could be said, to be compassionate, to act from care for a friend – but not *morally* good.

The complexities of the term "moral" and its variations need a more extensive exploration than I have seen, or can give here. The case for regarding Murdochian qualities of character and modes of being as part of morality stems from the following considerations: We admire and wish to emulate a compassionate and caring person, as we do a person who is conscientiously responsive to objective/impartial demands. Although we should be less likely to say of the former than of the latter that she is a "very moral" or "moral" person, we express a comparable thought by saying that she is a "good" or even a "morally good" person. Even without the use of the term "moral," it would be difficult to deny that calling someone "good" could be part of a moral judgment or a moral assessment of her character.[28] We include Murdochian traits (kindness, considerateness, compassion, and the like) in our ideals of human character. We wish our children to have these characteristics, and see their inculcation as part of moral education. Furthermore, none of the standard categories with which "moral" is employed as a contrast – aesthetic, political, legal, etiquette, personal – captures this sort of value.

Moreover, the Murdochian account of morality encompasses one feature present in ordinary consciousness but absent in the impartialist conception, and that is what Michael Slote calls "self-other asymmetry."[29]

27. *Sovereignty,* p. 43.
28. For further defense of the use of "moral" in these contexts, see Chapter 9, "Moral Development and Conceptions of Morality."
29. Michael Slote, "Self-other asymmetry," *The Journal of Philosophy* 81 (1984), and *Common-Sense Morality and Consequentialism* (London: Routledge and Kegan Paul, 1985), Chapter 1.

On the impartialist view, morality consists in taking up a perspective in which no one is favored over any other. This implies (more so in consequentialism than Kantianism) that there is no moral difference between benefiting myself and benefiting someone else, if every other feature of the situation remains the same, for example, if both alternatives maximize total benefit. But, as Slote points out, according to our ordinary moral intuitions, we are permitted to sacrifice a greater benefit to ourselves for a lesser benefit to someone else, while disallowing a greater sacrifice to someone else for a smaller benefit to ourselves (or to a third person).

Murdochian morality also embodies this self-other asymmetry, for it sees in action and attitude toward others moral value it does not accord in regard to the self. In this way, Murdochian morality is more in line with a basic moral intuition than is a pure impartialist conception of morality.

Yet it is worth noting a difference between the role of self-other asymmetry in Murdoch and in Slote's discussion of consequentialism. In the latter, self-other asymmetry is an explicitly anticonsequentialist principle of permissibility, allowing the promotion of another's lesser benefit at the expense of one's own greater benefit. Murdoch's view differs from this in two ways. First, and most obviously, Murdoch is concerned with what is morally good and not merely morally permissible, and would no doubt regard many cases of sacrifice on behalf of a lesser benefit to others as morally good.

Second, and more significant, Murdoch's view is not concerned with weighing up benefits and losses. It is, in fact, not concerned with the agent's own benefit at all. It bids us to focus on others not at the *expense* of the self, but, so to speak, without considering the self at all. The moral task is not self-negation but self-transcending. One way in which Murdoch's view captures an important part of moral action is that in many cases of acting for the sake of another, it could not meaningfully be said whether the agent had lost more than the other had gained or not. Both consequentialism and the anticonsequentialist view that Slote articulates presuppose that the agent's benefit and loss are something determinate prior to the situation at hand. But often when we do something for another, although we are not thinking about ourselves, we are not clearly giving something up of ourselves either. If, for example, I stay an extra hour in my office to help a student to whom I have already devoted a fair amount of time but whom I want to help, I am not necessarily giving up a potential benefit which is either more or less than what the student will gain. In fact, in some cases, to weigh the benefits and losses, even if one ends up giving more than the other gains, might betoken a failure of the focus on the other that Murdoch wants from us.[30]

There is, then, a prima facie case for according moral value to the phenomena which Murdoch articulates. The challenge can be thrown back to the impartialist: Outside of an exclusive prior commitment to impartialism, what grounds are there for restricting the concept of morality solely to the objective/impartial domain of action?

Yet ultimately it is not the term moral itself but rather the place and importance in human life which the moral domain is thought to have which is fundamentally at stake here. My concern is only to accord to loving attention, care, and the Murdochian qualities generally that same importance ordinarily thought to attach to the "moral."

30. I do not mean to imply, however, that the failure to focus on the self at all is entirely a *strength* of the Murdochian perspective. It can also be a weakness in not making clear that the self has some moral standing, so that servility is a moral defect, and standing up for one's rights can be a virtue. It is not that Murdoch takes the explicit position, found say in Kierkegaard's *Works of Love,* that the self has no such moral standing. Murdoch is not attempting to state a comprehensive view of morality, and it is compatible with her view that there are self-regarding virtues. Her perspective, however, gives no articulation of or even distinct conceptual space for those virtues. My point in this discussion is only that there are elements of our moral experience that, while according with a self-other symmetry in general, are better captured by Murdoch's lack of self-focus than by the anticonsequentialist weighing of the self's and the other's benefits and choosing the other's lesser benefit over the agent's greater one.

3

Moral perception and particularity

Iris Murdoch's series of essays *The Sovereignty of Good*[1] and her novels call our attention to the important role of *moral perception* in the moral life. How do agents come to perceive situations in the way they do? How does a situation come to have a particular character *for* a particular moral agent? What is the relation between our moral-perceptual capacities and other psychological capacities essential to the moral life? These questions have drawn scant attention in contemporary ethical theory.[2] Moral philosophy's customary focus on action-guiding rules and principles, on choice and decision, on universality and impartiality, and on obligation and right action have masked the importance of moral perception to a full and adequate account of moral agency. Yet although an agent may reason well in moral situations, uphold the strictest standards of impartiality for testing her maxims and moral principles, and be adept at deliberation, unless she perceives moral situations as moral situations, and unless she perceives their moral character accurately, her moral principles and skill at deliberation may be for naught. In fact, one of the most important moral differences between people is between those who miss and those who see various moral features of situations confronting them.

In discussing moral perception here, I relate it to the phenomenon of *moral judgment,* understood as the process that bridges the gap between

Earlier drafts of this essay were presented at Sonoma State University, to some students and faculty at the University of California at Berkeley, and at the Conference on Impartiality at Hollins College in 1990. I wish to thank those audiences for stimulating discussions. I wish also to thank Stephen Darwall for his comments on my presentation at the Conference on Impartiality. I wish also to thank Marcia Homiak, David Wong, Owen Flanagan, Stephen Nathanson, and Margaret Holland for very helpful comments on various drafts.

1. Iris Murdoch, *The Sovereignty of Good* (London: Routledge and Kegan Paul, 1970).
2. Important exceptions to this claim – and works to which I am indebted – are Martha Nussbaum, "The Discernment of Perception," in *Love's Knowledge* (New York: Oxford University Press, 1990) and *The Fragility of Goodness* (Cambridge: Cambridge University Press, 1986), pp. 298–306; Charles Larmore, *Patterns of Moral Complexity* (Cambridge: Cambridge University Press, 1987), Chapter 1; Nancy Sherman, *The Fabric of Character* (Oxford: Clarendon Press, 1989), especially Chapter 2; John Kekes, *Moral Tradition and Individuality* (Princeton: Princeton University Press, 1989), Chapter 7.

moral rules (and principles) and particular situations.[3] I show that, like moral perception, the phenomenon of moral judgment does speak to an important lacuna in principle-based theories of morality. Yet I also explore the limitations of that very metaphor of "bridging the gap between the general and the particular" as a way of capturing what is missing in theories which focus only on the general or the universal.

Thus moral perception, I argue, cannot be identified with moral judgment. In a given situation, moral perception comes on the scene before moral judgment; moral perception can lead to moral action outside the operation of judgment entirely; and, more generally, perception can involve moral capacities not encompassed by moral judgment. I argue also that moral perception should not be conceived of as a unified capacity, but that it involves multifarious moral and psychological processes.

Finally, although I criticize principle-based theories for failing to recognize the importance of the operation of moral perception and moral judgment, the boundaries are not sharp between those capacities and processes involved in moral perception and judgment and those more commonly associated with moral agency as portrayed in principle-based theories (rationality, commitment to principles, sense of duty, testing maxims for moral acceptability, and the like). My language may sometimes suggest this, but I am not conceiving of moral perception, moral judgment, and moral reasoning as anything like wholly distinct psychic functions. Indeed, although I do not explore this here, the moral principles we consciously adopt are in part a reflection of our moral perceivings, and conversely our moral perceptions are in part shaped by our consciously adopted moral principles.

I begin with three examples of the operation of moral perception in particular situations. These examples help me introduce some basic terminology and set the stage for the theoretical argument in the main body of the essay.

I

Example 1: John and Joan are riding on a subway train, seated. There are no empty seats and some people are standing; yet the subway car is not packed so tightly as to be uncomfortable for everyone. One of the passen-

---

3. The notion of "moral judgment" is frequently used in philosophical contexts to refer to the selection of the right action or principle in situations of conflict of principle. This may be the most frequent use of this notion, but it is not the one I will be employing here. For more on this point see the Postscript to this chapter.

gers standing is a woman in her thirties holding two relatively full shopping bags. John is not particularly paying attention to the woman, but he is cognizant of her. Joan, by contrast, is distinctly aware that the woman is uncomfortable.

Thus different aspects of the situation are *salient* for John and Joan. That is, what is fully and explicitly present to John's consciousness about the woman is that she is standing holding some bags; what is in that same sense salient for Joan is the woman's discomfort. That an aspect of a situation is not salient for an agent does not mean she is entirely unaware of it. She could be aware of it in a less than fully explicit way. One can imagine, for example, that Joan asks John, "Does that woman seem uncomfortable to you?" This question might have the effect of making John realize that at some level he had been aware of the woman's discomfort all along, but that he had failed fully to take it in. This might be because he was not paying more attention to the situation.

It seems natural here to talk of awareness of a situation, or of an aspect of it, existing "at different levels." An aspect or feature can be more or less salient for, or "taken in" by, an agent. Thus the notion of salience admits of degrees; by contrast, that of "perceiving situations under different descriptions" – sometimes used to express the way the same situation can be seen differently by different perceivers – does not readily leave room for this degree aspect. (This is not meant to deny that some aspect of a situation not encompassed in an agent's salience-consciousness could be totally outside the perceiver's awareness.[4])

In this situation, the difference between what is salient for John and Joan is of moral significance. Joan saliently perceives (hereinafter I shall just say "perceives") the standing woman's good (i.e., her comfort) as a stake in a way that John does not. Joan perceives a morally relevant value in the situation that John does not.

One morally significant aspect of this difference is the way that perception is the setting for action. John's perception provides him with no

4. Note that to speak of a feature of a situation as "salient" for an agent does not (necessarily) mean that the agent takes that feature to be action-warranting. It only means that the given feature occupies the agent's most explicit level of consciousness concerning the situation. I mean for perceptual salience to provide the setting in which an agent decides to act, but not to be definitionally tied to action or reasons for action. A salient perception of some morally significant aspect of a situation could in some situations inform sympathy, indignation, or regret yet not action.

It might be misleading to refer to the "agent" as I am doing (but I can think of no better single term). For the aspect of the individual as a full moral person with which I am concerned here is not so much her *agency* as something that takes place before she takes herself to be called on to exercise that agency. Unless she already perceives her situation in a certain way in the first place, she will not engage her agency. (See Postscript.)

32

reason to offer to help the woman.[5] Whereas, in involving the woman's good, Joan's perception of the situation already provides her with a reason for action not based in her self-interest or projects.

But the moral significance of the difference between John's and Joan's perceptions of the situation lies not only in the relation between that perception and the taking of beneficent action. It lies in the fact of perception itself. We can see this more clearly if we imagine John's and Joan's perceptions to be fairly typical of each of them. John, let us say, often fails to take in people's discomfort, whereas Joan is characteristically sensitive to such discomfort. It is thus in character for the discomfort to be salient for Joan but not for John. That is to say, a morally significant aspect of situations facing John characteristically fails to be salient for him, and this is a defect in his character – not a very serious moral defect, but a defect nevertheless.[6] John misses something of the moral reality confronting him.

Again, the deficiency lies not only in his failure to *act*. For we can contrast with John someone, say Ted, who perfectly clearly perceives other people's discomfort but is totally unmoved by it. Ted simply does not care, and this is why he does not offer to help. John, as I am envisioning him, is not callous and uncaring in this way. We can imagine him as someone who, when others' discomfort is brought to his attention, is as sympathetic and willing to offer help as a person of average moral sensitivities. John's failure to act stems from his failure to *see* (with the appropriate salience), not from callousness about other people's discomfort. His deficiency is a situational self-absorption or attentional laziness.[7] So

---

5. This may be overstated. John might believe that out of politeness he as a male should give up his seat to a female, or to an older female, and he might offer her his seat for this reason. One might or might not call such an act of politeness morally significant, but in any case it would represent a different moral significance than if he offered her the seat out of a perception of her discomfort.

6. This is not to imply that a failure of moral perception is morally significant only as a revelation of a larger defect of character. The failure of perception can be significant in its own right within the given situation, just as a motive can be bad in itself on a given occasion, *as well as* in its revealing of a general defect of character. Instances of perception and motives in specific situations can be morally criticizable even when they are out of character for the agent, as well as when they are neither in nor out of character.

Regarding the subway example, however, it may be misleading to say that it is morally criticizable for a passenger to fail to perceive the discomfort of a passenger on a particular occasion; the failure may be too insignificant, and the moral relationship between the seated and the standing passenger too attenuated, for it to count as a moral failure. It may, however, still be criticizable insofar as this failure is expressive of a general failure to perceive discomfort.

7. Another case would be someone who "tunes out" in crowded, overstimulating environments like subways but is quite sensitive in one-on-one interactions.

there is a different moral significance to failing to act depending on the character or explanation of that failure. (To say that moral perception is of significance in its own right is not to take a stand on whether it is better to perceive and not to act than not to perceive in the first place. Accurate moral perception is a good in its own right, but like other moral goods it is so only ceteris paribus.)

Example 2: Theresa is the administrator of a department. One of her subordinates, Julio, has been stricken with a deteriorating condition in his leg causing him frequent pain. He approaches Theresa to help work out a plan by which the company, and in particular their department, can accommodate his disability. Theresa is unable to appreciate Julio's disability and the impact it is having on his work. Although in principle Theresa accepts the company's legal obligation to accommodate Julio's disability, in fact she continually offers him less than he needs and is entitled to.

More generally, Theresa makes Julio feel uncomfortable in approaching her and gives him the impression that she thinks he may be too self-pitying and should just "pull himself together." It is not that Theresa fails entirely to see Julio as "disabled" and "in pain," but she does fail to grasp fully what this means for him, and to take in or acknowledge that pain. The level of Julio's pain and its impact on his mental state is insufficiently salient for Theresa.

Theresa is failing to perceive or acknowledge something morally significant – namely Julio's physical pain and his distress at the impact of his condition on his work situation. Let us imagine further that Theresa has a distinct personal *resistance* to acknowledging Julio's pain. It is not simply a matter, as it is for John (as I am envisioning him), of situational self-absorption, or of something that could be corrected simply by calling Theresa's attention to it. (Julio has repeatedly tried to do precisely this.) Perhaps Theresa unconsciously identifies pain with weakness. When people evince pain in her presence, or describe pain which they have had, Theresa becomes uncomfortable. She is inclined to think they are overdoing it; she finds herself having feelings of contempt toward such persons, though perhaps she is not aware of this. (One can imagine various psychodynamic accounts of this; Theresa may have an irrational fear of pain herself, and may have developed a defense against this fear by not wanting to acknowledge pain in others.)

The failure to be in touch with part of the moral reality[8] that con-

8. I mean to be using the notion of "moral reality" pretheoretically, without taking any stand on current debates regarding "moral realism," such as whether there are moral facts or whether moral judgments are best thought of as truth claims. My notion of "moral reality" is, however, in some degree inspired by Iris Murdoch's work, so I want

fronts her is a deficiency in Theresa's response to this situation (bound up with a deficiency of character as well). Note that in this situation adequate moral perception is not only a matter of making "moral discriminations," a term often used to express a moral process involved in moral perception, that is, noting a morally significant feature of a situation. It is also a matter of that moral aspect of the situation – here, Julio's disability – weighing adequately within the agent's view of the situation. Theresa must have a certain degree of empathy for Julio in his situation in order for her to perceive his pain with an appropriate degree of salience and it is this empathy that is lacking. The notion of "moral discrimination" overintellectualizes Theresa's lack (and failure) in the situation, and omits the necessarily affective dimension to the empathic understanding often (though by no means always) required for fully adequate moral perception.[9]

Theresa's deficiency is bound up with, but not exhausted by, her failure to take adequate steps to provide accommodation for Julio's disability. Theresa and Julio have a role relationship which grounds her obligation under the law or company policy to provide accommodation to Julio. But I think we regard their role relationship as involving more than this. It also grounds the thought that Theresa ought to be able to respond appropriately to Julio's situation, and explains why her not appreciating (with the appropriate salience) his disability is a morally criticizable failure on her part. Because of their work relationship, Julio's state of being is very much part of Theresa's moral reality.

Can it be replied to the claim that perception of morally significant aspects of situations is of moral value in its own right that in fact this perception is morally neutral, since a person could have accurate moral perception, yet misuse what she perceives to harm the other person, or otherwise to commit a wrong act? But even if the premise of this argument is true, the conclusion does not follow. Any moral/psychological phenomenon can be put to bad use, including devotion to duty or principle (the principles might be bad ones), compassion or sympathy (which may lead someone to neglect moral requirements). But we do not say that devotion to duty or principle is morally neutral just because it can be

to make clear that I am not accepting the Platonic cast of her view of moral reality. I would argue that there are two somewhat distinct pictures of "moral reality" in Murdoch – the first quite Platonic, and the second meaning something like "other persons and their situations." My own sense of the term is closer to the latter Murdochian notion.

9. On the role of emotion in understanding the situation of others, see Nussbaum, "Discernment of Perception," Sherman, *Fabric of Character,* and Blum, "Emotion and Reality," Boston University Colloquium for the Philosophy of Science, 1986 (typescript).

put to bad use. Accurate moral perception is, ceteris paribus, a good thing.

What it would take for Theresa to allow others' pain to be salient for her in the appropriate way (and circumstances) would involve coming to grips with and working through her resistances. Why does she identify pain with weakness? She would have to come to understand herself better in these areas. Self-knowledge would be integral to her moral improvement. Although such self-reflection would involve thinking about herself in relation to others, it is not a form of thought characterized by the attempt to arrive at principles. It is rather reflection that tries to understand a particular individual (herself) with regard to her moral character. This point may seem obvious, but is worth mentioning as one sometimes finds the acknowledgment of a need for moral reflection cited as an argument in favor of principle-based or impartialist views of ethics as against one more strongly centered in virtue or emotion. In fact moral reflection by itself is neutral as between such theories.

Example 3: Tim, a white male, is waiting for a taxi at a train station. Waiting near him are a black woman and her daughter. A cab comes by, passes the woman and her daughter, and stops in front of Tim, who, with relief, gets in the cab.

Tim's relief at having secured a cab might block from his full awareness the cab driver's having ignored the black mother and child in favor of him. Salient in Tim's perception might simply be the presence of the cab.

But suppose that once in the cab Tim, idly ruminating, puts the pieces of the situation together and comes to see it, in retrospect, in a different way. He sees the driver as having intentionally passed up the woman and child. Suppose he also infers that the driver did this out of racism – because he just prefers not to have blacks in his cab, or does not want to go into the sort of neighborhood where he imagines the woman will ask him to go. (Although these are morally distinct reasons, both involve racism, perhaps in different ways.) Whether Tim is correct in this inference is not so important to my current purposes as whether the inference is a plausible one, which I am assuming it to be. This perception of racism now becomes Tim's "take" on the situation. He now sees in the situation an issue of injustice he did not at first see. He gains moral insight regarding the situation. He wonders why he did not recognize the injustice before getting in the cab. Regardless of any action Tim might now take, it is (ceteris paribus) a (morally) better thing for him to have recognized the racial injustice than not to have done so.

Note some features of moral perception in this situation that contrast with examples 1 and 2. First, Tim's (ultimate, though not initial) perception of the situation involves both *construal* and *inference* in a way that Joan's and Theresa's perceptions do not. Tim has to construe the situation in a certain way to see it as "the cab driver passing up the woman and her child." And he has to infer the racist motive. Both these processes involve some degree of imagination, not necessarily required in the other two cases, though the difference may well be only one of degree.

This example also indicates how perception depends on the agent's already possessing certain moral categories. Let us imagine (although this would be implausible) that Tim had never before heard of or experienced racial discrimination, so that, although he might come to think it unfair of the driver to have passed up the woman and her daughter, he would nevertheless fail to grasp the further wrongness of racial injustice. Lacking the moral concept of "racism" (or "racial discrimination"), he would not have been able to perceive the racism in the situation. (Of course, the agents in examples 1 and 2 must have the morally significant concepts of "discomfort," "pain," and "disability" to gain an adequate moral perception of their situations too.)

I want to count Tim's construal of the driver's action and his inference of racism under the rubric of "perception," for I am including under "perception" anything contributing to, or encompassed within, the agent's salience-perception of the situation before he deliberates about what action to take. Tim is not led to suppose the racist motive as a result of deliberating on how to act in the situation; he is merely idly focusing on the situation, not necessarily intentionally or even fully conscious that he is doing so. The point is (and this will be discussed in more detail below) that perception occurs prior to deliberation, and prior to taking the situation to be one in which one needs to deliberate. It is precisely *because* the situation is seen in a certain way that the agent takes it as one in which he feels moved to deliberate.[10]

II

One familiar line of criticism of a principle- or rule-based ethic — at least with regard to its completeness as a conception of moral agency or the

10. Note that this definition of situational perception is relative to a deliberative event. Once an agent begins deliberating in a situation, the process of deliberation can further affect her perception of the situation. (If I am remembering accurately, I am indebted for this point to Michael Slote and Margaret Walker at the Conference on Impartiality at which an early draft of this paper was presented.) It can lead her to see different aspects, to see as applicable moral concepts that she initially did not, and to see previous aspects with a different degree of salience. That perception will then provide the context for the next level of deliberation.

moral life itself – emphasizes the particularity of (moral) situations. It is not the rule but some other moral capacity of the agent which tells her that the particular situation she faces falls under a given rule. The accurate or adequate assessment of particular situations – a knowledge or perception of particulars – is not accounted for, or guaranteed by, the mere possession of rules themselves.

This perception of particular situations is taken up by Charles Larmore in his book *Patterns of Moral Complexity,*[11] where he points out that Kant recognized the need for something to bridge rule and particular situation, something he called the power of "judgment."

> Judgment will be the faculty of subsuming under rules; that is, of distinguishing whether something does or does not stand under a given rule.... Judgment is a peculiar talent which can be practiced only, and can not be taught ... [A]lthough admirable in understanding [an individual] may be wanting in natural power of judgment. He may comprehend the universal *in abstracto,* and yet not be able to distinguish whether a case *in concreto* comes under it.[12]

Larmore rightly credits Aristotle with having more to say than Kant about the need for such judgment, for emphasizing the particularity involved in exercising it, and for delineating its place in ethical deliberation and conduct.

I will discuss further the nature of such "judgment" as a moral operation seemingly required by, yet often omitted in, the accounts of moral agency in principle-based ethical theories. Then I will argue that what I have called "moral perception" incorporates moral operations and capacities that are not captured by this notion of "judgment." Moreover, I will argue, some aspects of moral perception – and of the particularity connected with them – become invisible if we think that an adequate ethical theory consists solely of rules and principles supplemented by the moral capacity that allows us to bring those rules to bear on particular situations. Finally, this discussion will yield a complex and multifaceted understanding of the role of "particularity" in ethics.

There are two distinct features of judgment conceived as Larmore (following Kant) does, as linking rules and particular situations. One is to know what a given rule calls upon one to do in a given situation. Many rules or principles are formulated in too coarse-grained a fashion to capture the

11. See footnote 2.
12. Kant, *Critique of Pure Reason,* trans. L. W. Beck (New York: St. Martin's Press, 1965), p. 177:A133–A134. See also Kant in *Foundations of the Metaphysics of Morals,* trans. L. W. Beck (Indianapolis: Bobbs-Merrill, 1959), p. 5:389: "No doubt these laws require a power of judgment sharpened by experience, partly in order to decide in what cases they apply."

relevant moral detail in particular situations, and thus require something beyond the rule itself to apply them adequately to the particular situation. Larmore rightly points out that some principles require a greater role for the exercise of this function of judgment than do others.[13] For instance, in example 3, suppose Tim, the rider, holds the principle that one should take a stand against racism. How best to do this – or even discerning which of the actions that he can think of would count as taking a stand against racism – is no simple matter. For example, should he try to make the driver go back to the train station on the off chance that the woman and her child have not yet gotten a cab; tell the driver he disapproves of what he assumes to be the driver's racism; make the driver stop so he can get out of the cab; engage the driver in conversation about why he passed up the woman and child? Discerning which action best instantiates a given principle requires judgment about the particularities of the situation.[14] The power of judgment thus presents at least a necessary supplement to traditional principle-based ethics. For knowing how to apply the principle, how to pick the best among the possible actions instantiating the principle, involves a moral capacity (or capacities) beyond the adoption of, or recognition of the validity of, the principle itself (e.g., the principle of trying to counter racism or injustice). Tim could be entirely and sincerely committed to opposing racism and injustice (and for the right reasons), yet be a poor judge of what implementing his opposition would actually involve in this or another particular situation.[15]

One can see the need for this aspect of judgment to fill out the conception of moral agency in a principle-based ethic by considering Kant's notion of "imperfect duties."[16] In contrast to "perfect" duties,

13. *Patterns of Moral Complexity*, p. 5.
14. Discussing Aristotle's account of deliberation, David Wiggins points out that much deliberation is not an attempt to find the best means to a given end, but a search for the "best specification" of that end. David Wiggins, "Deliberation and Practical Reason," in *Essays on Aristotle's Ethics*, ed. A. Rorty (Berkeley: University of California, 1980), p. 228. My point here is that knowing how best to apply a principle (which one already sees as applicable to a given situation) to the situation requires a kind of moral judgment neither encompassed nor guaranteed by the possession of the principle itself. It is a form of judgment involved with grasping the morally significant particulars of a given situation. (For further remarks on the notion of specification and on Henry Richardson's important discussion of it in "Specifying Norms as a Way to Resolve Concrete Ethical Problems," *Philosophy and Public Affairs*, 19, 1990, 306–31, see Postscript.)
15. For a more detailed argument for the view that different moral capacities may be brought into play in applying a principle than in coming to hold the principle, see Chapter 10, "Gilligan and Kohlberg: Issues for Moral Theory."
16. My delineation of imperfect duties is drawn from Thomas Hill's oft-cited account in "Kant on Imperfect Duty and Supererogation," *Kant-Studien*, 62. Jahrgang, Heft 1, 1971. This account is followed in Marcia Baron, "Kantian Ethics and Supererogation," *Journal of Philosophy*, vol. 84, no. 5, May 1987.

imperfect duties (such as beneficence) do not prescribe a specific action in a specific situation; they prescribe the adoption of a general end (e.g., the happiness of others) but do not specify how or toward whom the beneficent actions are to be carried out. According to one interpretation, it is morally indifferent when and how one carries out the duty – beneficence, for example – as long as one does so on some (appropriate) occasions.[17] Such a view would appear to imply that there is no distinctively moral work to be done in choosing when to act from imperfect duty and in knowing how to do so. Since the scope of imperfect duties is great, this could be taken as a defense of the view that an ethic of principle is adequate to cover virtually the entire domain of the moral life.

But this view of duty neglects the fact that it is a moral matter, and not merely one of personal preference or moral indifference, *how* one carries out a duty or precept. It involves moral capacities, sensitivities, and judgment (1) to know which acts count as exemplifying particular moral principles, (2) to know how to carry out the act judged to be specified by the principle, and (3) to know when it is and isn't appropriate to instantiate given principles. These capacities go beyond possessing the principle (plus the strength of will to act on it); they are neither guaranteed nor encompassed by the commitment to the principle (plus strength of will) itself.

My argument is not meant as a critique of the notion of an "imperfect duty" but only to show that distinct moral processes and capacities are involved in bringing principle to bear on particular situations, and that these are required in order for moral agents to produce action in accord with imperfect duties. As we have seen, Kant recognized the need for judgment, but he did not appear to regard this capacity as a distinctly moral one, and, at least as far as I am aware in his major ethical writings, Kant seemed to think his moral theory complete without an account of what is specifically involved in (moral) judgment.

A second feature of moral judgment not generally taken up by philosophers in the principle-based traditions in ethics is the recognition of features of a situation as having moral significance, and thus as being

17. See Hill, p. 64. In the same spirit, Onora O'Neill says, "What is left optional by fundamental imperfect obligation is selection not merely of a specific way of enacting the obligation but of those for whom the obligation is to be performed." "Children's Right and Children's Lives," in *Constructions of Reason: Explorations of Kant's Practical Philosophy* (Cambridge: Cambridge University Press, 1989). In a brief footnote giving a provisional definition of perfect and imperfect duties, Kant says that perfect duties allow no exceptions "in the interest of inclination," thus implying that imperfect duties do allow for such exceptions. *Foundations of the Metaphysics of Morals*, 39:422.

features which must be taken into account in constructing a principle fully adequate to handle the situation. If I am presented with a specific situation I must know for example that the fact that it involves promise-keeping and harm to an individual means that it involves two morally relevant features, whereas its involving taking a walk or eating cereal is morally irrelevant. This component of moral judgment is *antecedent* to the one just discussed. For before the issue of *implementing* a principle comes to the fore for the agent, she must know that specific features of the situation before her (as she characterizes that situation to herself) are morally significant ones, and hence "pull for" specific moral principles.

This feature of moral judgment, as an issue for Kantian ethics in particular, has been explored by Barbara Herman in "The Practice of Moral Judgment."[18] Herman says that if the categorical imperative is regarded as a testing procedure for already formed maxims of action, then (given that a proposed action may fall under several descriptions), how an agent knows which features of a situation are relevant and which irrelevant in constructing the to-be-tested maxim of her action is itself a moral matter. The moral knowledge involved in a commitment to the categorical imperative cannot *by itself* account for or guarantee this prior knowledge. For this feature of moral agency, Herman posits a different kind of moral knowledge, captured in what she calls "rules of moral salience."

To sum up, principle-based traditions have generally failed to note the specific moral character of either of the following aspects of moral judgment of particular situations: (1) knowing what counts as best exemplifying, and knowing how to apply, rules or principles and (2) before this, recognizing given features of a situation as morally significant.

III

I now suggest that the phenomenon of *moral perception* encompasses moral processes beyond these two features of moral judgment, and that discussions of judgment have often tended either to conflate these different phenomena, or to neglect those connected with moral perception entirely. (I shall not say much about the terms "judgment" and "perception" here. Either term can be used to refer to some of the processes I have included within the other. What is important is to recognize the range of distinct moral processes and capacities involved.)

For example, to know what to do about the cab driver's presumed racism, Tim must know that racism is a morally significant feature of the

18. Barbara Herman, "The Practice of Moral Judgment," *Journal of Philosophy,* vol. 87, no. 8, August 1985.

situation that he must take into account in figuring out how best to act. (This is Barbara Herman's point.) But such knowledge does not guarantee that Tim perceives the racism in the driver's behavior in the first place. Such perception involves a different kind of, or aspect of, moral sensibility or understanding. It means, as we have seen, that Tim must see the situation in terms other than personal relief at finding a cab. He must see the driver as having passed over the woman and child. He must use his knowledge and imagination to suppose a racist motive. Tim must recognize that what has transpired is in fact racism before he can get to the point of using his already present knowledge that racism is a morally significant feature of a situation to help him construct a principle to guide his action, and then to determine which action will best instantiate that principle.[19]

It is moral perception that constructs what an agent is faced with as "a (moral) situation" in the first place. The idea of moral judgment as bridging general rule and particular situation depends on a prior individuating of "the situation." It is moral perception which does that individuating or construing of the situation, thus providing a setting in which moral judgment carries out its task.

A second way in which moral perception is distinct from moral judgment is that some morally significant perception leading to action takes place outside the context of rules and rule application altogether. In the subway example (number 1), when Joan perceives the standing woman's discomfort, her offer to help need not be mediated by a rule, principle, or precept; she may be acting out of direct compassion, an emotion-based sentiment in which the woman's discomfort is directly taken as a reason for helping. So the role of moral perception here in tuning in to a morally significant feature of the situation is not to help the agent select the relevant rule (or construct an appropriate maxim) and then to (test it and) apply it. Rather, the morally charged description of the situation salient for that moral agent (e.g., that the woman is uncomfortable) itself already contains her reason for action, a reason that draws her to offer help without mediation by principle.[20]

A third and more encompassing way that moral judgment understood as the bridge between principle and action narrows the scope of morality

---

19. On pp. 423ff. of her article Herman refers indifferently to the perception of distress, and the recognition of distress as being morally significant. Thus she appears to recognize what I am calling moral perception, but seems not to appreciate its distinctness from the operation of moral judgment.

20. I cannot here join the complex question whether reasons of compassion such as Joan operates from can be derived from, are in some strong sense grounded in, or are required to be restricted by (impartialist) moral principles. I take up some of these issues in Chapter 2, "Iris Murdoch and the Domain of the Moral," and in my introductory essay.

is in its confinement to the task of generating moral *action*. Moral perception and moral understanding of particular situations are significant not only for their role in generating (right) action. Right action not informed by understanding of the moral realities confronting one (even when done from a morally good motive) loses some, and sometimes all, of its moral value. Suppose, for example, that Theresa (in example 2) is prevailed on by her superiors to grant Julio the accommodation to his disability that he requests. Perhaps she even becomes convinced that this is the right thing to do; yet she is still unable really to appreciate Julio's condition with the appropriate salience. Although she does the right thing (and may even do it for a moral reason, in coming to believe that it is her duty), her action is at least somewhat diminished from a moral point of view by lacking the appropriate moral understanding of Julio's condition. As argued earlier, Theresa *ought* to perceive and understand Julio's disability with the appropriate salience, as part of her work relationship with him; and this does not mean *only* (though it does entail) that she should engage in the correct behavior from the appropriate motive.

Moreover, as argued earlier, just or accurate moral perception is of value in its own right, not only in its informing of right action. We praise, admire, and encourage correct perception and moral insight prior to and partly independent of its issuing in right action. In the taxi cab example let us envision an observer of the scene, Yasuko, who sees the cab driver pass up the black woman and her child. Yasuko senses that the woman is not only irritated and angry at not having gotten the cab she had reason to expect would be available to her, but also experiences an affront to her dignity and a sense of being shamed (especially in regard to her child) because she too thinks the driver passed her up for racist reasons. (Let us suppose that Yasuko is correct in this perception.) Thus Yasuko sees – perceives – a violation of dignity that escapes Tim. Let us imagine that Yasuko's seeing the violation of dignity in this particular case is connected to a more pervasive characteristic of her moral sensitivities, namely, that she is more deeply concerned about, and tuned in to, issues of dignity in people's lives than are most people. She has a deeper understanding of and insight into injustice and dignity and why they are important. This sensitivity cannot be understood simply as a disposition to perform certain actions. It is more pervasive than that, informing her emotional reactions to things, what she notices, what is salient for her, and the like, and particular actions and emotions can be seen as stemming from this sensitivity.[21]

21. The collapsing of the significance of moral perception into judgment of right action – and a consequent masking of its full value – is particularly striking in John McDowell's influential article "Virtue and Reason" (*The Monist*, 62 [1979]: 331–50),

To summarize: Three importantly distinct moral operations are omitted from traditional principle-based accounts of ethics and are needed at least to supplement the latter. They are (1) accurate perception of a situation and its component morally significant features (including herein the perceptual individuating of the "situation" in the first place); (2) explicitly recognizing those features as morally significant ones, to be

where McDowell, citing Iris Murdoch, gives a central role to perception in ethics. He rightly connects the importance of perception to the limitations of an ethic of articulable rules or procedures, arguing (following Aristotle) that rules cannot capture the full moral sensibility of a person of good character. McDowell speaks of sensitivities to aspects of moral reality as (in a given situation) being "salient" for the agent. In doing so he points toward the Murdochian view that awareness of moral reality is a moral task and accomplishment in its own right and action is only one part of the appropriate response to the perceiving of moral reality.

As McDowell develops his argument, however, the notions of perception, salience, and sensitivity become defined solely in terms of the generating of right actions. What is to be perceived becomes, for McDowell, that consideration in a situation the acting on which will produce right action (cf. p. 331 and elsewhere). The notion of salience is cashed out as that moral consideration among all those present which would be picked out as the one to act on if the agent is to engage in right action. Lost is the idea of moral reality the accurate perception of which is both morally good in its own right and also provides the setting in which moral response in its broadest sense takes place.

Early in the article (p. 332) McDowell speaks of "specialized sensitivities" to different aspects of moral reality. (I discuss this issue later in more detail.) This conception promises a vision of a complex moral reality, sensitivity to different aspects of which (e.g., injustice, discomfort, physical pain, racism, dignity) is the setting for but is not definitionally tied to the production of right action. But McDowell does not deliver on this promise, for his idea that there is unity in the virtues is taken to imply that each "sensitivity" entails all the others (p. 333). This undermines the idea of a complex of sensitivities, reducing it to a unified awareness of the single rightness-generating characteristic in any given situation.

McDowell's defense of Aristotle's view that only judgment or discernment (perhaps guided by the idea of the mean) can tell us the right or noble thing to do *in the particular situation confronting the agent* is an important alternative picture, or at least a corrective, to a principle-centered view of ethics. Yet McDowell's notion of judgment is still confined to the discernment of right action rather than to the broader compass of right or good emotional, perceptual, and imaginative response to a situation.

Aristotle does not confine himself to right action; for him emotions are an integral part of virtue, as has been emphasized in both Nussbaum's "Discernment of Perception" and Nancy Sherman's *Fabric of Character.* Nevertheless, the sensitivity to moral features – to moral reality – which I have argued to be of moral significance in its own right is still not fully captured by supplementing the notion of right action with right emotion. It is not only a matter of having the right amount of anger (for example) toward the right person on the (appropriate) occasion in question, either by itself or accompanying a right or noble action. Such a view still confines moral life too much to specific occasions (calling for action or emotion), and fails to bring out (as discussed above) that both the action and the emotion appropriate on specific occasions are expressions of sensitivities and forms of moral perception that pervade the agent's view of the world. Sherman's account, and Nussbaum's to a slightly lesser extent, do in fact attempt to attribute to Aristotle the broader view of moral perception I am developing here.

taken into account in deliberating what to do – specifically, deliberating about which principles govern the situation; (3) knowing the best specification of, and how to implement, the principles one takes to be conclusive in determining what to do. And there are two ways that moral perception reveals a limit to principles themselves as a necessary feature of morality: (1) Moral perception, and action stemming from it, can go on outside the context of principles entirely; (2) accurate moral perception is good in its own right independent of its leading to action.

IV

Let us return to something that Charles Larmore says about "judgment." Larmore says that Aristotle himself had little to say about the way in which such judgment is exercised – only that it is acquired by experience and practice.[22] Yet Larmore does not regard this absence as a defect in Aristotle's view. He agrees that, "although we can understand what kinds of situations call for moral judgment, the kinds of tasks that moral judgment is to accomplish, and the preconditions for its acquisition, there is very little positive we can say in general about the nature of moral judgment itself."[23]

Perhaps one reason Larmore thinks that little can be said about moral judgment is the way he construes the "particularity" of moral judgment. He appears to be thinking that because judgment is particularistic, therefore nothing general can be said about it.[24] Particularity here seems to be taken implicitly as the inexpressible counterpart of general rules (as the earlier quote from Kant also suggests). Such a conception contributes to mystifying the operation of situational perception and judgment.

Our previous discussion suggests that the way people perceive particular situations, and their ability to discern the morally significant character of particular situations, is not mysterious and ineffable but is bound up with general features of their character and their moral makeup. This is partly because (as will be discussed in greater detail below) the perception of particularities is often a sensitivity to particular sorts of particular moral features – injustice, dishonesty, racism, physical pain, discomfort – and much can be said about what promotes those particular sensitivities, and about the obstacles to such sensitivities and how they can be overcome. Once particularity is broken down into particular sorts of moral features and sensitivity to their presence, the

22. *Patterns of Moral Complexity,* p. 19.
23. Ibid., p. 19.
24. Ibid., p. 15.

door is open to exploring the ways that imagination, attention, empathy, critical reason, habit, exposure to new moral categories, and the like contribute to the formation of those sensitivities.

Besides the implication of ineffability, a further way that Larmore's (and others') conception of moral judgment blocks inquiry into its operations – and the operation of moral perception as well – is the idea of "moral judgment" (alternative locutions embodying this same defect are "practical judgment," "situational intuition," "judgment of particulars") as a *unitary* faculty. This conception has been preserved, in fact, in the way I have up to now been talking about perception – as if "perceiving the particularities of situations" were *one* single kind of moral/psychological process.[25]

But situational perception is not a unified capacity. Different parts of one's moral makeup are brought to bear in "seeing" (and not seeing) different features of situations, of moral reality. Different aspects of one's moral reality can draw on different sorts of sensitivities or forms of awareness. In a way, it is misleading to speak of a particular individual as "sensitive to particulars" (or "good at perceiving the moral character of particulars") *tout court*, as the quotation from Kant does. The fact is, particular persons are better at perceiving certain *sorts* of particulars than other sorts.

Here are some morally distinct features of situations which some persons may be better at perceiving than others: suffering, racism, dishonesty, violations of someone's rights, temptations to compromise one's moral integrity. Even the subcategory of moral considerations concerning other people's well-being is not really unified. For example, Theresa's being "blocked" in her perceptions of physical pain would not preclude her from being sensitive to and understanding other sorts of needs or concerns, even in the same other persons. Another example: The hurt of being treated unjustly (as in Yasuko's perception of the black woman) is (in part) a kind of injury different from a hurt not necessarily connected with injustice (e.g., disappointment due to failure in a fair competition, or personal rejection where no one is to blame).

25. Note how Nussbaum refers to moral perception, in a discussion of the importance of such perception to an ethical life: "The subtleties of a complex ethical situation must be seized in a confrontation with the situation itself, by a faculty that is suited to address it as a complex whole" ("Discernment of Perception," pp. 172ff.). See also *Fragility*, p. 301. The idea of such perception as *a faculty* is precisely what I want to criticize here, though as I mention I too have been guilty of this mode of expression and conceptualization. (Nussbaum's excellent discussion of perception has been formative in my own thinking on these matters.)

In the same restricted area of moral considerations having to do with others' well-being, a moral agent's sensitivities can also fail to be unified across different types of persons who are objects of their perceptions. Some people are generally sensitive to the feelings of adults, but not of children; for others, the opposite. More generally, person A may be sensitive to the plight of members of certain groups, or people sharing a certain condition (e.g., blacks, Jews, the socially excluded), but less so, or not at all, to that of others.[26]

The complexity of the way that moral sensitivity and perception operate within persons – and the variety of processes involved in an individual's coming to have multifarious sensitivities – can also be seen in the variety of obstacles to accurate moral perception. For example, for John to see the subway woman's discomfort might simply entail attending to her without his usual self-absorbed distractions. For Theresa to acknowledge Julio's pain would require coming to terms with herself – working through her resistances. This would involve self-knowledge and self-exploration in a way perhaps not essential in John's case.

My view is not that there is some absolute number of distinct moral sensitivities. After all, the ones I have already mentioned could be broken down even further. I mean only to point to an oversimplification in the way sensitivity to particularity is portrayed when seen on the model of a unitary faculty. Such a view fails to reveal – and thus blocks further scrutiny into – the multiplicity of psychic processes and capacities involved in moral perception and moral judgment.

This oversimplification and overunification of moral/psychic phenomena is not confined to an ethic of rule and principle. One can see it also in philosophies which center on emotion-based phenomena such as compassion, sympathy, or empathy. (I here include my own book *Friendship, Altruism, and Morality.*) My discussion suggests that sympathy and empathy are in a sense not unitary phenomena but, rather, collections of at least somewhat distinct sensitivities to different aspects of other people's well-being (discomfort, physical pain, the hurt of injustice, the hurt of disappointment, and the like). One implication of this is that when moral philosophers and educators talk about cultivating sympathy and empathy, accomplishing this will in part involve nurturing or developing some distinct sensitivities, and may involve different tasks

26. The character of Mrs. Hoffman in Carol Ascher's *The Flood* (Freedom, CA: Crossing Press, 1987) is a wonderful example of someone compassionate toward anyone she is able to see as a victim of discrimination, or as a kind of refugee (from, e.g., the flood), but often uncompassionate, insensitive, and harsh to others.

and processes for different persons with respect to different objects of sympathy or empathy.[27]

Larmore's idea that "practical judgment" is a unitary faculty about which little can be said (since it depends on intuiting particulars) accompanies the idea that the only way one can improve one's capacity for such judgment is through practice and habit. (The same idea seems implied in the quote from Kant, above.) There is nothing one can tell people about how to exercise judgment; they simply have to "do it." But seeing the multifarious nature of practical judgment as perception of particulars throws light on the ways and extent to which practice and habit do teach practical judgment, and also broadens the methods by which people can learn to perceive particulars.

Iris Murdoch's notion of an "obstacle" (discussed above), which distorts or blocks accurate perception of moral reality, is helpful here. Such obstacles may prevent an individual from being able to learn from experience and practice how to perceive and judge well in some area of life. For example, Theresa may deal with many people who have physical pain, yet may never get any better at grasping their problem and judging what to do about it. Her own unconscious resistance to opening herself to others' physical pain may constitute an obstacle not only to accurate perception, but also to learning in the way suggested in Aristotle's idea of habit, practice, and experience.[28] Coming directly to grips with one's obstacles may in some cases be necessary for opening oneself to certain aspects of one's moral reality, as well as to learning from experience and practice. Theresa may need to work through – perhaps in some form of therapy – her deep and partly unconscious association of physical pain with weakness, though

27. E. V. Spelman, "The Virtue of Feeling and the Feeling of Virtue," in *Feminist Ethics: New Essays,* ed. C. Card (Lawrence: University Press of Kansas, 1991), develops this point in connection with race and class differences within the same gender. She argues that persons (and in particular women) who are caring and concerned toward others of their own race and class may yet not be so toward women of other races and classes. Owen Flanagan and Kathryn Jackson, "Justice, Care, and Gender: The Kohlberg-Gilligan Debate Revisited," *Ethics,* 97, no. 3, April 1987, make the point that several distinct moral capacities might well be part of what Gilligan calls the morality of care. See also Flanagan, *Varieties of Moral Personality: Ethics and Psychological Realism* (Cambridge, Mass.: Harvard University Press, 1991), Chapters 9–11, for an important assessment of Gilligan's work. In "Three Myths of Moral Theory," p. 291 (in Rorty, *Mind in Action* [Boston: Beacon Press, 1988]), Amelie Rorty notes the diversity of attitudes covered by concepts like "respect" and "love." In general, Rorty's work (in *Mind in Action* and elsewhere) is an important source of insight into the multifarious nature of moral sentiments, attitudes, and virtues, and a caution against the oversimplification of the realm of moral psychology found in much moral theory.

28. Sherman interprets Aristotle's notion of "habit" to include the kind of self-knowledge and redirection of emotion and perception that I am contrasting with a more mechanical conception of habit. See *Fabric of Character,* Chapter 5.

Murdoch herself would be suspicious of such therapy, and, more generally, of any attempt to come to grips with one's moral obstacles by focusing explicitly on them.[29] Yet Murdoch's pessimism about moral change in the face of such obstacles, though insightful about the dangers of self-absorption in the attempt to rid oneself of that very self-absorption, seems overdone. Progress in working through and mitigating these moral obstacles can be made.[30]

V

I want briefly to situate the criticisms I have made of principle-based ethical theories in relation to some other important and influential criticisms. In some cases, these criticisms concern "impartialist" theories, in others specifically principle-based theories, whether impartialist or not.

1. Those that challenge the (impartialist) form of moral principles – for example, by claiming that some principles require greater moral concern toward persons related to us[31]
2. Those addressing the relative force of moral and nonmoral considerations (e.g., connected with the notion of a "personal point of view"), criticizing impartialism for the assumption that an impartial moral point of view necessarily takes precedence over all other practical standpoints[32]
3. Those claiming that impartialism or principle-based theories deny, or at least cannot account for, the unique and irreplaceable worth of

29. I cannot find a citation for this wariness about therapy in Murdoch's *Sovereignty of Good,* and I suspect I may be remembering something said by a character in one of her novels. Many of her novels do exemplify this wariness or suspicion of psychotherapy as involving yet another form of diversion from the task of confronting the moral reality external to oneself.
30. In the section from which the passage from Kant cited earlier is taken – "Introduction to 'Transcendental Judgment in General' " – Kant seems somewhat contradictory in his views concerning the prospects for improving one's capacity for judgment of particulars. On the one hand, he agrees with Aristotle about the necessity for practice, and adds that lack of exposure to examples of particular kinds of situations is a remediable source of poor practical judgment. But in a footnote on the same page (178) he says "Deficiency in judgment is what is ordinarily called stupidity and for such a failing there is no remedy."
31. See, for example, John Cottingham, "Ethics and Impartiality," *Philosophical Studies* 43 (1983); Christina Hoff Sommers, "Filial Morality," *Journal of Philosophy* vol. 83, no. 8, August 1986: 439–58.
32. See, for example, Bernard Williams, "A Critique of Utilitarianism," in *Utilitarianism: Pro and Con,* ed. J. J. C. Smart and B. Williams (Cambridge: Cambridge University Press, 1973); Thomas Nagel, *The View From Nowhere* (Oxford: Oxford University Press, 1986), Chapter 10; David Brink, "Utilitarian Morality and the Personal Point of View," *The Journal of Philosophy* 83, no. 8 (1986): 417–38.

each individual (either within the context of personal relationships or in general)[33]

4. Those claiming that "the particular" – for example, particular judgment – is prior to and more significant in the ethical life than general principle[34]

I mention these familiar alternative criticisms of impartialism and principle-based ethics partly because they are often insufficiently distinguished from the criticism I am mounting in this essay (as well as from one another). I want to make clear that I do not take myself to be making *any* of these criticisms. My view neither entails nor is entailed by any of them, though I believe that my criticisms are consistent with all of them. I can only very briefly attempt to indicate these claims: Regarding (1), issues of perception and particularity arise no matter what the form ("partialist" or "impartialist") of moral principles. Number (2) deals with issues entirely distinct from perception and particularity (which apply in both moral and nonmoral domains). The issue of unique worth in (3) is not engaged by my notions of perception and judgment. Issues of moral perception and judgment obtain whether or not each individual has a unique worth. Regarding (4) I do not claim a priority for perception and particularity over principles. I am saying only that even if principles are taken as an essential feature of moral agency, perception and particularity are nevertheless both (partly) independent from it and no less essential to moral agency.

I do want, however, to focus on one further criticism of impartialist, principle-based theories, associated with the work of Carol Gilligan, Nel Noddings, and others.[35] This view alleges that impartialism is defective because it represents only one domain or "voice" within morality, the other being captured by what Gilligan and Noddings call the "morality of care," yet presents itself as covering the entire domain. Some elaborations of this view bring in notions of perception and particularity as integral to the morality of care. For care involves attention to and sensitivity to particular persons and their situations in a way (it is alleged) not fully recognized by impartialist, principle-based moralities.

33. See for example Martha Nussbaum, "Discernment of Perception," p. 178. Stuart Hampshire, "Morality and Convention," in *Morality and Conflict* (Cambridge, Mass. Harvard University Press, 1983), pp. 135–6.
34. See for example, Nussbaum, "Discernment of Perception"; Kekes, Chapter 7; and John Hardwig, "In Search of an Ethics of Personal Relationships," in *Person to Person,* ed. G. Graham and H. LaFollette (Philadelphia: Temple University Press, 1989).
35. Gilligan, *In a Different Voice* and *Mapping the Moral Domain,* ed. Gilligan, J. V. Ward, J. McL. Taylor (Cambridge: Center for the Study of Gender, Education, and Human Development, 1988); Nel Noddings, *Caring: A Feminine Perspective on Ethics and Education* (Berkeley: University of California, 1984).

This criticism is partially valid, I want to argue, but partially incomplete. We need to distinguish three types – or perhaps aspects – of "particularity." The first and second are involved in every situation, ones involving justice as well as care, impersonal ones as well as those within personal relations. By contrast, the third aspect of particularity is more significant in some moral situations than others.[36]

The first aspect of particularity – the one I have been most concerned with here – is the perception of particular situations. This is an issue for any moral principle or concept. There is a gap between an intellectual adherence to and grasp of principles of justice on the one hand, and the recognition of particular situations confronting one as violating (or otherwise implicating) those principles – just as there is a gap between holding the value of "caring for individuals," and recognizing a given situation as one in which that value is called for. In our cab driver example (number 3) Tim may well be a strong proponent of justice, but he initially fails to see that his own situation involves an injustice. What it takes to be sensitive to actual injustice as manifested in particular situations in one's life is not the same as what it takes to see the character and validity of principles of justice. These involve different (though of course related) aspects of one's moral being. It is not as if the principles themselves already fully contain the sensitivity needed to recognize their applicability, violation, and the like. This is true of any moral virtue or principle, not only ones involving care or compassion for particular persons. Hence, regarding perceptual particularity, proponents of a morality of care are wrong when they claim that "particularity" is involved only in a morality of care and not in an impartialist, principle-based domain or "voice."

Although perceptual particularity is involved in every situation, I have argued that what allows an agent to perceive appropriately and well are a variety of related psychic capacities – not a single monolithic faculty. To put it oversimply, different particularities are governed by different sensitivities.

A second aspect or mode of particularity is what might be called the "particularistic attitude," one which the responsible moral agent brings to every situation. It involves the following: being alive to the ways that a given situation might differ from others (to which it might be superficially similar), not being quick to assume that a noted feature of a situa-

36. Margaret Walker's "What does the different voice say?: Gilligan's women and moral philosophy," *Journal of Value Inquiry* 23 (1989): 123–34, credits Gilligan with at least a confused recognition of the broader scope of particularity for which I am arguing here. My discussion of different aspects of particularity in relation to care ethics is indebted to Walker's excellent account of different strands in Gilligan's thought.

tion correlates with others with which it has been correlated in the past, not being quick to assume that a principle which has been conclusive in similar situations will be conclusive in the current one, and the like. This attitude corresponds to an injunction to "keep in mind the particularity of situations." Such an attitude cannot guarantee accurate, good, or just situational perception. If a person is simply insensitive to certain types of moral features of situations, she may just not perceive them, even when keeping the particularistic injunction in mind. Nevertheless, this attitude is certainly an aid to good perception and can become deeply rooted in a moral sensibility so that it need not be appealed to explicitly in each situation.

In contrast to perceptual particularity and the particularistic attitude – which are implicated in every situation – there is a third aspect of particularity which (for a given, situated agent) some situations involve more than others. I call this "detail particularity." It is here that Gilligan's and Noddings's view of the specific connection of particularity with an ethics of care has merit. In general, (though certainly not always) adequate moral concern for intimates requires a more detailed understanding and sensitivity to such persons as particular individuals than does moral concern for strangers.[37] In general, one needs to know in more detail the friend's feelings, concerns, and interests, and must therefore be more alive to how these might differ from those of others in the same situation, than one does to act well toward a stranger.

Detail particularity differs from the *particularistic attitude* in that the latter bids us be alive to possibly relevant differences between the situation before us and others to which we might otherwise assimilate it, whereas detail particularity involves the process of actually gaining more specific and detailed knowledge about a particular situation. The particularistic attitude is required in every situation, but some situations require more detailed understanding of particularities than others.

Detail particularity differs from *perceptual particularity* in not being bound up so intimately with perception. Detail particularity becomes a factor subsequent to perceptual particularity's coming into play. Once one perceives a particular situation as a moral one, calling for moral response, there remains an issue of the degree of detailed understanding – a finer-grained as contrasted with a coarser-grained – that one needs to make an

37. See the fine discussion on this point by Seyla Benhabib in "The Generalized and the Concrete Other: The Kohlberg-Gilligan Controversy and Moral Theory," in Eva F. Kittay and Diana T. Meyers (eds.), *Women and Moral Theory* (Totowa, N.J.: Rowman and Littlefield, 1986); reprinted in her *Situating the Self: Gender, Community, and Postmodernism in Contemporary Ethics* (Cambridge: Polity Press, 1992).

adequate moral response. The particular moral issues raised in the situation, and the domain of moral concern, alert one to the degree to which one presses toward a finer-grained moral understanding.[38]

VI

Let us bring out more explicitly how the phenomena of moral perception and particularity constitute criticisms of principle-based ethical theories. I fear that many theorists of the latter mold will regard what I have discussed here as perhaps mildly interesting, but as involving nothing inhospitable to a principle-based account of ethics. And this will be correct if one conceives of the task of moral theory as consisting in no more than the working out of, and providing a theoretical rationale for, moral principles. This is certainly one important task of philosophical ethics, and perhaps some practitioners proceed as if it were the only one. Nevertheless, I believe that most adherents of a principle-based ethic have greater aspirations and want to see their approach as involving not only principles themselves but a conception of moral agency as well. Certainly this is true of Kant and Mill, the two forerunners of the still dominant theories on the contemporary scene.

Let me consider three different positions expressive of the view that the conception of moral agency in a principle-based ethic can incorporate moral perception, judgment, and particularity.

1. The conception of moral agency in a principle-based ethic already contains moral perception and particularistic sensitivities.[39]
2. The commitment to the primacy of principle entails a moral commitment to develop perceptual and particularistic sensitivities.
3. The conceptual resources of principle-based theories can be mustered to express what is involved in moral perception and particularistic sensitivity.

The view regarding (1) is that a moral agent cannot achieve a genuine understanding of and commitment to (universal, valid) moral principles without developing along the way sensitivity to situations in which those principles are to be applied, knowledge of how to apply them, awareness of relevant situational detail, and the like. But unless this is made to be

38. Distinguishing three aspects of particularity constitutes a refinement of the notion of particularity used in Chapter 9, "Moral Development and Conceptions of Morality," written earlier than this essay.
39. This position was suggested by Stephen Darwall in his remarks on my presentation at the Hollins Conference on Impartiality.

true by definition, it seems entirely implausible. Surely, as argued earlier, the moral capacities necessary to see the validity of moral principles (to be able to test them for universalizability, or for utilitarian validation), to appreciate why they should be adopted, and to sincerely adopt such principles – all these do not guarantee that one will not miss situations in which those principles apply, that one will know the best specification of those principles in a given situation, that one will have the requisite sensitivities to different aspects of one's moral situations. Certainly one would not say of someone that she had fully grasped the validity of a moral principle if she never noticed when the principle applied. The two sorts of capacities are therefore not entirely distinct. But position (1) requires a much stronger connection than this.

I consider position (2) in its Kantian version, drawing inspiration from Kant's *Doctrine of Virtue.* It says that, if Kant wanted people to adhere to their duty or duties, he must also have wanted them to recognize situations in which they had duties; hence he must have wanted moral agents to develop the capacities necessary to master such situational recognition.[40] That is, he must have wanted agents to develop the perceptual sensibilities and judgmental capacities I have been discussing here. It could also be said that according to Kant there is a duty to cultivate such capacities and sensibilities.

Earlier, I pointed to several problems with this view. Accurate moral perception – seeing injustice, distress, dishonesty where it occurs – has (or can have) moral worth in its own right, not only as a means (even a necessary means) to performance of principled action.[41] And not all morally good action is done from, or covered by, principle or duty.

But even within the domain of principle-based action, position (2) is inadequate. For if one acknowledges the need for a full picture of moral agency – or moral personhood – then my argument has been that situational perception, judgment, and particularistic sensitivities are as central to that agency as is commitment to principle. One gets a significantly

---

40. I take this position to be in the spirit of parts of Herman's "The Practice of Moral Judgment." See, e.g., p. 424: "Might not the ability to discern distress require the development of affective capacities of response? . . . Then we will have found a Kantian argument for the development of the affective capacities, and Kantian grounds for valuing them. Not, of course, valuing them for themselves, but as morally necessary means." See also Rorty, "Virtues and Their Vicissitudes" in *Mind In Action,* pp. 320ff.: "Consistent rationality recognizes that in order for moral intentions to issue in well-formed actions, the will must be supported by the virtues. Since Kantian morality commands the acquisition of the several virtues . . ."

41. This point is argued in Nancy Sherman, "The Place of Emotions in Kantian Morality," in *Identity, Character, and Morality: Essays in Moral Psychology,* ed. Owen Flanagan and Amelie O. Rorty (Cambridge, Mass.: MIT Press, 1990).

different picture of moral agency if one sees the complexity of these capacities and their central role in good character than if one pictures moral agency on the model of the possession of principle (perhaps plus strength of will to carry it out). So, unless the principle-based theorist can show that these capacities can be accounted for within the conceptual resources of the principle-based theory, it is no defense of that theory to say that it can recognize the need for – and even that there is a duty to produce – these particularistic perceptual and judgmental capacities.

This leads us to position (3), which claims just this – that whereas principle-based theories as traditionally understood may not incorporate perception and judgment, they provide the conceptual resources to do so. This position cannot be evaluated in abstraction from a particular principle-based ethic and its resources; so let us consider Kantianism.[42] There are two versions of (3). First, the concepts of Kantianism – rationality, universality, ends – can be used to capture the (proper) objects of perception, judgment, and particularity. That is, the capacities one needs to perceive, to judge, and to be sensitive to are themselves Kantian phenomena.

Even if this were true (which I do not believe), it would not be sufficient to ground the claim that one has accounted for perception (for example) within Kantian categories. Suppose that treating someone as an end encompassed relieving her distress; that is, the Kantian notion of an "end" would have encompassed the object of situational perception (namely distress). It would not follow that holding the principle that one should treat others as ends encompasses the psychic capacity that leads the agent to perceive distress when it is present. Hence Kantian conceptual resources would not have fully accounted for moral perception.

Second, the structure of perception, judgment, and particularistic sensitivity *as moral/psychological capacities* can be accounted for by Kantian concepts.

Yet, if position (1) is abandoned, it is difficult to see the plausibility of this view. Rationality in one's maxims, testing for universalizability, and the like do not capture what it is about someone that makes her sensitive to other persons' distress, or able to discern the best specification of a principle of justice. These seem distinct (though related) aspects of an individual's moral psychology. Perhaps a better candidate would (again) be treating someone as an end. Yet if what one means by this is commitment to the principle of treating others as ends, then such a commitment will guarantee neither seeing when the principle is applica-

42. Position (3), as well as (2), can be found in Herman, "The Practice of Moral Judgment." See pp. 426–8.

ble (i.e., moral perception), nor knowing the best way to implement that principle even when one sees that it is applicable (i.e., moral judgment). On the other hand, if one includes the capacities of perception and judgment within the very notion of "treating as an end," then one will have made the second version of position (3) true only by definitional fiat, rather than by demonstrating the Kantian character of the capacities of perception and judgment.

It might be worth exploring, in the context of a specific example, problems with the idea that sensitivity to an issue of principle guarantees perception of all significant moral features of situations.

In the cab driver case let us imagine that as Tim thinks about the driver's action he comes to see it as racist, unjust, and wrong. He sees that the action violates principles of justice. Contrast Tim here with Yasuko who like Tim perceives the wrongness of the cab driver's action, but in addition directly perceives the indignity done to the black woman passed up by the driver. Tim perceives the injustice – the violation of principle – without perceiving the indignity to the person who suffers the injustice. As this example illustrates, it is possible to grasp the wrongness of an unjust action without actually registering the affront to dignity sustained by the sufferer of the injustice.

This calls into question the idea that sensitivity to actions as violating principle (e.g., a principle of injustice) guarantees or can account for sensitivity to the indignity suffered by the persons who are victims of the violation of that principle. Thus it calls into question the idea that the Kantian capacity for recognizing violations of principle encompasses or guarantees the perceptual sensitivity to the morally significant feature, the suffering of indignity.[43]

One might reply that the notion of dignity is itself Kantian. But one may be sensitive to violations of Kantian principle (e.g., a principle of racial justice) with no guarantee that one is sensitive to issues of dignity. In addition to throwing into question whether – or what it means to say that – the universalizability formulation of the categorical imperative is equivalent to its "end" (or "dignity") formulation, this is further encour-

43. What this argument suggests, I think, is that if the Kantian notion of (respect for) dignity is understood as (respect for) rational agency, then this notion is inadequate to the understanding of "dignity" involved in the thought that the black woman's dignity is affronted by being passed up by the cab driver. On this overrationalistic conception of dignity in Kant see Victor J. Seidler, *Kant, Respect, and Injustice: The Limits of Liberal Moral Theory* (London: Routledge and Kegan Paul, 1986), and Chapter 3, "Mortal Men and Rational Beings," in Raimond Gaita, *Good and Evil: An Absolute Conception* (London: Macmillan, 1991).

agement for the view that commitment to principles does not guarantee situational perception.

I have argued in this section that the phenomena of perception, judgment, and particularistic sensitivities constitute a significant critique of principle-based theories. I also want to emphasize a less combative point. Until recently, the Kantian – and more generally the principle-based, impartialist – traditions have failed to acknowledge and explore those capacities of perception and emotion that neo-Kantians (and many utilitarians and consequentialists) are now acknowledging as essential to a moral life and to an adequate picture of moral agency. My purpose here has been first and foremost to give those capacities their due, to point out something of their complexity, and to indicate the need for further exploration of their nature. If philosophers identifying with Kantianism or with the impartialist tradition share these concerns, then the differences between us seem much less significant than they once did.

POSTSCRIPT

This essay presents itself as concerned with moral perception and moral judgment. In retrospect, I now prefer to think of its central argument in sections II and III in more general terms, as being an account of how a person comes to act on a particular principle in a given situation. In part, this account can be thought of as a theory of "moral agency," but for two reasons that terminology is misleading. First of all, as mentioned in footnote 21, I am concerned not only with *action* but also with (morally appropriate) nonactional responses, such as emotions, attitudes, and the like. Second, as will be discussed below, part of what gets us from situation to action is judgment about whether agency itself is appropriate in that situation, or whether it is better to do nothing, and it may or may not be misleading to see an account of the preconditions of agency as an account of agency itself.

I would now say that there are *seven* steps that take the person from a given situation to action based on moral principle. (I refer to these as "steps" both to emphasize their analytical separateness and also to leave their psychic nature open – for example, whether they are to be thought of as processes, events, faculties. In any case, some of them can go on simultaneously, and situations are often grasped in a gestalt that encompasses several of them.) In one way or another many of these steps are mentioned in the original essay, but I would like to lay them out more systematically here.

The first step is the accurate recognition of a situation's features. Here the situation itself is initially (as the person/agent comes upon it) inchoate – not even yet a distinct "situation" – and the person then takes it to be a situation of a certain character, that is, possessed of certain features (section III).

The second step is to recognize the features of an already characterized situation as morally significant (section III). Putting steps one and two together yields the idea of a person coming upon a situation and perceiving its morally salient features. This is usefully thought of as "moral perception." The two steps are distinct, however, in that in the second the person is confronted with a situation as described, and it is the first step that supplies that description. So Joan's perception of the woman on the subway as suffering (where "suffering" counts as a moral feature) breaks down into the recognition of suffering as going on, and then the taking of suffering to be morally significant.

Whereas the two steps together can usefully be thought of as moral perception, the second by itself might as naturally be thought of as an exercise in judgment – judging a situation's features to be morally significant.

The third and fourth steps involve the matter of whether to engage one's agency in the situation. Taking a situation before one to have a moral character (step 2) does not guarantee that one decide to take action in the situation, nor that it is either appropriate or possible to do so. Often we see that something morally unfortunate or wrong is going on, yet were we to intervene we would only make it worse. In other situations it might not be possible for agent X to act, though if she could it would be good for her to do so. None of the examples presented in the chapter bring this feature out clearly.

I will call steps 3 and 4 together "agency engagement." There are two distinct elements to this, though distinguishing between them in a particular sitaution is not always possible. Step 3 involves moving from the moral characterization of the situation (in step 2) to raising the question of whether one should take some action in the situation. For example, in the cab driver case, when Tim comes to see an injustice as having taken place, he may nevertheless think of that injustice as over and done with, with nothing for *him* to do about it. That is, he may not even raise the question of whether his agency should be engaged by the situation.

It is striking how little attention has been paid within mainstream moral theory to this issue of "agency engagement." Why do some people remain passive – not even raising the issue of taking action – in the face of situations they themselves take to be morally significant, whereas others routinely engage their agency? What are the different moral psychologies operating? More thought needs to be given to these issues.[44]

Step four is the subsequent step of judging whether or not one should in fact take action (or whether doing so is possible) once one has raised the question in the first place. It seems appropriate to think of this step as involving a kind of "judgment," and possibly a kind of moral judgment; but the question raising in step three does not seem usefully characterized either as perception or as judgment. It is, however, a crucial step in the transition from situation to action-on-moral-principle, contrary to the essay's implication that everything in this territory is either "perception" or "judgment."[45]

The fifth step is the selection of a rule or principle that one takes to be applicable to the situation. In the example of Tim and the cab driver, the principle Tim selects is "one ought to take a stand against racism." In the essay I do not conceptualize this as a separate step or process (hence I do not discuss how one comes to pick the principle, or what an appropriate method for doing so would be). To some extent the range of relevant principles will be given by the moral characteristics one attributes to the situation. If there is suffering, one natural principle is "relieve suffering." But there is wide scope for judgment here, for there are several different kinds of principles governing what to do about moral bads (or moral goods) that one has identified in a situation. Hence this step is more than an adjunct to the previous ones, but a process in its own right.

The sixth step is discussed in the essay – determining the act that best instantiates the principle one has selected (section II). I make this step a bit easy for myself by not looking at cases of conflict of principles. As mentioned in footnote 3, what to do when principles conflict is often thought of as paradigmatic of "moral judgment." Yet even if one conceives of the outcome of the latter process as a single, weightiest principle (and it can be a somewhat complex principle, building in qualifications motivated by the competing principles), the task of step six still remains – selecting the act that best specifies this principle. (Moreover a notion of "moral judgment" as selecting among competing principles

44. Carol Gilligan's Chapter 3, "Concepts of Self and Morality," in *In a Different Voice* (Cambridge, Mass.: Harvard University Press, 1982) is an empirical study of these issues. Among other things, Gilligan talks about how women are often socialized for passivity in the face of moral challenges. One of her subjects says, "As a woman, I feel I never understood that I was a person, that I could make decisions and I had a right to make decisions. I always felt that that belonged to my father or my husband in some way, or church" (p. 67).

45. For more clearly distinguishing the issue of "agency engagement" from those of moral perception and moral judgment, I am indebted to a conversation with Bernard Williams (in the context of an NEH Summer Institute in July 1992).

finesses the issue of agency engagement.)[46] Both steps five and six can be thought of as forms of "moral judgment."

The seventh and final step in the situation-to-action-on-principle process is figuring out how to perform the act specified in step six. (This step is not clearly identified in the essay.) For example, although Tim might identify "engaging the cab driver in conversation about the racial incident (with a view to having some impact on the driver's racial attitudes)" as the best specification of his original principle, he might not know how

46. A combination of steps five and six has been called "specification" in an excellent article by Henry Richardson ("Specifying Norms as a Way to Resolve Concrete Ethical Problems"), mentioned in footnote 14. Richardson counterposes specification to two other models of bringing general principles to bear on particular cases. One is "application," in which one directly subsumes a case (a situation) under a given rule by a kind of deductive inference (p. 281). This model is unsatisfactory because the rules so often conflict; so Richardson explores a second model, "intuitive balancing." This involves recognizing the applicability of several principles, and a scrutinizing of all to see which seems to have the greater force in the situation. Richardson criticizes this model for its arbitrariness and for "lack[ing] rational grounding" (p. 287).

Richardson favors a third model, that of "specification," in which an initial general norm is brought to bear on the specific situation in question by means of a more particularized norm that both counts as a modification of the original one (preserving its original moral thrust), and at the same time makes it clearer than the original norm which act should be performed in the current situation. Richardson's model shows how thinking about specifying a norm can help one to clarify and/or modify what one took one's moral commitment to the original norm to be. In some cases this process leads to replacing the original norm with another that, on reflection, one finds more appropriate; this process is distinct from specification itself, in which the moral commitment to the original norm as it stands is retained (though clarified in the new norm).

In the cab driver case, specification might work this way: Tim's initial choice of norm is "take a stand against racism." Tim might decide that "take a stand against racism by trying to prevent the injustice caused by it" is the situationally appropriate specification of this principle, and that it implies that he should make the cab driver return to the train station to see if the woman and child are still there. Alternatively, Tim might decide that he should take the opportunity to engage the cab driver in conversation about this incident, that to do so would best meet the moral concern underlying his original principle ("take a stand against racism"), yet the principle implied in engaging the cab driver is not best seen as a specification of that principle, but rather as a different principle (perhaps "do what one can to lessen racist attitudes and behavior in the world").

Richardson presents his theory as addressing the issue of how rationally to resolve moral dilemmas. As noted earlier, this framing bypasses (by presupposing) all the issues of moral perception and agency engagement (steps one through four) that are implicated prior to the agent's taking herself to be facing a dilemma with its moral description already given. Yet sometimes Richardson implies that his is a theory about the more general matter I am concerned with – getting from the particular situation to the general principle and then to the particular action. In bypassing one through four, however, his account omits too much of the moral processes involved therein to be adequate to this larger task. As an account of steps five and six (rule selection and act specification), however, Richardson's theory is an important contribution to understanding crucial elements in that overall process.

to accomplish this. That is, his attempts to engage the driver might fall entirely flat, produce resentment, or fail to engage the driver's racial attitudes. This gap between act identification and act performance is to be distinguished from weakness of will, in which the agent identifies the act and would be able to accomplish what it specifies were she to perform it, but cannot bring herself to perform the act in the first place.

It would be odd to call step seven either *judgment* or *perception.* In many situations this step presents no problem at all, but where it does the psychic process involved seems morally significant, if not straightfor-wardly moral. It certainly concerns the full functioning of moral agency. A person who consistently selected the right act to perform but could never work out how to succeed in performing the act would be morally incomplete, if not decidedly deficient. Here, too, mainstream moral theory has given us little illumination.

I have attempted in this postscript to clarify the process of a person's moving from a particular situation to action on principle in that situation, but this issue forms only part of the overall argument of the essay. An important part of that argument is that not all moral action does involve "action on principle." Some acts grounded in moral perception, and per-haps judgment as well, are morally good although they do not involve principles.

PART II

Moral excellence

4

Moral exemplars:
reflections on Schindler, the Trocmés, and others

In *The Sovereignty of Good*[1] Iris Murdoch berated Anglo-American philosophers for failing to describe a moral ideal which is of unquestionable excellence and which has the power to inspire us to be better than we are. Murdoch assumed that such a task would involve a fuller moral psychology than the resources of philosophy had at that time been able to provide.

Although the beginnings of such a moral psychology have begun to show themselves in work done within virtue theory, at the same time there has been an attack on moral excellence itself, an attack which has had two sources. The first questions the traditional view that moral considerations – generally associated with an impersonal, impartial, and universal point of view – take automatic precedence over any other action-guiding considerations. Thomas Nagel and, more radically, Bernard Williams argue that considerations of personal satisfaction or self-realization should in some circumstances be allowed to outweigh moral considerations (as defined by an impersonal point of view), while Philippa Foot argues more generally that moral considerations do not always override nonmoral ones.[2]

This attack on the priority of the moral has spawned a second, more direct, attack on moral excellence itself, that is, on the supreme value of a morally excellent life. A weaker form of this attack has it that since many

A small part of this is essay is drawn from a short panel presentation at the Institute on the Virtues at the University of San Diego (February 1986). Earlier drafts were presented at the philosophy departments of Wesleyan University and the College of William and Mary; I thank members of those departments (especially Noel Carroll, then of Wesleyan) for useful feedback and criticism. I wish to thank David Wong for very useful and perceptive comments on a later draft, and, especially, Margaret Rhodes and Owen Flanagan for marvelously detailed and acute readings of the penultimate draft.

1. Iris Murdoch, *The Sovereignty of Good* (London, 1970).
2. Thomas Nagel, *The View From Nowhere* (New York, 1986); Bernard Williams, *Moral Luck* (Cambridge, 1981) and "A Critique of Utilitarianism" in *Utilitarianism Pro and Con* (Cambridge, 1973); Philippa Foot, "Morality as a System of Hypothetical Imperatives" and "Are Moral Considerations Overriding?" in *Virtues and Vices* (California, 1978), and "Morality and Art" in *Philosophy As It Is*, ed. T. Honderich and M. Burnyeat (New York, 1979).

human goods – for example, aesthetic, scientific, athletic – lie outside morality, lives devoted to morality exemplify only one of the many types of human good, and one which cannot be given a general priority over all others. A stronger form of the attack on moral excellence has questioned the human worth of a life centered on moral concerns itself, and has suggested that such a life involves various important deficiencies. Both these lines of argument have been taken by Susan Wolf in her influential article "Moral Saints," but they have been echoed by others as well.[3]

These criticisms of moral excellence raise Murdoch's challenge once again. They remind us how devoid of attempts to articulate the contours of an admirable and worthy life most recent moral theory has been since Murdoch lodged her challenge in the late 1960s. Utilitarianism, and to some extent contemporary Kantianism, although purporting to defend the supremacy of moral considerations in a human life, have given surprisingly little indication of what a person would actually be like who lived a life according to their recommendations. It is especially striking that utilitarianism, which seems to advocate that each person devote his or her entire life to the achievement of the greatest possible good or happiness of all people, has barely attempted to provide a convincing description of what it would be like to live that sort of life.[4] Wolf's article, though largely critical of utilitarianism, has provided more in this direction than have most utilitarian theorists themselves.

This essay attempts a beginning of a psychology of moral excellence, with the ultimate goal of showing that moral excellence is worthy of our highest admiration and, appropriately understood, our aspiration. I will argue here that morally exceptional persons – whom I will call "moral exemplars" or "moral paragons" – are of irreducibly different types (some of which share features in common); and that a recognition of these differences is the first step in a realistic moral psychology of excellence. In the first section of the paper I will consider in some detail one example (Oskar Schindler) of a type of moral paragon or exemplar which I will call the "(moral) hero." The second section will examine the complexi-

3. Susan Wolf, "Moral Saints," *Journal of Philosophy* 79 (August 1982). Foot and Williams make some of these points also. Owen Flanagan, "Admirable Immorality and Admirable Imperfection," *Journal of Philosophy* 83 (January 1986) makes the weaker criticism of moral excellence.

4. A significant and impressive step in that direction, though to my mind an unsatisfactory one, is Peter Railton's "Alienation, Consequentialism, and the Demands of Morality," *Philosophy and Public Affairs* 13 (Spring 1984). Some such attempts in a Kantian direction are Marcia Baron, "The Alleged Moral Repugnance of Acting from Duty," *Journal of Philosophy* 81 (April 1984); Barbara Herman, "Integrity and Impartiality," *The Monist* 66 (April 1983); and Adrian Piper, "Moral Theory and Moral Alienation," *Journal of Philosophy* 84 (February 1987).

ties of determining unworthy motives and their relationship to moral excellence. The third section will distinguish from the moral hero another type of exemplar I will call the "Murdochian exemplar." The fourth section will consider the role of risk and adversity in the determination of moral excellence, primarily in connection with the hero and the Murdochian. The fifth section will distinguish two more types of moral exemplar – the "idealist" and the "responder." (None of the distinctions among types of moral exemplars is meant to be exhaustive, and the discussions will point to other varieties as well.) The sixth section will briefly raise some questions, based on the typology of moral exemplars developed in previous sections, for Susan Wolf's description and assessment of moral excellence. The final section discusses the extent to which ordinary persons can and ought to imitate, emulate, and learn from moral exemplars.

In partially defending moral excellence against various charges of deficiency and unattractiveness, I will not, however, be disputing the reservations which Foot, Williams, Nagel, and Wolf have expressed concerning traditional Kantian and utilitarian assumptions about the supremacy of the impersonal point of view. Rather I will want to show that some of the reasons why Wolf is able to depict moral paragons as unappealing and unworthy is because she, like Williams and Nagel, too fully accepts the identification of morality with an impersonal, impartial, and universalistic point of view. I will thus be suggesting that the conception of morality in terms of which the different types of moral exemplars are seen to be excellent is *not,* or not primarily, that of Kantianism or utilitarianism.

SCHINDLER AS MORAL HERO

I will first discuss in some detail a fascinating character whom I take to be an example of a "moral hero" – Oskar Schindler, portrayed in Thomas Keneally's book *Schindler's List.*[5] Schindler was a German industrialist who ventured to Poland in the late 1930s as an agent of the German intelligence service, in order to avoid duty in the German Army, and with the intention of going into business there. During the Nazi occupation of Poland (1939–1945) Schindler saved the lives of thousands of Jews, at great personal risk to himself (he was arrested several times), and with the ultimate result of losing the entire personal fortune which he had made, primarily from his war-related businesses. Schindler accomplished this feat primarily through employing Jews as workers in his enamelware

5.   Thomas Keneally, *Schindler's List* (New York, 1983).

factory; by cajoling and tricking Nazi officials, he managed to employ many more Jews than were in any way necessary to production, and also to keep them in reasonably good health. He thereby protected all of them.[6] In addition, toward the end of the war Schindler managed to keep his own workers from being shipped to death camps, while also securing the release of three hundred other Jews from Auschwitz, the largest and most notorious of the concentration camps.

This description alone means that Schindler accomplished something morally notable and extraordinary. But accomplishing a great good or preventing a great evil, such as the death of many people, even at great risk to oneself, is not sufficient for moral heroism or excellence. During the war some Jews were saved by Poles who sheltered them in exchange for payment.[7] Although humanity can be grateful for those choosing to take this path rather than (what a much larger number did) to denounce Jews to the Nazis or to fail to provide any help whatsoever when they were in a position to do so, such activity does not constitute moral heroism or excellence, no matter how many endangered Jews an individual saved in this manner (which did generally involve substantial risks). Because such a rescue effort was carried out primarily from the motive of self-interest our moral approval of the act does not lead to a judgment that the agent was morally heroic in performing it.[8]

Oskar Schindler was different from these financially benefiting rescuers in that he saved Jews because he cared about the Jews – at least about the particular Jews he came to know – and because he believed the Nazi

6. Protecting one's Jewish workers was itself a remarkable feat during the Nazi era. During the war the use of Jews as labor for the German war effort normally involved literally working them to death, then replacing them by new, healthier ones; for example, at one IG Farben plant in Germany 25,000 of 35,000 workers died (Keneally, *Schindler's List*, p. 203).

7. A moving account of one such sheltering – of her own family – is described by Nechama Tec in her memoir *Dry Tears* (New York, 1983). Tec describes and analyzes different moral types of Christian rescue of Jews in *When Light Pierced the Darkness* (New York, 1985).

8. In her memoir, Tec relates how, at the end of the war, the family which had sheltered her family did not express satisfaction at having been able to help; they were concerned that their neighbors not realize that the family they had been sheltering (Tec's family) was Jewish. This demoralized Tec's family, and reveals how far from a moral concern was the Polish sheltering family's financial motivation in helping them.

   My brief discussion of nonmorally heroic rescue masks many important distinctions in the motivations of paid rescuers, some of which Tec discusses in *When Light Pierced the Darkness*. For example, some persons may have initially sheltered Jews for money, which they in fact received, but then developed a concern for those or other Jews which led to engaging in riskier activities than they would have taken on merely for the financial reward.

policies abhorrent. These sentiments and moral attitudes, rather than any expectation of reward, prompted his actions.

Yet more seems necessary for moral heroism than accomplishing a great good at great risk to oneself and from morally worthy motives, as we can see by contrasting Schindler during the later period of the Nazi occupation of Poland with the Schindler of 1939 and 1940. In those early years, although Schindler already wanted and intended to help Jews, he did not think that such efforts would result in great losses and risk to himself. Failing (along with many others) to grasp the extraordinary power and evil of the Nazi regime, Schindler seemed to have believed that he would be able to help the Jews *and also* make a great fortune from his manufacturing operations, and that he would escape from the war unscathed. Though Schindler's acts of helping Jews during this period were morally motivated and morally praiseworthy ones, he was not then, or yet, a moral hero. For all one could tell at that point, Schindler might *not* have engaged in a rescue effort if he had realized its financial consequences for himself. Moral excellence seems to require, in addition to a morally worthy motive, some degree of depth of moral commitment, in relation to other desires, dispositions, and sentiments operating in the person's psychological economy. Even though there was no definite point at which Schindler's desire to save Jews did become paramount in his motivation – far outweighing any concern with his own fortune – by the final two years of the war his commitment to saving Jews had certainly attained the requisite depth and centrality in Schindler's scheme of commitments. The morally good rescue efforts of the earlier years had turned into full-fledged moral heroism.[9]

Our discussion of Schindler so far has yielded three criteria of "moral heroism": (1) a moral project – bringing about a great good or preventing a great evil; (2) morally worthy motivation; and (3) deep rootedness of that morally worthy motivation in the individual's system of motivation. But what counts as "morally worthy motivation"? I cannot give a full account here, but want to make clear that I am rejecting a purely Kantian conception of that category, which restricts it to "doing what is right because it is right" or "acting from (a sense of) duty." The sense of duty seems to me insufficiently broad to encompass the full range of moral motivation involved in morally excellent activities and lives. I want to suggest that other morally worthy motives include: direct concern for

9. I have no general account of how one discerns "depth of moral commitment," nor of the degree of such commitment requisite for moral heroism or moral excellence more generally.

the well-being of individual persons or groups of persons; personal and communal ideals not (necessarily) seen as duties.[10]

In addition to these three criteria, a fourth seems involved in the form of moral excellence which Schindler seems to exemplify – the facing of risk or danger. It is not only that the facing of risk can be one way of testing for the presence of the third criterion – depth of moral motivation.[11] But there seems, in addition, an element of admiration attached in its own right to the doing of good in the face of risk, an admiration captured, as J. O. Urmson suggested in his seminal article on this subject, by the notion of "hero."[12]

UNWORTHY DESIRES

The portrayal of Schindler so far may seem to omit what to many readers of Keneally's book is one of its most striking features – the moral *ambiguity* of its central character. There are aspects of Schindler's life and character which could be thought to render him less than morally excellent or exemplary. Discussing some of these will help us to examine Schindler in light of the second criterion (morally worthy motives), and also to confront a fifth criterion of moral heroism, namely "faultlessness," or the relative absence of unworthy desires, sentiments, and attitudes. Moral exemplars must have not only morally good desires as their primary motives, but must also *not* possess too much in the way of unworthy states of consciousness, to some extent independent of their direct motivational role. Discussing Schindler's possible faults and foibles will help us to see how far from moral faultlessness or purity of consciousness someone must be for us no longer to regard him or her as a moral exemplar.

I shall discuss five aspects of Schindler's behavior or motivation which arguably detract from his moral excellence: (1) Schindler's love of pleasure, especially sex and drink; (2) his unfaithfulness to his wife; (3) his

10. A defense of part of this broader conception of moral motivation is given in my *Friendship, Altruism, and Morality* (London, 1980) and in other essays in this volume.
11. However, willingness to take risks is neither necessary nor sufficient for depth of moral commitment or motivation. It is not necessary because a person may be deeply committed to a moral project which perhaps does not involve great risks, but commitment to which can be shown by the conscientiousness and dedication with which the project is pursued in the face of competing pulls. It is not sufficient, for even the willingness to take some particular risk (in service of a moral project) could itself be a relatively ephemeral element in a given individual's life or character, for example in an individual for whom taking risks had a psychological appeal in its own right.
12. J. O. Urmson, "Saints and Heroes," in *Essays in Moral Philosophy*, ed. A. I. Melden (Washington, 1957).

ready ability to lie, when doing so furthered his ends; (4) his adventurousness or attraction to taking risks; and (5) his apparent attachment to his power and self-image as a kind of "savior-father" of the Jews in his factory.

1. Keneally portrays Schindler as a *bon vivant,* almost a libertine. He was a sensual man, and seemed entirely unashamed of his devotion to sex and the pleasures of food, drink, and fast cars. These features certainly do not sit well with a common understanding of what it is for someone to be "highly moral," or a "very moral person." For many persons the notion of "moral" excludes a full sensuality (or perhaps much sensuality at all), and especially excludes a valuing of sexual pleasure purely for its own sake, in no particular connection with marriage.[13]

As Alasdair MacIntyre and others have pointed out, the notion of "moral" encompasses several traditions of thought; and we are familiar with one which connects it intimately with sexual prohibitions.[14] I would suggest, however, that such a denial of sensuality and sexuality would be difficult to further justify in terms of the broader perspective of concern for human well-being characteristic of other traditions and elements within our honorific concept of "moral."

2. Schindler's infidelity to his wife Emilie is another matter, though as Keneally describes it (and this aspect is not really much discussed in the book), Schindler's open sexuality was closely connected with his seeming lack of concern for sexual fidelity. It is difficult not to regard this as a moral deficiency in Schindler – it certainly appeared to cause his wife some degree of pain – though one would have to know more about the specific nature of Emilie and Oskar's relationship (as well as his relationships with his two mistresses in Poland) to know precisely how to assess it. There is no suggestion that Oskar otherwise mistreated Emilie, and it is relevant that they lived apart during Oskar's years in Poland, and that when Oskar returned to Germany in the final year of the war Emilie worked closely with him in his rescue activities.

This infidelity certainly renders Schindler *less* of a moral paragon than he would otherwise be; but he remains, I think, a moral hero.

3. Schindler's lying and deception were integral to his project of saving Jews. He could succeed in the complex and risky project of inefficiently and wastefully employing more and more Jews and keeping

13. Margaret Rhodes has suggested to me that the troubling element in Schindler's sensuality is that he continued his sensual enjoyments in the face of the material deprivation that the Jews who worked for him suffered (though there is no suggestion that by depriving himself of these pleasures Schindler could have rendered their lives any better). This interesting point raises issues I am unable to pursue here.
14. Some part of the history of the relations between morality and sexuality is discussed by Michel Foucault in *The Use of Pleasure* (New York, 1985).

71

them reasonably healthy and out of the clutches of the Nazis only by a deep and continually maintained deception that he was devoted to production for the war effort. When inspectors came to visit his factory "he would play the somber, baffled, manufacturer whose profits were being eroded."[15] Schindler was clearly aware of his ability to strike up relationships with all sorts of people and make them think him an affable fellow. He had to maintain a semblance of friendship with morally repulsive characters, such as Amon Goeth, the head of the local labor camp, who would shoot inmates at random. Although all would agree that even paragons of honesty ought to lie to Nazis if this is necessary to save lives, only certain kinds of personalities could have pulled off the sort of vast and intimately maintained deception that Schindler did; and a person considered to be devoted to truthfulness would probably not have been such a one.[16]

It is significant, however, that there is no suggestion that Schindler was a generally dishonest or untrustworthy person, for example, in relationships with those he respected or from whom he needed nothing for his rescue efforts, nor that he enjoyed deception for its own sake (though he may have enjoyed deceiving Nazis). Thus, although it might be that Schindler lacked the highest embodiments of the virtue of honesty, it would not be true to say that Schindler's lying and deception to the Nazis constitute a moral *deficiency,* and certainly not one which detracts from his moral heroism. What this indicates (contrary to a strong "unity of the virtues" view) is that not all virtues can be combined within one person in all situations, and that moral excellence does not require possession of every virtue; further, it suggests that there will be irreducibly different types of moral excellence.

4. In his study of some Christian rescuers of Jews, Perry London finds a "spirit of adventurousness" in many of them;[17] one certainly sees this in Schindler. Such a spirit may draw some people to the risky activity of

15. Keneally, *Schindler's List,* p. 343.

16. On the matter of the sort of personality needed to carry out a morally necessary but complex and long-term deception, it is noteworthy to contrast Schindler with Magda Trocmé, a prominent rescuer of Jews and deceiver of Nazis, who will be discussed further below. Magda never became emotionally reconciled to the deceptions – e.g., the making of false ration cards – which she had to practice during the Nazi occupation of France, and clearly kept them to a bare minimum. (See Philip Hallie, *Lest Innocent Blood Be Shed: The Story of the Village of Le Chambon and How Goodness Happened There* [New York, 1979], p. 126.) Being deceptive, even to Nazis and when necessary to save lives, disturbed Magda Trocmé in a way it did not disturb Schindler.

17. Perry London, "The Rescuers: Motivational Hypotheses About Christians Who Saved Jews From the Nazis," in *Altruism and Helping Behavior,* ed. J. Macaulay and L. Berkowitz (New York, 1970).

rescue of threatened persons or refugees (e.g., in the "underground rail-road" at the time of slavery, or helping to provide sanctuary for Central American political refugees).

To assess this "attraction to risk," we must distinguish between a person who gets positive gratification from risky activities, and one who does not but who is not so *averse* to such activities that she is unable to engage in them when she has a strong moral impulse to do so. Schindler certainly falls within the former category, but the distinction is important, since it might be a psychologically necessary condition of engaging in risky, long-term rescue operations that one not be too averse to taking risks, that one can accept risk. We can perhaps put this point by saying that one must have a "spirit of adventurousness" to *some degree* in order to exemplify that form of moral excellence.

Further, among those who, like Schindler, possess that spirit of adventurousness not minimally but more fully, one must distinguish between the spirit of adventurousness being motivationally *necessary* to get the rescuer to act, and it being an element of attraction of the endeavor but not actually necessary to get the rescuer to act. Yet this distinction begins to break down somewhat in regard to long-term activities such as Schindler's. Certainly his primary motives in *planning to undertake* rescue of Jews seemed entirely moral ones (concern for those Jews; belief that the Nazi policies were wrong); there is no suggestion that love of adventure or risk constituted a distinct, initial, direct motivation toward the activities in question. Nevertheless what motivates the initiating of a long-term project is different from the various motives which over time sustain the complex activities that constitute the project. Perhaps this can be put by saying that for Schindler the concern for Jews' lives was a necessary condition for his spirit of adventurousness playing a motivational role in sustaining his risky activities of rescue; without the former the latter would not have moved him toward rescue at all.

If this is right about Schindler, then his love of adventure is not a moral deficiency, nor does it detract from his being a moral hero. "Love of adventure" is not itself a morally *unworthy* motive, and if it is not playing an autonomous motivational role, then its presence should not be seen as a moral deficiency.

Accepting this, however, one might yet say that love of adventure is not itself a positively morally *worthy* motive; so Schindler represents a less pure case of moral excellence than someone for whom moral projects are animated by purely moral motives. Such a purer case of moral excellence seems represented by Magda Trocmé, described in Philip Hallie's book, *Lest Innocent Blood Be Shed.* [18] Magda was one of the two guiding spirits of an extraordinary rescue effort during the Nazi occupation of France. Under the leadership especially of Magda's husband André, the French Protestant village of Le Chambon sheltered thousands of refugees (mostly Jews) from the Nazis during the war years; Hallie claims that Le Chambon was the safest place for Jews in Europe. During that time Magda Trocmé worked tirelessly in caring for the refugees who arrived at Le Chambon. She exhibited great courage and resourcefulness in finding shelter for them and helping to sustain the village's system of rescue; she fed them and took some into her own home. These were all very risky activities for her; yet there is no suggestion of an attraction to risk itself such as was involved in Schindler's courage in facing similar risks.

At the same time Magda Trocmé managed to hold together her family – her husband and four children – with love and understanding, and with attention to their individual needs, in the midst of the tension and danger occasioned by the rescue effort. Her husband André thought of her thus, "Here is a person who cares for others on their own terms, not in order to parade her own virtues, but in order to keep them well. . . . She cared for others . . . both emotionally and in action" (64–5). There is no suggestion in Magda Trocmé of any less than morally worthy motive, such as one sees in Schindler.

Magda Trocmé does seem a more admirable character and a purer case of moral excellence than does Schindler. She combines the bringing about of a great good or the prevention of great evil, at risk to herself, performed from moral motives rooted deep in her character, and with an absence of less than morally worthy motives. (Magda Trocmé will be discussed further below.) But it does not follow from this that Schindler's love of adventure (in the particular role it played in his motivation) either disqualifies him from moral excellence (of the morally heroic sort), or constitutes an actual moral deficiency.

5. Schindler's attitude toward his own role as the central figure in the rescue effort presents a more complex matter. Schindler was able to help the Jews who worked for him only because of his position of power, his contact with various German officials (locally and in the armaments administration), and his ability to pull strings. In itself this fact does not detract from his moral accomplishment, but Schindler's attitude toward that power is significant. There is some suggestion at various places in the account of Schindler's life that he was a bit too taken with his role as savior of his Jews.

18. All subsequent page references concerning Magda and André Trocmé and Le Chambon will be to this book.

There are some parallels here to our discussion of the spirit of adventurousness. Schindler's attachment to his power is not an autonomously operating motive; it is only his power *as a helper* that he is attached to. So the concern to save the lives of Jews is a necessary condition for that motive to operate. Nevertheless there seems an important moral distinction between the two motives. For whereas love of risk or adventure seems morally neutral, attachment to power seems morally unworthy. Thus the degree of this motive's role in Schindler's motivational system seems a significant issue for determining his moral excellence.

A full treatment of this complex point is not possible here. Because of Schindler's unique situation, it is very difficult to discern the degree to which his desire that-Jews-be-saved-by-him corrupted his desire that-Jews-be-saved. But it is relevant to note that Schindler deeply respected several of the Jews with whom he worked closely in the financial and administrative end of the enamelware company; he was clearly aware of his reliance for the success of his projects on these Jews and their own virtues of courage, resourcefulness, and moral strength. Moreover, it seems significant that when the Allied armies finally gained control of the German territory where Schindler had moved his operations, roles were completely reversed, and Schindler became entirely dependent on the Jews to protect him from being killed or taken prisoner. Although Keneally does not delve into Schindler's emotions at the time, Schindler did seem to accept this situation of dependency, and continued throughout the rest of his life to remain in personal and emotional contact with several of his former workers. These events suggest, though by no means conclusively, that Schindler's attachment to his sense of power over the Jews did not run nearly as deep as his concern for their welfare.

I claim, then, though acknowledging uncertainty about this, that Schindler meets the five criteria for the moral hero: (1) bringing about a great good (or preventing a great evil); (2) acting to a great extent from morally worthy motives; (3) substantial embeddedness of those motives in the agent's psychology; (4) carrying out one's moral project in the face of risk or danger; and (5) relative "faultlessness," or absence of unworthy desires, dispositions, sentiments, attitudes.

MURDOCHIAN MORAL EXEMPLARS

We have no trouble seeing Magda Trocmé and (though perhaps to a lesser extent) Oskar Schindler as living morally worthy lives, as being extraordinarily admirable. And yet there exists a very different picture of the moral exemplar in the history of moral thought. This is a picture articulated, though somewhat sketchily, in Iris Murdoch's writings, including her novels but especially the philosophical essays in *The Sovereignty of Good.* It is a picture of the good, humble, selfless person, an inheritor of a familiar Christian conception, and one perhaps closer to what people mean when they refer to "saints," taking this term in a not necessarily directly religious sense, and yet a sense strongly influenced by that religious heritage.

An example of the Murdochian paragon can be drawn (with one significant variation, which will be discussed below, footnote 26) from the character of Ed Corcoran in Mary Gordon's *Men and Angels.*[19] Ed has a young son and a wife with a terrible disease, contracted during her pregnancy with their son, which has distorted her body, made her generally unable to take proper care of herself, and unbalanced her mentally. Rose Corcoran says horribly embarrassing and hurtful things in front of other people; she is evidently a terrible trial to live with; yet Ed seems to care for her without resentment or bitterness, yet also without illusion. Rather than dwelling on how terrible her condition is, Ed chooses to view her in relation to the progress she has made since an earlier time, when for example she could not even walk. Ed's admirable character is shown also in his relationship with his son, for whom he is the primary parent and whom he takes with him when he does electrical work in people's houses. Ed has managed through his love and understanding of his wife and his child to shield the boy, at least to some extent, from his mother's terrible behavior and to help him to be reasonably happy. Ed treats other people too (though in the book one sees only the people he works for) with kindness and respect. He is generous and warm-hearted, where one might have expected bitterness, resentment, and envy. He is responsible and conscientious. He leads an admirable life in the face of a great tribulation. He exemplifies many significant virtues and appears to lack what Murdoch calls "the avaricious tentacles of the self": self-pity, envy, overconcern with the opinion of others, self-absorption, concern for power.

In contrast to the moral hero, the Murdochian moral exemplar is not necessarily engaged in a "moral project," a bringing about of great good or preventing a great evil. That there can be this sort of moral excellence is especially significant in light of Susan Wolf's portrayal of what she calls the "moral saint." Wolf gives two different descriptions of that figure – first, that the person has the virtues or excellences of character to an extraordinary degree; and second, that the person is devoted to

19. Mary Gordon, *Men and Angels* (New York, 1985).

maximizing the good of others or of society. It is the second of these descriptions – maximizing overall good – which in fact plays the larger role in Wolf's argument, though she implies that the two descriptions correspond. But as Robert Adams points out in his reply to Wolf,[20] these two descriptions are by no means identical. A person who has the virtues to an extraordinary extent is not necessarily someone devoted to doing good (much less to *maximizing* the amount of good in the world). The converse is true as well; as the example of Schindler shows, a person sincerely devoted to a moral, good-producing project can well lack certain important virtues.

(From this point on I will, for stylistic reasons, sometimes refer to the Murdochian paragon as the "saint," attempting to use this concept without its religious overtones, without the connotations of self-sacrifice which it often carries in common parlance, and also as distinct from Wolf's characterization, especially those aspects connected with Kantianism and utilitarianism.)

The moral saint and the moral hero share three features in common – they are animated by morally worthy motives, their morally excellent qualities exist at a deep level of their personality or character, and they meet the standard of relative absence of unworthy desires.

But there is another difference between them besides the absence of "moral project" in the Murdochian paragon: the standard of "absence of unworthy states of consciousness" is more stringent for her than for the moral hero. In a sense the moral project of the moral hero can be seen (as in the case of Schindler) as counterbalancing a somewhat less-than-pure consciousness. For the saint, by contrast, it is precisely the higher standard of faultlessness which is salient, though this does not mean that the moral saint is to be pictured as, so to speak, spiritually excellent but remote from engagement with the world of action. Part of severing this notion of saint from its religious roots is to ensure that the sense of excellent motivation and excellent form of moral consciousness in the Murdochian paragon not be seen on the model of a purely inner spiritual purity, but precisely that it concern the way one acts within the world of other persons. It is the greater absence of unworthy or suspect elements of consciousness, not a greater remoteness from the world, which distinguishes the saint from the hero.

So far I have discussed the moral hero and the moral saint as if they were entirely parallel types of moral exemplar. But there is an important disanalogy between them, though the difference is perhaps only one of degree. To call someone a moral hero is not necessarily to refer to more

20. Robert Adams, "Saints," *Journal of Philosophy* 81 (July 1984).

than a specific, time-limited (though necessarily substantial) slice of her life. Thus (as we will discuss further below) Schindler's heroism lasted only the length of the war. He did not seem to continue being "morally excellent" after that. The notion of moral heroism allows for that time limitation; the notion of moral saint, or Murdochian paragon, does not. A person cannot be a Murdochian paragon for three or four years, reverting then to moral mediocrity. Although the moral commitments and relatively faultless motivation characteristic of the moral hero must also be deeply rooted, they do not need to be *as* deeply rooted in the moral hero's character as in the Murdochian paragon's. The Murdochian paragon must be more resistant to change. If someone who appears to be a saint begins to act, and continues to do so, in a morally nonexcellent manner, this generally indicates that we were wrong to think her a saint in the first place.

But this does not mean that the Murdochian paragon's character must be *totally* resistant to change or undermining. In very extraordinary situations, under extreme sorts of pressures, a person who is good can become mediocre, or even bad, without this showing that she was never really good in the first place. Where to draw this line is a difficult matter; distinguishing cases of change of character from variations within the same character will be a difficult task.[21]

The positive features of the saint and hero can be combined in one individual. Magda Trocmé appears to meet the Murdochian standard of faultlessness, yet she also brought about a great good. Obviously such a person is rarer than either of the single types alone.

The absence of a single picture of the moral exemplar may in part be a reflection of the different traditions of moral thought mentioned earlier. According to ordinary usage it may even be more natural to see the Murdochian paragon than the moral hero as "very moral" or "morally virtuous." It would be intelligible to say that Ed Corcoran was a "better person" than Oskar Schindler. Certainly a recognizable tradition within our own thinking does in fact connect the term "moral" more closely with an excellence and purity of inner motivational state than with the bringing about of good. In a certain sense this is a point on which the Kantian emphasis on inner motivation comes together with the Aristotelian emphasis on individual character, virtue, and motivational state, despite their differences in other important respects. Both contrast with a

---

21. The argument of this paragraph concerning the degrees of vulnerability and invulnerability of different types of morally excellent characters is influenced by Martha Nussbaum's Chapter 11 of *The Fragility of Goodness* (Cambridge, 1986), on character and vulnerability in Aristotle.

tradition such as the utilitarian which, while requiring appropriate motivation in its assessment of character, connects moral excellence more closely with the production of good. Schindler's form of moral excellence might more naturally be expressed by saying that his *life* (or an important portion of it) exemplifies moral excellence, or that he led a *morally exemplary life,* than by locutions (such as "morally virtuous") which emphasize *state of character,* and apply more naturally to the moral saint.

Apart from these considerations, is there more to be said about whether we should attach more value to the moral saint or to the moral hero? There is one popular tradition of thought ("charity begins at home") which would aver that virtue in one's personal and domestic life is more fundamental than concern for those unrelated to oneself; this tradition might, for that reason, accord greater moral merit to Ed Corcoran than, say, to Schindler. But the overly privatized vision of morality expressed in that sentiment may itself be a socially and historically limited one; a society and moral culture in which concern with the wider communities of city, nation, and humanity in general are seen as fundamental to a morally responsible life would reject such a prioritizing of the "private" to the "public" (which is not to say that it would *reverse* that prioritizing).[22]

In light of this argument, can one say that the more privatized moral saint (such as Ed Corcoran) cannot be morally exemplary if, although generous, loving, courageous, and understanding toward those close to him, he evinces no concern for wider communities of persons? Both Bishop Butler and J. S. Mill appear to vindicate, if not actually to justify, the more limited scope of moral concern, by saying that many, even most, people are never or virtually never in a position to take the public good as their province.[23] But modern civilization has undercut the support for that position; there are now ways for most individuals to have an impact on their wider communities, and even on the world as a whole, unimagined in the periods when those philosophers lived.

At the same time, it would be going too far in the other direction to say

22. A recent current of thought, represented for example by Alasdair MacIntyre, *After Virtue* (Notre Dame, Ind., 1982), Robert Bellah et al., *Habits of the Heart* (Berkeley, 1985), Michael Sandel, *Liberalism and the Limits of Justice* (Cambridge, 1982), has argued that we live and are formed in our essential being by wider communities than just our family and friends; so that moral responsibilities toward those wider communities are as important as are the responsibilities of private life.
23. Joseph Butler, Sermon 5, section [3], in *Five Sermons* (Indianapolis, 1983), p. 58. J. S. Mill, Chapter 2 of *Utilitarianism* (Indianapolis, 1979), p. 19. In the latter passage, Mill is trying to show that utilitarianism does not have the consequence that each individual must take the good of all persons, or all of society, as the goal of his every action.

that a person who evinces no concern for the wider community cannot be a moral exemplar. Whether some such individual can be an exemplar depends very much on the particular circumstances, the degree of exposure of the individual to the concerns of the wider community, the ethos of the person's own community, and the like.[24] But I think we have to allow that often we properly do have great admiration for the Ed Corcorans of the world, and regard them as moral exemplars.

Thus, both moral heroes and Murdochian moral paragons seem to be exceptionally admirable and exemplary persons, and are so in a way recognizably moral – as opposed, say, to exemplifying nonmoral excellences, such as artistic talent, personal charm, athletic ability, physical beauty, theoretical intelligence.[25] Both involve morally excellent motivation as well as good action in the world; but the differences between them may reflect an irresolvable difference in understandings of notions of morality or different interests involved in what it is to assess someone as "morally excellent."

RISK AND ADVERSITY

I have described the Murdochian exemplar without mentioning the element of risk, which was central to the merit of the moral hero. Urmson

24. One factor which seems to affect our assessment of persons in light of the "wider/narrower concern" issue connects with the way in which a given person is, in Michael Sandel's term, "encumbered." (See Sandel, *Liberalism and the Limits of Justice.*) A slightly happier term for the same concept is "implicated," used by Philip Selznick in "The Idea of a Communitarian Morality," *California Law Review* 75 (1987). Consider an individual who is "encumbered" or "implicated" as a member of an oppressed group, and whose morally excellent life is devoted to the welfare of that group only, evincing no concern for wider communities. I think we are more willing to regard such a person (for example, Harriet Tubman) as a moral exemplar (provided that she meets the other requirements) despite that limitation than we would someone with a similarly limited scope of moral concern but not so encumbered.

25. This is not to deny the difficulties in drawing a firm distinction between moral and nonmoral excellences; the existence of distinct traditions concerning morality would lead one to expect such difficulties. Certain excellences – for example, perceptiveness, understanding, resourcefulness, even sense of humor – seem to me to strain that distinction.

At the same time I very much want to resist attempts, such as one finds in Aristotelian-influenced writers, to eschew or greatly minimize the importance of the moral-nonmoral distinction altogether; see for example Martha Nussbaum, *Fragility of Goodness*, pp. 4–5, 28–30, and Amelie Rorty, *Mind in Action* (Boston, 1988). And I wish to resist the move of those who construe morality as the perspective of the practical "all things considered" (a view vigorously defended by Lawrence Becker in Chapter 1 of his *Reciprocity* [London, 1986]). I am aware, however, that I have done little by way of explaining that distinction, though I mean "moral" to have more in common with what Bernard Williams means by "ethical" than what he means by "moral" in his *Ethics and the Limits of Philosophy* (Cambridge, 1985).

distinguished a "saint" from a "hero" in that the former performed great morally worthy actions at great *cost* or *sacrifice* to himself, whereas the latter performed these actions in the face of *danger* or *risk* to himself. Urmson was correct to link our idea of heroism to danger and risk, and to distinguish it from another kind of moral excellence which did not involve these elements. But was Urmson correct to see cost or sacrifice playing an analogous role in the saint? Certainly the adversity constituted by Ed Corcoran's wife's illness, and Corcoran's ability to live with this honorably, is an important element in the exceptional merit which we see in Corcoran's character and life.

But although adversity in the saint's life can play a role analogous to risk in the moral hero's, adversity cannot be identified with sacrifice and cost. "Sacrifice" and "cost" are concepts to a significant degree (though by no means entirely) internal to or relative to a particular person's conception of value in his or her life; this is much less true for adversity and risk. There can be no doubt that Ed Corcoran's wife's illness constitutes adversity for him, but Ed's own sense of identity and value may well be so bound up with his marriage to her, with his sense of the value of marriage and faithfulness, and with his family, that the notion of Ed's sacrificing himself for his wife, or the marriage involving a cost to him, seems not the best way of expressing the fact that there are possible goods in life which Ed cannot pursue because of this marriage.[26]

Thus, contrary to Urmson, "cost" and "sacrifice" do not play the same role with regard to saints (Murdochian paragons) as risk and danger do with regard to heroes. But in addition, although the one example we have given of the Murdochian paragon (Ed Corcoran) does involve adversity, and that adversity is part of its moral excellence, in fact confronting adversity can by no means be seen as a *requirement* of this form of moral excellence. A person's motivational system can be built around morally worthy motives without her really facing any significant adversity. A person can be exceptionally generous, caring, honest, and kind in the absence of adversity. (However some virtues – such as courage – seem by

---

26. I would like to mention here the element in Mary Gordon's portrayal of Ed Corcoran which I am leaving out in my own version of "Ed Corcoran." Late in the book Gordon portrays Ed's devotion to his wife as resting on an unconscious regarding of Anne Foster – the woman for whom he has been doing some work, and the novel's central character – as a "charade wife, someone doing in another house all the things that were not done in his" (p. 371). It would be fascinating to explore how this unconscious motivation affects our moral assessment of Mary Gordon's Ed Corcoran: Does it, for example, make of his devotion to his actual wife a sham, and deprive it entirely or at all of moral value? I am assuming, however, that we can imagine an "Ed Corcoran" such as I have described him but without this self-deceptive element in his character (important as that element is for Gordon's fictional personage).

81

definition to require adversity.) This does not mean that such a person would never face some kind of temptation to act contrary to those virtues – that situation is unimaginable. But conflicts from various personal interests or inclinations are not the same as genuine adversity, and in fact many persons' lives, including those of Murdochian paragons, can fortunately be spared adversity such as Ed Corcoran's.

Something analogous is true of risk as well. A person may exhibit the form of moral excellence (to which we have not given a name) which is like moral heroism but without the element of facing risks. A person can have the required depth of moral commitment to a moral project, act from worthy motives, and have the requisite degree of absence of unworthy ones, without facing serious risks or adversity. This is very nicely illustrated in John Berger's *A Fortunate Man*,[27] a nonfiction account of a doctor, John Sassall, who chooses to establish a medical practice in a poor remote village in the north of England. Sassall is acutely aware that the villagers have few resources to develop themselves, and his choice of where to set up his practice stems importantly from an ideal of service to the needy villagers. At first he is attracted by the excitement of emergency medicine (and is somewhat impatient with patients presenting lesser complaints) and by its sense of concrete accomplishment. But gradually Sassall comes to realize that in order to attend fully to the health of the villagers, he must understand them as whole human beings, beyond their medical condition narrowly defined, and must expand – one might say "morally expand" – his sense of what it means to be a doctor in that village. Berger describes how Sassall comes to care for the villagers in a fuller way than the ideal of "service," admirable as that is.

Although occasionally frustrated and despondent at what he is unable to do to make the lives of the villagers better, Sassall retains a belief in the worth of each life he tends. He emerges from the book an excellent man (at least in relation to the villagers – Berger does not deal with his family life at all), exemplifying many virtues, and bringing great benefit to his patients and to the village in general. And we learn how Sassall came to develop his greater depth of moral character in the process of his work. We can think of Sassall as (or as close to being) a moral exemplar (though neither a hero nor a saint).

Yet the burden of the title of the book – "a fortunate man" – is that Sassall is a man for whom life has worked out very well. In contrast to most of the people in the village, he has had options and has ended up with what he knows that he values; and he lacks few goods that he

27.   John Berger, *A Fortunate Man* (Harmondsworth, 1969).

genuinely wants. He is part of a community within which he has an honored and meaningful place. In contrast to Schindler, Magda Trocmé, and Ed Corcoran, Sassall does not face serious risks, danger, or adversity; in a straightforward sense he has much more in the way of well-being than they. Yet like them he is morally excellent.

Thus it is possible for morally excellent qualities to exist and to inform a good part of a life, yet without being tested in the face of grave adversity or risk. This is not to deny that we may feel of some persons that their lives have been too sheltered to count them unequivocally as exceptionally virtuous, even though they give evidence of being so. And there may be persons of whom we think that if they *did* face certain moral challenges they would be unable to meet them, and that this counts against saying, now, that they are exceptionally good persons. Nevertheless, it cannot be a *general* test of the attribution of virtue, or of exceptional virtue, that one be confident that it not weaken in the face of various situations the person has not faced and is not likely ever to face. This is partly because, as I have tried to indicate, there are different kinds of moral excellences; and while it is unlikely that Schindler would have maintained the virtue of an Ed Corcoran in the sort of situation Ed faced, this does not count against Schindler's being himself morally excellent.[28]

"IDEALIST" AND "RESPONDER"

Another distinction among moral exemplars, which cuts across that of hero and Murdochian paragon, I will call "responder" and "idealist"; as in the case of saint and hero the difference may not be a sharp one, and is also not meant to be exhaustive. The idealist is someone who consciously adopts general moral values and principles, ones which, from the outside, can be regarded as high or demanding moral standards (though they need not be seen that way by the idealist herself); she then goes about attempting to live up to these ideals, and searches for ways to implement them. To be an idealist, the agent must see these ideals as more than merely personal goals or a personal conception of the good. They must be formulated as general values, and regarded by the agent as having some kind of intrinsic worth or general validity.

The idealist must in some way believe that it is *possible* for her ideals

28. On my penultimate draft of this paper, Owen Flanagan rightly pressed the point that an attribution of moral excellence has, at least in many instances, something to do with an assessment of how a person *would* act in various hypothetical situations. I have not been able to think this important issue through systematically, and am aware of the sketchiness of my few remarks on it here.

to be implemented in the world, or at least possible for the world to be made to correspond substantially *more* to these ideals than it does currently. Thus the idealist is characterized by a quality of hopefulness. A person who guided her life by general and honorable values but did not really believe that the world could in any significant way be brought more into line with these values would not be an idealist (though she might be admirable, and even a moral exemplar). The idealist's life has a quality of conscious self-creation and self-direction; the idealist chooses her ideals and explicitly guides her life according to them.

Even assuming that the idealist meets other requirements of moral exemplariness, an idealist as so far defined is not necessarily a moral exemplar. Only a successful idealist – one who truly lives her ideals – is a moral exemplar. But there can be persons who genuinely hold worthy ideals and (what is not the same thing) attempt conscientiously to live up to them, but who do not succeed in doing so. Such persons may be in some ways admirable, but they are not moral exemplars (or anyway, not the sort of moral exemplars I mean by "idealist").

A fine example of an idealist moral exemplar is André Trocmé, Madga's husband and the pastor of the village of Le Chambon. Prior to his arrival in Le Chambon, André came to develop, adopt, and live out a moral outlook centered on the principles of resistance to evil, of nonviolence, and of the cherishing of each individual human life. In his years at Le Chambon, André continually looked for ways to implement these ideals. He wanted to go beyond helping refugees who happened to arrive in the town, conceived of turning the village into a haven for refugees, and organized the town in this endeavor. This rescue effort manifested André Trocmé's ideals; it was a form of resistance to the Nazi evil which, in contrast say to the armed resistance (with whom André had an uneasy relationship), could remain nonviolent; and it involved the cherishing of refugee and other lives through sheltering them from likely death.

In contrast to the idealist, the "responder" moral exemplar does not, prior to confronting the situations in which she manifests her moral excellence, possess a set of moral principles which she has worked out explicitly, committed herself to, and attempted to guide her life by. Nevertheless the responder responds to the situations she faces and to individual persons in a morally excellent way. Whereas the idealist is concerned to ensure that her behavior meets a predetermined standard or principle (which does not, however, require that she consult the principle on every occasion), the responder just, as it were, *does* the morally good thing, without having the further project of ensuring that she lives up to specific standards.

This does not mean, however, that the responder acts impulsively, irrationally, inconstantly, or unreliably. His or her behavior manifests a perceptive understanding of particular situations. Consistency of moral behavior is no less correlated with responderness than with idealism.[29] To be *morally excellent*, both idealists and responders must act from dispositions, sentiments, and traits of character which lie at a fairly deep level of their psychological economy.

Schindler illustrates the "responder." His awakening to the plight of the Jews was wholly surprising and (morally) unprepared for. In the 1930s Schindler seemed entirely morally unexceptional, and for a time even flirted with the Nazi party, not from any firm convictions but simply because it was opportune to do so. Prior to his coming to Poland, Schindler had already become leery of Nazism, but he gave no evidence of seeking to resist it, or of trying to do anything morally good with his own life. He sought only to wait out the Nazi period and make a fortune in some business venture.

But when Schindler came to see what was happening to the Jews in Poland – the seizure of property, the raids, then the ghettos, then the round-ups for the camps – he *responded* to the situation. As related earlier, he showed exceptional powers of perceptiveness and imagination in figuring out how to shelter substantial numbers of Jewish workers. Nothing in Schindler's previous life would have led one to expect this from him.

Schindler *never* really formulated an explicit moral outlook to anything like the extent that someone like André Trocmé did. To be sure, he was engaged in a project which he took to be a moral one – saving particular Jews. But a personal commitment to aid specific persons does not constitute an "ideal," which must be formulated as a general value. Moreover, it was only gradually, toward the end of the war, that Schindler even came to expand his moral horizons to include Jews he did not know (or about whom he was not personally informed). Yet even then this value ("saving Jews from the Nazis," not just saving a particular group of Jews) did not seem to be held by Schindler in the form of a general guiding principle; his own actions continued to be governed more by responding to opportunities to rescue particular Jews he knew of than to a sense of living up to a general principle of saving Jews.

The contrast between Schindler's and André Trocmé's lives after the war is instructive in regard to the contrast between responder and idealist. André continued to work for the ideals of nonviolence, becoming the

29. These points are defended (though without using the term "responder") in Chapter 2 of my *Friendship, Altruism, and Morality*.

European secretary of the Fellowship of Reconciliation, an international organization devoted to nonviolence.[30] Schindler, by contrast, led a relatively morally unexceptional life, attempting several unsuccessful commercial ventures but never finding a place for himself. His experience during the war had undermined a comfortable relationship to Germany and to the values of his youth, but had not replaced them in the depths of Schindler's character with a set of higher values – much less ones explicitly articulated as ideals – capable of carrying Schindler into the postwar situation and providing him with some purpose in life. (His case is quite distinct from that of someone who once had ideals but then lost them.) Schindler's moral excellence remained localized to the particular situation of the war.

Magda Trocmé, though less so than Schindler, was more of a "responder" than an "idealist." She intentionally shunned her husband André's somewhat grand and sometimes grandiose ideas and ideals (especially their religiously inspired aspect). She responded to people individually and in terms of their particular need. She did not come morally armed with a worked out set of general ideals which she searched for ways to implement. Looking back on the Le Chambon period Magda expressed what, in retrospect, she thought herself to have been like at the time, and characterized her involvement in the rescue effort: "I try not to hunt around to find things to do. I do not hunt around to find people to help. But I never close my door, never refuse to help somebody who comes to me and asks for something" (pp. 152–3). André Trocmé understood his actions as instantiating his formulated ideals; by contrast Magda understood her actions in terms of helping the particular refugee who presented himself at her door.[31]

Though both were responders, Magda differed from Schindler in important ways. Magda had a clearer and more consistent moral self-identity than did Schindler. The traits of character (compassion, caring, courage, understanding of individual needs) which constituted her form of responsiveness were more deeply rooted in her character than were Schindler's

30. At the same time, Hallie documents a sort of moral decline in André after the (probably) accidental death of his son; he became more authoritarian and more self-absorbed (p. 263).

31. The distinction between "idealist" and "responder" has some kinship with the distinction between "justice" and "care" which Carol Gilligan has developed in her various writings, most famously *In a Different Voice* (Cambridge, 1982). Gilligan sees a gender link here, though not a simple one, with men tending to favor a "justice," and women a "care," approach. Such a gendered perspective regarding moral excellence and its modes seems to me a fruitful approach to connect with an appreciation of different types of moral exemplars and their respective moral psychologies. See Chapter 10, "Gilligan and Kohlberg."

morally heroic traits within his. (This is one reason why Magda is a Murdochian paragon as well as a moral hero, whereas Schindler is only a hero.)

But doesn't Magda's self-characterization ("I never close my door," etc.) represent a kind of ideal of behavior? To this suggestion two things can be said. First, Magda's having given this formulation retrospectively does not mean that the value expressed in it played a role in *guiding* her actions at the time. The later formulation might rather be seen as a kind of in-retrospect summary of what Magda did at the time, rather than a general rule or value which she sought to ensure that she lived up to.

Second, even if we take Magda's self-characterization to reflect how she did think of herself at the time (during the war), the characterization is meant by her precisely to distinguish her own morality from the "morality of ideals" of her husband. In order to function *as* ideals, and as guides to action, ideals (such as André's: "Cherish every human life") must be formulated at a level of abstraction somewhat removed from the concrete particularity of individual situations; moreover, they necessarily speak to only some aspects of the full moral reality of individual situations. Both of these features allow for a gap between an attachment to an ideal, and a full moral response to a situation. Magda perceived this gap in André. She felt that his ideals often threatened to make him lose touch with particular individuals and their perhaps mundane needs, for food, for a coat.[32]

It is not that Magda chose a moral outlook specifically to correct for what she saw as the deficiencies in André's. Rather it seems clear that she was already very much someone who cared about individual persons, who felt a responsibility toward individuals who crossed her path. These dispositions were deep within her character, and for herself she was not particularly drawn to formulating them as general values to guide her, nor did she need to do so. However, an awareness of the potential limitations of André's particular form of moral goodness made Magda more aware of the differences between his mode of moral being and hers. Without the interaction with him, she may never have formulated, even to the extent she did, the self-characterization given retrospectively to Hallie. The continuation of the quote from Magda cited above is revealing: "When things happen, not things I plan, but things sent by God or by chance, when people come to my door, I feel responsible. During André's life during the war many many people came, and my life was therefore complicated" (p. 153).

---

32. See Hallie, pp. 65, 67, 153.

Magda is not a case of a pure responder; but this passage contains hints of what a pure responder's mode in this situation would be: A refugee shows up at her door, and she helps him. But she does not think about what she would do if another refugee shows up. Then another refugee does show up, and she helps her too. But she still does not formulate any general intention, or principle, of helping refugees. Perhaps each time she thinks there will be no more, or perhaps she just does not think one way or the other about it. But she continues to help each refugee who comes across her path until she is no longer able to do so.[33]

Magda and André Trocmé were morally complementary. Magda's responder's grounding in the concrete present helped to keep André's ideals more in touch with reality. At the same time this very rootedness in the concrete present can have its own limitations.[34] It is not an accident that it was André's moral vision and long-term perspective, rather than Magda's outlook, that led to the plan of organizing Le Chambon as a haven of refuge. Some moral situations require a degree of

33. This account is not a fanciful one. Pierre Sauvage's film, *Weapons of the Spirit*, a documentary on Le Chambon, involves interviews with several peasants who sheltered refugees during the German occupation (perhaps exemplifying the "virtuous peasant" about whom Iris Murdoch occasionally speaks). Some of their retrospective account accords fairly closely with the description of the "pure responder" given here.

I am grateful to David Wong for pressing me to provide greater clarification than an early draft contained of the contrast between responder and idealist, in regard to the role of guiding principles. I am aware that there is a good deal more to be said on this point, which involves central and much-debated issues in moral theory concerning the adequacy of a principle-based ethic. I have tried to show that a caring responsiveness to particular persons in particular situations constitutes a genuinely alternative form of moral consciousness to one grounded in appeal to principle in other essays in this volume, especially Chapters 1, 9, and 10. On these same issues in connection with Aristotle's emphasis on the concrete particular in deliberation, see Martha Nussbaum, *The Fragility of Goodness,* especially Chapter 10, and "The Discernment of Perception: An Aristotelian Conception of Private and Public Rationality," in *Love's Knowledge* (Oxford, 1990). Nel Noddings's *Caring: A Feminine Approach to Ethics and Moral Education* (Berkeley, 1984) contains some criticisms of a principle-based ethic which accord with some of the pitfalls of idealism mentioned in the essay, though Noddings tends to underplay the strengths of a principle-based ethic.

34. Keneally relates an incident which illustrates the moral pitfalls of Schindler's form of responder morality in the complex and dangerous situation in which he operated. Schindler responded to his worker/prisoners' hunger by feeding them illicitly; but in the summer of 1943, other worker/prisoners (in other establishments) were so visibly suffering from hunger that the contrast with Schindler's prisoners was "dangerously visible." Schindler thereby risked SS retaliation, though in fact this never materialized.

It is noteworthy, however, that Schindler engaged in this sort of risky activity relatively infrequently. The general goal of saving Jews (while not, as I have argued, rendering Schindler an idealist) served to temper the pure responder's morality of reacting to each individual situation and person. (I am unsure, however, whether to see this tempering purely as a corrective of a responder morality, or as a possible mode of it.)

distancing from the situation at hand, which the idealist may be in a better position to deal with than the responder. Better than either would be some kind of synthesis – an extremely difficult one to achieve – of the positive features of both the idealist and the responder. But it is nevertheless significant that either moral type by itself can exemplify moral excellence. (And it is also possible for someone who is one to become the other.)

As mentioned earlier, the distinction between idealist and responder cuts across that of saint, or Murdochian exemplar, and hero. André Trocmé is an idealist hero (and, perhaps, a saint as well); Schindler is a responder hero, Magda Trocmé a responder saint-hero. And a Murdochian exemplar could be either a responder or an idealist. In some way perhaps the Murdochian paragon has more affinities with the responder than with the idealist – this is certainly so in Murdoch's own account, in which the paragon is understood as "responding to individual reality." However, idealism and Murdochian excellence are not really incompatible either. For one can hold explicit and idealistic values but seek to apply them in only a limited realm. Someone might, for example, hold as a general ideal that one should love one's neighbor, but apply this value only to those with whom one comes in personal contact rather than seeing it as encompassing all of humanity.

It is noteworthy, however, that Ed Corcoran, the Murdochian exemplar, is *not* an idealist in this limited realm sense. His loyalty to his wife, his generous spirit, and his exceptional family love and understanding are not (as I am conceiving him) a reflection or application of general ideals. He is not being portrayed as someone dedicated to the ideal of greater marital fidelity and/or love of neighbor, seeing his own actions as contributing to realizing these ideals. He is, I think, better seen as operating with some purely personal values (of fidelity and the like) which give moral substance to his life, but which he does not formulate as general and objective values.

CRITIQUE OF WOLF

The intent of my typology of moral exemplars is primarily a constructive one, to begin to map out a psychology of moral excellence; but it can also help to indicate (though I can do so here only briefly) some limitations of some previous influential attempts at a moral psychology of moral excellence. In particular one can see that three characterizations given of the "moral saint" by Susan Wolf, and not challenged by Robert Adams in his partial critique of Wolf, do not apply to all instances of moral exemplars.[35] These characterizations are (1) the moral exemplar as striving to maximize the good; (2) the moral exemplar as striving after moral perfection; (3) the moral exemplar as denigrating the pursuits of others.

We have already seen that the Murdochian paragon cannot be characterized as striving to maximize the good, since, for one thing, she is not characterized in terms of undertaking to realize specific goals, or a "moral project." The point can also be seen in relation to the responder (hero or saint). Even if the responder's excellence can be characterized in terms of attention to the needs of particular persons (as Magda's, for example, can be), in seeking the well-being of particular persons the responder does nothing like seek a *maximizing* of the good. As described, Magda's helping particular individuals is not seen by her, even implicitly, as a way of bringing about the most overall good that she can (though perhaps what she does may *be* virtually the most good that she could do).

Though perhaps less obviously so than the responder and the Murdochian paragon, neither does the idealist fit the characterization of "striving to maximize the good." He comes *closer* to doing so in that, in contrast to the responder, his way of being is characterized by explicitly striving to realize certain goals which are seen (by him) as good. The idealist-hero (André Trocmé for example) does aim to promote what is in fact a great good, and this is an important element in his moral excellence. But this is a far cry from striving to *maximize* good. The idealist's goals are importantly more particular than this. André sees the rescue of refugees as a project at the intersection of his three moral ideals – nonviolence, resistance to evil, and cherishing of each individual life – and it is this feature which grounds its hold on him. He does not necessarily see this project as a way to maximize the good.[36]

35. Adams's critique of Wolf primarily, though not entirely, takes the form of agreeing with Wolf's characterization of the secular moral saint, and accepting the negative assessment of the figure thus characterized, but denying that either those characterizations or those negative assessments apply to what he (Adams) regards as actual, i.e., religious saints, such as Gandhi or St. Francis. To a secular moralist such as myself, Adams's criticisms seem to concede too much to Wolf's denigration of a purely moral, non- (or not necessarily) religious excellence. At the same time some of Adams's defense of religious saints can, as I will argue below, be appropriated to defend secular moral saints.

36. Michael Slote has usefully distinguished a "satisficing" from a "maximizing" form of consequentialism (in *Common-Sense Morality and Consequentialism* [London, 1985], Chapter 3). Slote's point is, roughly, that sometimes an agent has, from a moral point of view, "done enough," and no *further* justification need be given for *not* doing more. Although this point supports my argument that moral excellence does not require maximizing the good, my argument is not that moral heroes do enough already, and need not be held to any more demanding standard. For this way of putting

Nor can moral exemplars be characterized generally as seeking moral perfection. This is especially evident with regard to responders, whose moral excellence is not characterized by the explicit seeking of any distinct set of moral goals; in particular it does not involve taking as a goal a morally characterized state of themselves.

The characterization "striving for moral perfection" might seem better to fit the idealist, who does attempt to guide his actions by explicit moral ideals. However even here Wolf's characterization does not do justice. Striving to implement ideals cannot be identified with striving for perfection. For one thing, if the notion of "perfection" here is meant to imply that every moment of life be thought of as in some way needing to contribute to one's goal (if only as necessary preparation for the effort required, and the like), then, as Adams points out, those whom he might actually regard as saints (e.g., Albert Schweitzer), do not do this; they give some time to purely personal pleasures and pursuits not seen as having moral import whatsoever. And yet we do not see this as detracting from characterizing them as saints;[37] and the same point holds for idealist moral exemplars more generally.

Further, the ideals which the idealist strives for are not necessarily, or typically, seen by himself as exceptionally high, heroic, or perfection-grounding moral standards. To the idealist these standards can and often do seem merely right or necessary, even in a sense ordinary. To André Trocmé the ideals of love, nonviolence, and resistance to evil seemed not exceptional or exceptionally demanding ones but necessary and proper concerns in the light of his own experience. The moral exemplar (of either responder or idealist type) does not typically regard himself *as* a moral exemplar; and in fact there seems an inherent contradiction, or at least a tension, in doing so, for one is then in danger of the pride, self-aggrandizement, and a sense of superiority, which detract from moral excellence. Hallie's respondents in the village of Le Chambon, and especially Magda, to whom he spoke while researching his book, emphasize that helping the refugees seemed to them *not* extraordinary or worthy of exceptional praise, but rather something entirely unremarkable. The villagers were greatly perplexed at the notion that there was anything particularly worthy of note,

the point still sees the "enough" in the context of some implicit "maximizing" standard; it is as if the notion of "enough" involves a distinct rejection of "maximization." My point, by contrast, is that the way the good done by the idealist moral hero figures into our assessment of him as excellent is *not* as the thought that it is "less than the maximum but still enough" (for moral excellence), but only that it is a great good (or prevention of a great evil).

37. Adams, "Saints," p. 398.

much less of extraordinary praise, in sheltering persons whose lives were in danger.[38]

But the Trocmés' own rejection of moral exemplariness as applying to themselves does not detract from the appropriateness of that attribution. Rather it points to a lack of connection between *regarding* oneself as morally excellent and *being* morally excellent.

I would like, finally, to address the charge that the moral exemplar is self-righteous and judgmental toward others less morally virtuous. Wolf implies that because the moral exemplar holds herself to such a high standard of morality, she will make others feel that they are being judged as wanting, that the exemplar believes that their less morally impressive pursuits lack value.[39]

But what someone may feel in the face of the moral exemplar is a different issue from whether the moral exemplar is actually judging that person negatively. On the former point, it may well be true that in the presence of a moral exemplar one may come to feel that one has been caught up in less valuable and significant endeavors than one might be, or that one has been more self-absorbed and insensitive than one ought to be. And it may also be true that, because of this, some will steer clear of the exemplars in their vicinity, in order to avoid having such matters brought to their attention. It is not evident, however, what kind of objection it is to moral exemplariness that we may not wish to be reminded of our own moral shortcomings and mediocrity. Certainly this does not render the moral exemplar in some way inherently unattractive or defective, as Wolf implies.

In any case moral discomfort is not the only effect moral exemplars can have on others, as we can see by considering the matter of self-righteousness, a genuine charge of deficiency in the moral exemplar.[40] Here the thought is that the moral exemplar *means* to have the effect on others which we acknowledged above that she may in fact have.

38. See for example Hallie, pp. 20–1 and 154. The same moral outlook of the villagers emerges from Sauvage's film *Weapons of the Spirit*. Hallie partly connects the rejection of the ascription of great moral merit with Magda's (and perhaps the other villagers') Protestantism, in which sainthood and "moral nobility" are eschewed (p. 154). And Sauvage and Hallie also suggest that Le Chambon's geographical isolation kept the villagers from being confronted in a direct day-to-day way with the shameful treatment of Jewish refugees elsewhere in France, a confrontation which might have made their own exceptional behavior more manifest to them.
39. See Wolf, "Moral Saints," pp. 424, 428.
40. It should be said that while Wolf charges that the "moral saint" will devalue nonmoral pursuits engaged in by others, she does not, as far as I am aware, say explicitly that the moral saint is self-righteous. Nevertheless this is certainly a charge which popular thought often associates with moral exemplariness.

In this regard it is striking that the moral exemplars I have discussed here have not possessed these deficiencies. André Trocmé, in particular, seemed to have quite an opposite effect on other people. He was able to reveal to them and to encourage them to develop their own capacities for a stronger moral goodness. He made people feel that he was indebted to them for whatever they were able to do. A truly morally excellent person is more likely to have the generosity of spirit and "love" of others which is able simultaneously to accept others for what they are, not to make them feel condemned for how they choose to live, yet also to spur them to their best efforts.[41] Self-righteousness is a serious moral deficiency, involving a sense of moral superiority to others and often accompanied by contempt; a truly morally excellent person does not possess it.[42]

The thought that someone whose life embodies an exceptionally high moral standard must necessarily think ill of others who *fail* to live up to that standard stems perhaps partly from an overemphasis on moral universality – the Kantian thought that what is right for the agent must be, and must be thought by him to be, right for everyone else. In fact moral exemplars are no more likely, and may even be less likely, to think of their own standards and commitments as setting a standard for, or for assessing, others. It is true that a moral idealist devotes himself to a goal which he regards as not merely personal but as expressing some intrinsic good, but this is a far cry from his thinking that everyone else must or ought to do so as well, and thinking ill of them for failing to do so.[43]

41. Adams, responding to Wolf's charge that saints are bland and unappealing, cites the "charisma" that many actual saints had which induced many persons to find them fascinating and to follow them ("Saints," p. 393). But the quality of generosity of spirit and affirmation and love of others which I am speaking of here cannot be identified with charisma, but is an attitude taken by the moral exemplar explicitly toward others.

42. Self-righteousness is perceptively discussed in Robert Adams's "Involuntary Sins," *Philosophical Review* 94 (January 1985): 4–6. Marcia Homiak has plausibly maintained (in personal conversation) that self-righteousness quite often stems not from moral excellence but from insecurity and lack of confidence.

43. That holding oneself to a moral standard does not morally or conceptually require holding others to it is argued for in the following: Michael Pritchard, "Self-Regard and the Supererogatory," in *Respect For Persons: Tulane Studies in Philosophy* (1982): 147ff., argues that while there is a sense or use of the moral "ought" which does carry universalistic implications, there is another which does not. Gregory Trianosky, in "Supererogation, Wrongdoing, and Vice: On the Autonomy of the Ethics of Virtue," *Journal of Philosophy* 83 (January 1986): 39, argues that "legitimate moral standards or principles can be private at least some of the time." Thomas Hill, Jr., in "Self-Respect Reconsidered" in *Respect for Persons: Tulane Studies in Philosophy* (1982): 132, argues that even a universalistic moral judgment often commits the speaker to no specific judgment about any particular other person, since the speaker may not see "relevant similarities" between himself and any actual others. A. I. Melden, in "Saints and Supererogation," in *Philosophy and Life: Essays on John Wisdom,* ed. Ilham Dilman (The Hague, 1984), argues that saints

It may well be that a person lacking in virtue or any pretension to it is, ceteris paribus, less likely than someone of genuine moral standards even to be tempted to apply such standards to others. But this temptation is in any case less likely to arise in someone possessing the virtue of "acceptance with understanding" than, as suggested above, in the person who is insecure regarding her virtue. Moreover, self-righteousness can be found in the morally mediocre as well as in those of more moral substance.

EMULATING MORAL EXEMPLARS

Inquiring about the attitude moral exemplars take toward others raises the question of the extent to which moral exemplars provide appropriate models of aspiration and emulation for others. There are several questions here. I hope that my descriptions of the moral exemplars discussed in this essay have shown them to be appropriate objects of an all-things-considered *admiration;* to do so has been an important part of my task in countering Wolf's suggestion that they might well not be.

This admiration might naturally, though not with conceptual necessity, incline some to wish to be like the moral exemplar. It is important to accept that for most persons this could not be accomplished, no matter how conscientiously one set oneself to become anything like the moral paragons one admires. In this sense moral excellence is not within the scope of the will, of choice; it is a dimension of morality which is simply not up to us.

This may be particularly evident in the case of those exemplars who functioned in what might appropriately be thought extreme circumstances, such as the Nazi terror. Qualities needed for moral excellence in such circumstances may be very different from those needed in more ordinary ones. And those who are excellent in one setting may not easily be so in others. Oskar Schindler's wife Emilie, interviewed after his death, perceptively and poignantly said of Oskar: "He was fortunate, therefore, that in the short fierce era between 1939 and 1945 he had met people who summoned forth his deeper talent" (Keneally, p. 397).

That moral excellence may often be tied to particular circumstances is, then, a matter of what Bernard Williams and others have called "moral luck" (though Williams does not use the concept in this particular connection). But the specialness of the circumstances in which Schindler and the Trocmés operated should not be overstated either. There is surely enough oppression, horror, injustice, and just plain pain and suffer-

properly speak of themselves as having "duties" even though they do not regard others as having such duties.

ing in our world to render that difference in circumstances at best one of degree (which is not to minimize that degree). Some people experience an urgency about addressing various of these ills of our own world which is comparable to the Trocmés' and Schindler's about saving the lives of Jews; and it is not certain that they are wrong to do so.

In addition to the dependence of some sorts of virtue on circumstances, there are other kinds of moral luck in operation here as well. It is simply not within our power to bring about in ourselves the psychological make-up constituting moral excellence. We cannot get to be courageous, compassionate, principled, kind, loving, or honest – much less some very difficult-to-achieve combination of these virtues required for excellence – merely by trying to do so, nor by any other method; nor can we similarly rid ourselves of various unworthy desires, sentiments, and dispositions.

What might seem open to all, however, is to adopt certain ideals, and thus to strive directly to be an idealist. This is in a way true and will be considered further in a moment. But while one can *try* to adopt ideals, one cannot ensure success in doing so; sincerely *professing* ideals is not equivalent to adopting them. Moreover (a different point) even if one succeeds in genuinely adopting ideals, one cannot ensure that one comes fully to *live* them, in the way required for moral excellence. Finally, one surely cannot by effort alone, or in any other way, simply bring it about that those ideals become deeply rooted in one's character in the way required for true moral excellence.

I wish to emphasize these limitations on the extent to which everyone, or even everyone who wanted to, could become a moral exemplar, in order to counter views of morality which tie it too closely to the will and to universal accessibility. I also wish to bring out the distance between admiring something and being able to take it as a direct model for one's own action or life.

Yet this is all meant only to clear the way for a realistic picture of what *can* be learned from moral exemplars which *can* affect one's own values and mode of life, and of how emulating exemplars can be a force for one's own moral growth. I have argued only that it is given to very few to *be* moral exemplars. Yet, for one thing, as the example of Schindler shows, we do not always know who those potential moral exemplars are. Robert Adams is no doubt right when he says, "In all probability there could be more Gandhis than there are, and it would be a very good thing if there were."[44]

44. Adams, "Saints," p. 397.

Moreover, though most of us could not become moral exemplars, we can all learn something from them – something about what is really of value in life. As Philippa Foot says, "It makes good sense to say that most men waste a lot of their lives in pursuit of what is trivial and unimportant."[45] And this formulation accords with Iris Murdoch's characterization of moral excellence in terms of seeing the right relationship and priority between different human values.

Although we cannot all be moral exemplars, what we all can be is *better* than we are. For each of us there are surely *some* virtues that we could come to possess in greater degree than we now do, no matter what circumstances we are in. The existence of moral exemplars can help to keep this possibility alive for us, and in some cases to suggest particular directions we might take in our own moral improvement.

The standard focus of moral theory on choice situations particularly ill suits what is to be learned from a discussion of moral paragons. The task of moral improvement, of changing our character for the better, cannot be understood if every individual is thought of as faced with an array of options of modes of life and character, among which he or she must choose. Genuine moral change is much more individualized and particular, and much more limited in its possible goals, than that picture suggests.

Returning to Wolf, I have not here disputed that there might be such figures as the Kantian or the utilitarian moral paragon. But it is noteworthy that the types of moral exemplars discussed here, and the individuals I have used to exemplify them, do not correspond to Wolf's portrayal of either of these. The exemplars are not characterized by the continual adoption of an impersonal and universal view on the world, by a striving for maximal good, or for personal moral perfection. So at least many actual moral exemplars are not properly understood in terms of a moral psychology built around such conceptions of "the moral."

Finally, perhaps the very disjunction between moral exemplars I have discussed and Wolf's conception of the moral saint means that in a sense my argument is irrelevant to hers. Perhaps Wolf's criticisms should be regarded as aimed only at the particular kind of Kantian and utilitarian moral exemplars she describes. Yet clearly Wolf wants in addition to cast some aspersions on the higher reaches of morality in general, and to suggest reasons why we need not be so concerned about morality as some (myself among them) would want us to be. Despite the skeptical eye that some first-rate contemporary philosophers have turned on morality, I myself have never been fully able to shake the conviction that Iris

---

45. Foot, "Virtues and Vices," in *Virtues and Vices,* p. 6.

Murdoch is right when she suggests that moral goodness is properly regarded as the central value in a human life, and that the questions, "What is a good man like? How can we make ourselves morally better? *Can* we make ourselves morally better?"[46] should be one of, or even *the*, central preoccupations of moral philosophy.

46.   Murdoch, *Sovereignty of Good,* p. 52.

5

Vocation, friendship, and community: limitations of the personal-impersonal framework

The conflict between personal projects and the impersonal demands of morality has been an important focus of recent moral theory. The writings of Thomas Nagel (1986), Susan Wolf (1982), Norman Care (1984, 1987), and others concern themselves with whether, and the extent to which, morality understood as impersonal, impartial, universal, and rational does, or ought to, constrain personal projects and satisfaction.[1] These writers appropriately question the unexamined presumption of traditional moral theories, especially of a Kantian or utilitarian stripe, that the impersonal demands of morality ought always and automatically to take precedence over personal pursuits. However, they also make the further assumption that ethical reflection must take place within a framework defined solely by the personal-impersonal dichotomy.

A second currently prominent issue is the communitarian critique of liberalism. An important strand of this critique is that because of its (alleged) bias toward individualism, liberalism cannot account for, nor can a liberal polity sufficiently foster, communalist social and political values such as a sense of community, citizen participation, the integrity of distinct cultures, specific shared goods as constitutive of political community, and the like.

The communitarianism-liberalism dispute has operated primarily in two philosophic domains – political philosophy and the "metaphysical" theory of the self. Regarding the latter, for example, Michael Sandel (1982) argues against John Rawls (1971) that the identities of selves are

I wish to thank members and students of the philosophy departments of the University of Maryland (especially Michael Slote and Patricia Greenspan), Arizona State University, and Darmouth College for their intelligent and sympathetic reactions to presentations of earlier versions of this essay; Pauline Chazan for a very acute reading of an early draft, especially concerning the portions on friendship; David Wong for a very helpful discussion of the relations between general category and particular relationship, especially in the context of friendship; Judith Andre for a very helpful conversation concerning different forms of caring; Susan Wolf for stimulating and clarifying conversations on the personal-impersonal framework; and Owen Flanagan for excellent suggestions on late drafts.

1. Other philosophers dealing with the personal/impersonal dilemma include Bernard Williams, Owen Flanagan, Michael Slote, Samuel Scheffler, Peter Railton, and Harry Frankfurt.

in part constituted by their communal attachments (to nation, ethnic group, family, class, and other such communal entities) and that this feature of the self is denied by Rawls's liberalism. Rawls (1985) replies that his liberalism requires no theory of the self at all and that the real question is whether a liberal polity can accommodate legitimate communitarian values. The dispute shifts back and forth between the metaphysical level and the political level.

Seldom is the liberalism/communitarianism dispute fought out on the turf of moral theory per se. Communitarians have not, by and large, attempted to develop a moral psychology for communitarianism. What kinds of motivations, attitudes, sensibilities, and virtues are involved in the attachments, and the actions flowing from such attachments, to various communitarian entities? How do communitarian attachments in their various modes generate responsibilities and actions?

I will try to bring the communitarianism-liberalism debate into closer relationship with moral theory by arguing that the "personal-impersonal" framework that forms the context of the debate about the legitimate scope of the personal domain presents a substantial obstacle to developing the kind of moral psychology capable of illuminating the liberalism-communitarianism controversy.

I will suggest that although philosophers working on the personal-impersonal issue have, for the most part, rejected Kantianism as a moral theory, they have insufficiently broken with Kant's moral psychology – his portrayal of morally significant motivation as either the desire for personal happiness or respect for the impersonal demands of morality.

Against the moral psychology implied in the personal-impersonal framework (as exemplified in the work of Thomas Nagel, Susan Wolf, and Norman Care, described below), I will argue the following:

> · There is a large range of types of action and motivation which fall neither on the side of the personal and nonmoral nor on the side of the purely impersonal and moral. I will be discussing in particular (1) actions of compassion for an individual outside a specific moral relationship, (2) actions stemming from one's social role, (3) actions of friendship, (4) actions issuing from one's understanding of one's vocation, and (5) actions stemming from one's attachment to a particular community. Actions in categories (3), (4), and (5) can in turn be broken down into three types: care, guidance by the general category of the relationship (friendship, vocation, or community), and guidance by the specific relationship.
> · Although an attempt can be made to capture these nonpersonal,

nonimpersonal actions within the personal-impersonal framework, this attempt distorts the phenomena in question.

· There are morally and psychologically distinct uses of "impersonal" that are also different from the notion of impersonality employed in the personal-impersonal framework.

· The personal-impersonal framework operates with a conception of personal good or flourishing that is excessively privatized and hence that fails to see how our personal good is bound inextricably to specific persons in personal relationships, to vocations, and to communities that give our lives meaning.

I

Thomas Nagel in *The View from Nowhere* (1986) sees "the central problem of ethics" as "how the lives, interests, and welfare of others make claims on us and how these claims . . . are to be reconciled with the aim of living our own lives" (p. 164). He characterizes the impersonal standpoint of morality as one from which all choosers can agree, as seeing oneself as merely one among others, and as seeing the world from nowhere within it. He looks forward to a world in which the impersonal demands of morality are met largely by impersonal institutions, leaving individuals "free to devote considerable attention and energy to their own lives and to values that could not be impersonally acknowledged" (p. 207).

Susan Wolf in her article "Moral Saints" (1982) expresses what she sees as the limitations of morality's hold over us and our practical deliberations, by speaking of two "points of view" from which choices and actions can be approached – the moral point of view, involving the impersonal demand that we consider other persons as "equally real" or equally important as ourselves, and "the point of view of individual perfection," in which the individual agent's making the most of herself, striving toward individual nonmoral perfection, is the salient consideration.

Wolf's distinction between these two perspectives is set in the context of a detailed criticism of a life centered on moral pursuits. Although her rich and complex argument cannot be summarized briefly, one important overall strand in it is that the "moral saint" neglects the perspective of the point of view of individual perfection and tends to devalue it. (A fuller critique of Wolf's argument is given in Chapter 4, "Moral Exemplars".) In this way the moral saint is importantly defective and unworthy of full (or perhaps even much) admiration and emulation.

A similar distinction between a purely personal good and the imper-

100

sonal concerns of morality is put to a quite different use by Norman Care in his excellent and challenging book *On Shared Fate* (1987) and earlier article "Career Choice" (1984). Care notes great inequities within the world in regard to life chances and to the means to personal self-realization. Drawing on this empirical fact, Care argues that a reasonably advantaged person living in an advanced country such as the United States ought to sacrifice some (and perhaps a great deal) of her own self-realization for the sake of promoting the self-realization of others. Care discusses self-realization specifically in the context of career choice, which is the choice of a central project and mode of one's life. Care's argument is based on what he calls "shared fate individualism," in which securing the bases for everyone's individual self-realization is a task for each.

In this way Care gives the moral priority over the personal. This is denied by Wolf and partially denied by Nagel. Yet, like Nagel and Wolf, Care frames his concerns in terms of an opposition between two mutually exclusive and seemingly exhaustive desiderata – a personal good (or self-realization) and an impersonal morality.

II

To explore the large domain of actions and motivations that are neither personal nor impersonal, I begin with an example taken from Herbert Kohl's *Growing Minds: On Becoming a Teacher* (1984). Kohl, then a secondary school teacher, was asked by some parents in a school in which he was teaching if he would give special tutoring to their son. The boy was 14 years old and did not know how to read. He was a large boy, angry and defiant; his teachers did not know how to handle him. Kohl agreed to work with the boy two days a week after class.

Kohl worked with the boy for several months. He found him extremely difficult and never grew to like him personally. But eventually he helped the boy to begin reading. Kohl describes how he came to take a personal interest in the boy's progress as a learner and to find satisfaction in what the boy was able to accomplish under his tutelage.

This activity on Kohl's part does not come under the rubric of purely personal good as this is understood in the literature I have referred to. Kohl was motivated neither to undertake helping the boy nor to persevere in doing so by a desire to promote his own personal benefit or self-realization. The request from the boy's parents was essentially an unsought and quite probably unwelcome intrusion into, in Nagel's words,

Kohl's "living his own life." And Kohl's inability to like the boy prevented the activity from being an enjoyable one for Kohl.

At the same time, the activity does not fall under the rubric of an accession to an impersonal moral demand either. For one thing, Kohl was not *required* to help the boy, and he does not describe himself as experiencing such a requirement. More important (since not all moral pulls from the side of the impersonal domain express themselves in the form of strict requirements), Kohl did not look at the situation, even implicitly, in an impersonal way. He did not step back to adopt a standpoint reflecting a universal, impartial perspective, figuring out what that standpoint urged on anyone situated similarly to himself, or looking at the situation from the viewpoint of any rational being. Rather, Kohl's motivation was of a more particularistic nature. He responded to, was moved by, the particular boy's plight, namely his being 14 years old and unable to read. Kohl experienced this as a terrible condition for the boy himself and was aware how damaged the boy would be if the school system continued to be unable to teach him to read. Perhaps Kohl was moved also by sympathy for the parents in their distress and despair. It is to the particular boy that Kohl responded, not to an impersonally derived value generating a reason for all.

The same could be said of many acts of compassion that presuppose no prior morally structured relationship between the agent and the sufferer. (In Chapter 2, "Iris Murdoch and the Domain of the Moral," I argue in greater detail that acts of compassion are typically neither "personal" nor "impersonal" according to the literature discussed here.) But it is significant in this situation that it is not simply as a human being or as an individual that Kohl takes on the tutoring, that he responds to the boy's plight, but specifically *as a teacher.* It is as a teacher that he sees the boy's need clearly, appreciates its significance, and is in a position to do something about it.

As Kohl is at pains to point out throughout his book, particularly in the chapter describing his interaction with the 14-year-old boy, Kohl's understanding of what it is to be a teacher is an important part of what meaning this particular activity has for him. In bringing this category (teacher) to bear on the situation, Kohl in a sense invokes the entire structure of social meaning and tradition within which the concept of teacher gets its significance. He sees that significance as involving certain values and ideals – promoting the intellectual growth of his pupils, teaching them habits of mind and a love for learning, which, as he sees it, will serve them in certain ways within society.

It is not that it would be *incorrect* to say that Kohl responds to the boy "as an individual." This could be a way of saying, for example, that he sees the boy as a whole individual person and not merely, say, as a member of a disadvantaged group or as a "problem case." And as a characterization of Kohl himself in this situation, to say that he acts "as an individual" could perhaps be to say that he is not acting merely from a narrowly circumscribed sense of his role. But in getting clear on the contours of the vast territory outside of the personal and the impersonal, there is an important distinction to be made between the kind of care, compassion, or concern appropriate to persons standing in no structured relationship to one another and those motives and sentiments as mediated by such structured relationships as teacher to student or parent to child.

III

I want to distinguish two forms of such structured mediating relationships. One draws on the idea of teacher as a role. Dorothy Emmet's account of this concept in her excellent book *Rules, Roles, and Relations* (1966) involves the imposition of a specific set of obligations on an occupant of the role – a set of obligations that applies in the same way to *anyone* occupying the role but not to those who do not occupy it. Thus the role obligations of a college professor might include holding a certain number of office hours, grading students fairly, teaching one's material in a professionally responsible way, and the like. This conception of role sees it as something like a job description. If you take on the job, such and such are your responsibilities.

The morality of a specific role in Emmet's sense is not wholly impersonal in the "view from nowhere" sense. It is not a universal morality but applies only to occupants of the role. It would be an impersonal morality in the sense of the personal-impersonal framework only if it could be further shown that the existence of that specific role with its specific responsibilities could be directly derived from (and not merely shown to be compatible with) such a purely impersonal point of view. Because of the historical contingencies bound up with the morality of virtually any given role in a particular society, this seems highly unlikely. (For a discussion of the relation between role and impartiality, see Chapter 9, "Moral Development and Conceptions of Morality.")

Thus action taken from a sense of role responsibility, even when done from obligation, is distinct from both personal and impersonal action. While in Kantian morality the notion of duty or obligation is identified with the universal and impersonal standpoint of the categorical imperative, role duties are not impersonal in that sense.

Nevertheless, in a different sense, role morality *is* impersonal. It is impersonal in the sense that the morality in question applies to *any* occupant of the role, independent of the occupant's particular personal characteristics. The obligations of a role are set (if not totally fixed) and are externally placed on anyone who comes to occupy the role. This is a familiar and significant sense of "impersonal," and is distinct from the view-from-nowhere sense.

IV

If "role" is understood in Emmet's sense (as I will understand it from here on), then Kohl probably had *no* role obligation to help the illiterate boy, since doing so was not part of his specific job responsibilities as a teacher in the school. But for Kohl in this situation, the notion of teacher functions as a much richer concept than role does in Emmet's sense. It invokes a general place and purpose within society and carries with it certain values, standards, and ideals. In fact, one of the burdens of Kohl's book is to exhibit teaching *not* simply as a job with a job description (that is, as a role in Emmett's sense) but as a *vocation.*

The notion of a vocation implies that the ideals it embodies are ones that speak specifically to the individual in question. There is a personal identification with the vocation, with its values and ideals, and a sense of personal engagement that helps to sustain the individual in her carrying out the activities of the vocation. These aspects are generally not present in the case of roles that are not also part of vocations. An individual needs to be in some way especially personally suited to a type of work in order for it to be a vocation, whereas this is not so for a role. Beyond this (since an individual could be suited to an occupation yet not experience it as a vocation) an individual with a vocation must believe deeply in the values and ideals of the vocation and must in some way choose or at least affirm them *for herself.*

(There are some wider issues about vocations that go beyond the scope of this essay but that might be briefly mentioned. Not all vocations are service vocations in the way teaching and medicine are, that is, serving, at least ideally, the good of individuals or of society as a whole. Science and art, for example, can certainly be vocations but are not necessarily service vocations in that sense. Perhaps there are even morally bad vocations, such as hit man or burglar. If so, then what would make a type of activity a vocation would be connected with the possibility of realizing various excellences, even if those excellences serve a countermoral end. This possibility implies that a paradigm vocation is one that both realizes excellences and also serves a good end or ends, even if these are not necessarily *moral* ends.)

The differences between roles and vocations yield a further sense in which vocations are nonimpersonal beyond the sense in which roles are nonimpersonal. Roles do not necessarily reflect the individual occupant's sense of personal value. This is why the moral pull exerted by role obligations as a moral requirement of the *position* can be experienced as entirely external to the person. In this sense the pull is impersonal. By contrast, when a vocation exercises moral pull – for example, the moral pull Kohl feels toward helping the illiterate boy – it is not in this sense impersonal, for it is experienced as implicated in the individual's own sense of personal values (as embodied in the vocation).

Related to this difference between role and vocation is that the particular way that the individual agent understands the values, ideals, and traditions of her vocation yields what she experiences as its moral, or valuational, pulls. Perhaps another teacher, for whom teaching was a calling, would show her particular dedication and sense of teaching ideals in what she did during official class time but, for personal reasons, would make a decision never to take on after-hours work. (It may, however, be inconsistent with treating an occupation as a calling that one *never* contravened such personal rules.) She would have a different interpretation of what teaching involved than does Kohl. The values and ideals that inform teaching, or any sufficiently complex and rich profession, as a vocation, and how to apply these values and ideals will inevitably be matters for dispute and personal interpretation. This fact does not, however, entail subjectivism, since argument can be given for the superiority of at least some interpretations over others, and some interpretations can be ruled out as too far from what any reasonable person could take the ideals and values of a particular profession to entail. (The latter implies that an individual could mistakenly believe herself to regard her profession as a vocation; her interpretation of it could be so defective or minimal in its demands as to be inconsistent with truly regarding it as a vocation.)

The existence in vocations of such personal variability contrasts with the case of roles. Although there is inevitably *some* room for interpretation with regard to almost any set of definite rules or job specifications, it is less than in the case of vocations, partly because the statement of ideals and values is at a much greater level of generality than a statement of role responsibilities. (Note, however, that the line between strict role obligation and ideal cannot be firmly fixed. It is subject to alteration, so that what one individual regards as required by her conception of a given vocation beyond current role obligations can come to be generally accepted and institutionalized as constituting the actual role obligations of that profession. For example, in a specific school a certain amount of after-class work could be or become mandatory as part of the role obligations of being a teacher in that school.)

We have, then, two distinct senses of "impersonal" of decreasing scope:

1. Applying to all persons independent of personal characteristics or personal values (view-from-nowhere impersonality)
2. Applying to a restricted group of persons (role occupants) independent of personal characteristics or values

Actions done from a sense of one's vocation are impersonal in *neither* of these senses, whereas role action is impersonal in sense (2) but not sense (1).

Although vocational action involves the element of personal value and personal interpretation rendering it nonimpersonal in the two senses mentioned, neither is it *personal* in the senses given to the term by Care, Wolf, and Nagel. The vocational agent does not take herself to be pursuing a goal simply because of its value to *her*. It is not *because it is part of her project* that she is impelled to help the pupil, to give extra tutoring to the student, and the like. Rather, the vocational agent takes herself to be responding to a value outside of herself, following (what she takes to be) its dictates. She is not pursuing a merely personal value either in the sense of something unconnected with the claims of other persons or in the sense in which she sees the reason for its pursuit as being conferred by its place in her own personal goals.

It is true that the vocational agent perceives this value, is sensitive to its force, is aware of its implications, and understands its dictates in the way she does *because* of her values, which she does not necessarily regard as incumbent on all others similarly situated. This is what is involved in the concept of a vocation developed here. This means that acting from one's own values can precisely be a way of responding to the plight of others or of responding to the dictates of an "external" value. This point will be explored further below, but at this juncture I can say that part of what it means that Kohl (for example) has the vocation of a teacher and affirms its values (as he understands them) as his own is that he appreciates the damage caused by illiteracy and is moved by the plight of an illiterate boy. It is part of his identity as a teacher (as he understands it) that he possesses these sentiments, understandings, appreciations, and the like.

This analysis of vocational action as not personal and also not impersonal in the two senses above yields a third sense in which it *can* be said to be "impersonal," namely that it is and is regarded by the agent as a response to some external, objective, or real value. It has value transcending the merely personal.

Vocational action is not what Norman Care means by "self-realization," inasmuch as he counterposes that to "service to others," for a service vocation does involve service to others. It is not what Susan Wolf calls "individual perfection," since its aim and motivation are not to perfect the person as individual but to respond to the values one sees as implicated in one's understanding of one's vocation. It is not what Thomas Nagel means by "living one's own life," as that is counterposed to acknowledging the claims of others as setting limits on such pursuit, since service occupations do acknowledge the claims of others.

To summarize the argument up to this point, there are three dimensions of action and motivation – direct individual-to-individual care, Emmetian role action, and action from vocation – that fit neither the model of purely personal or private good nor that of purely view-from-nowhere, impersonal morality.

V

Though neither personal nor impersonal, vocational action itself is not all of one motivational type. I will distinguish three different types, or dimensions, of vocational action. (They often operate together and on many occasions are only analytically separate.) These differ in regard to the different ways that particularity and generality come into their characteristic motivational sets. I will argue also that the same trichotomy applies to communal action, actions stemming from the agent's involvement with (certain kinds of) communities.

I will explain the three modes by drawing an analogy between vocation and friendship, arguing that friendship (and personal relationships in general) lend themselves to the same trichotomy. Friendship shares with vocation the quality of being a social category involving values, norms, or standards of action, attitude, and sentiment. It also shares these features with roles that are not vocations, but it lacks the definite structure of roles and leaves room for and even requires personal variability and individuality. The latter quality makes friendship more like vocation than role.

I will refer to the three modes of vocation, friendship, and community as care, generality, and particular relationship.

Care

A friend can act from a direct concern for her friend, without appeal to the norms of friendship, without a sense that the fact that the other is a friend renders her under an *ought* (which is not necessarily an obligation) to be helping her friend. She may simply be moved by her friend's suffering, danger, or unhappiness to comfort her, to help her out, and the like.

Friendship care is not the same as the pure individual-to-individual compassion discussed earlier. The spontaneous unmediated act of friendship is not the act of a pure individual toward another individual but of a friend to another friend. The friend would not have that same spontaneous reaction to a nonfriend. This is partly because in general (though not always) one cares about one's friends more than about nonfriends. But it is also because one cares about friends in a different way than one cares about strangers. One notices different things about friends than about others (though one also notices different things about different friends). Friendship care is characteristically more bound up with intimacy and with trust than stranger-to-stranger caring or compassion.[2]

Like pure individual-to-individual care, however, friendship care is neither personal nor impersonal. Similarly, we can speak of a kind of care attaching to vocations, especially service vocations. Kohl exemplifies a kind of teacher caring in his dealings with the illiterate boy. He responds directly to the boy without consulting the norms of his vocation to see what they prescribe. (Nor does Kohl seem to be drawing on them implicitly either. Caring is often distinct from even implicit guidance by norms or principles. On this, see Chapter 9, "Moral Development and Conceptions of Morality.")

At the same time, Kohl's caring is a specific *form* of caring (and this is not inconsistent with its being spontaneous and unmediated by principles). It is a caring especially focused on the aspects of the pupil that concern his *learning* and thus especially attuned to and understanding of

2. The notion of care in this section is meant to be that of Gilligan (1982, 1988), of Noddings (1984), and of the many others who have further developed the notion of a "morality of care." My somewhat critical remarks are meant to apply to them as well. (The criticisms apply also to my own *Friendship, Altruism, and Morality* [1980].) Although Noddings, Gilligan, and other writers show some recognition that caring means different things in different contexts, the implications of this for a theory of a morality of care are not developed, and the different virtues and sensitivities appropriate to the different contexts are not articulated. The criticisms made here echo Flanagan and Jackson's (1987) suggestion that there may be more than one distinct moral psychological competency encompassed by Gilligan's notion of care. (For more on this issue see Chapters 10, "Gilligan and Kohlberg," and 11, "Gilligan's 'Two Voices.'")

those aspects of his pupil. This is different from the more all-embracing concern for the other's good involved in friendship and parenthood (though these may themselves differ in that parental care is infused with a sense of *responsibility for* the child's good that is not, typically, present in friendship). And it differs from other, more specialized carings such as those of a nurse, doctor, athletic coach, or lawyer. (I refer to the persons cared for in these "vocational carings" – pupils, patients, clients, budding athletes – as "charges.") These different carings involve different kinds of sensitivities, and thus (to some extent) different virtues. If the *only* object of a teacher's concern is making sure that a pupil understands a certain subject matter, then this teacher does not exemplify teacher caring. To be caring, the concern must involve some regard for the pupil's overall good and a sense of how the good of learning the specific subject matter fits into the pupil's overall good. Without this, one can infer that the teacher values her subject matter but does not seem to have a clear sense of the value of her pupils as persons in their own right.

Caring must involve more than merely taking into account other aspects of one's charge's life. For example, suppose a college athletic coach concerned herself with her charges' family lives but *only* because and insofar as it impacted on their playing ability. While this would be an improvement over having no concern for her charges' life off the playing field, it would not count as caring in my sense, since the attention to the charge's family would be (for the coach) only a means to her sole ultimate concern, which is not for the athlete as a whole person but only for her athletic prowess and accomplishment.

Different sensitivities and virtues are required for dealing with charges who are extremely vulnerable and dependent, such as therapy patients and some medical patients, than with charges who are (in general) much less so, such as college students and athletes. Vocations that deal with individuals in the context of groups, such as classroom teachers, require (for the associated caring) a sensitivity to the ways that charges' self-esteem and motivation are affected by the group and individuals in it and an ability to act within this group setting to foster that self-esteem. Vocations taking place on a more individual-to-individual basis (e.g., doctor, lawyer, individual therapist) do not require this kind of sensitivity. A sensitivity to issues of trust, confidentiality, and betrayal is also differently required in different vocations, depending partly on the intimacy of revelation by the charge (e.g., in therapy), though almost any service vocation will involve these issues to some extent.[3]

3. See Churchill (1989) for an argument that medicine be seen as having distinctive (what he calls) moral ideals, values, and sensibilities not derivable from a universal ethic. This

Yet all the carings with which I am concerned here involve caring about a person *in her totality*, in contrast with caring *only* about the particular *aspect* of her good that I am referring to as specialized caring's "focus." Perhaps in some of these cases the differences between the virtues and sensitivities involved in vocational caring is only a matter of degree. But the point still remains that the moral character of the caring itself within different vocations is to some extent distinct. Note that vocational carings (or vocations as loci of caring) will not be *as* distinct as they would be in conceptions of professions as role definitions. Some such conceptions would justify a teacher, for example, in not concerning herself with a pupil's personal problems on the grounds that "that is for therapists, not teachers." Such rigid role definition is prevented by vocation as involving care, since the charge's whole good must be the object of care.

In fact, many of the divisions between vocations, although explainable historically, have the character of little more than pragmatic and provisional adjustments to human nature and time constraints. Teachers would in some ways be better *as teachers* if they were also (in part) counselors, therapists, friends – if they had the virtues, skills, and sensitivities involved. It is unrealistic to expect teachers (and this holds for other professions) fully to be all these things; the role would be too demanding for most people, and many people otherwise suited to teaching would not be able to take on these other sensitivities and their exercise. Nevertheless, it must also be kept in mind that the accepted definitions of vocations – with their specific norms, virtues, and ideals – are subject to contestation and change, and there are in fact currents afoot within teaching, law, and medicine to make them more caring and thereby to some extent to blur some of the divisions between these professions.

Recent discussion of a morality of care (see footnote 2), especially in the context of general talk of a morality of principle or morality of justice, has generally failed to explore the possibility that care can take significantly different forms in different contexts and thus can draw on significantly different virtues and sensitivities. But philosophical tradition – with its use of the very general and vague terms "beneficence," "benevolence," "altruism," "well-being," and the like – has been no better in this regard. Neither has appreciated the ways that caring about the good of others involves several distinct modes, sensitivities, and the like. Being able to

sort of argument also applies (though Churchill does not do so explicitly) to a distinctive form of medical caring, since medical caring can be seen as part of the general distinctive ethic of medicine.

perceive that someone is depressed and knowing how to bring her out of it is a different kind of quality than always being available to others when explicitly called on. Yet both can be expressions of caring, and both count as benevolence. Generosity, kindness, and compassion are all distinct virtues concerning others' good, involving (perhaps clusters of) distinct sensitivities.

I mean my remarks here not primarily as a criticism of the notion of a morality of care but as a contribution to its further development. For seeing how caring can be different in different contexts actually gives a morality of care a greater power and scope than it has seemed to have (especially to some of its detractors, but to some sympathizers as well). That is, many have taken a morality of care to apply solely to the domain of personal relations and have thought that once one leaves this territory – moving to more "public" domains such as professional life, for example – another ethic will be necessary. It may be true in some sense that caring within personal relations is *less* specialized, and thus seemingly less restricted and more total, than vocational caring. But some degree of differentiation is present in personal relations as well. Caring for children is different from caring for friends. And caring for different friends can involve different sensitivities, depending on the particular friend and friendship. I may display some caring virtues with one friend and others with another friend; the two friends might need very different kinds of things from me. In any case, there are ways in which a teacher cares for a pupil and in which a parent does not for the child who is that pupil – virtues displayed by the teacher toward him that the parent does not need to display or has not the occasion to.

Recognizing that there can be caring in nonintimate relationships – less "personal" ones – thus can have the effect of broadening the scope of an ethic of care.

Generality

The next two modes of actions in friendship and vocation involve making explicit appeal to the existence of the friendship as a guide to action, trying to figure out what the norms of friendship bid of one in the particular situation. Thus these modes involve an ought – though not necessarily a *requirement* or an *obligation* – that need not be present in the first mode (caring) of action of friendship or vocation.

Not every such appeal will have the right to be called an act of friendship, however. The appeal has to be for the sake of the friend himself in order to count as a genuine act of friendship. Thus if I appeal to the norms of friendship as a way of ensuring that I am able to regard myself as a good friend, I am not really acting for my friend's sake. It can even be argued that appealing to the norms of friendship out of a genuine desire to *be* a good friend is too distant from a concern for the specific friend himself. The appeal to the norms of friendship must be a way of ensuring that I am doing what needs to be done *for, and for the sake of, that specific friend,* in order to count as an act of friendship. When this is so, acting from the norms of friendship can be a genuine and authentic act of friendship.

Yet within the category of the appeal to the norms of friendship there is a further distinction – that between the thought that friendship bids me to do a certain thing and the thought that *this particular friendship with this particular person* bids me to do a certain thing. The former thought – that of friendship in general – might for example restrain me from doing something incompatible with the very idea of friendship. For example, suppose a Chinese student, Da-Wei, studying in the United States at the time of the crackdown on the student democratic movement in China in spring 1989 is pressured by agents of the Chinese government to reveal the identities of Chinese student-movement activists in the United States. If a friend of Da-Wei's is among those sought by the government, part of Da-Wei's motivation in not acceding to the pressures might well be the thought that one simply does not betray a friend in such a way. This is a type of action that the agent regards as prohibited to *any* friend toward any other friend.

This seems a case of a genuine act of friendship. However, appeal to the general category of friendship will sometimes be inappropriate to the situation and deficient as an act of friendship precisely *because* it abstracts too much from the particularity of the friendship.

Generality is like a role obligation in the respect that its moral pull applies to any occupant of the role (e.g., to any friend). But it need not always be impersonal the way roles are – sense (2) in section 4. For the role obligation is generally spelled out explicitly as a rule, whereas in friendship the norm the agent draws on depends on her particular understanding of friendship and of the norms and values that she sees implied in it; and that personal understanding will draw on cultural and other social differences in conceptions of friendship. Sometimes that understanding will be one that – at least it could be argued – *anyone* understanding the concept of friendship would have to accept. But other times there may be personal variability. The latter case will then be closer to the way vocation is impersonal (responsiveness to a value external to the agent) than to the way in which role is.

Particular relationship

The category of friend is invoked not only in general form but also explicitly as the particular relationship with a specific person. Each relationship has a unique, nonreplaceable value to its participants. Each has a unique history. And each involves the accumulation of specific understandings, both explicit and implicit, which reflect that value and that history. Because of this, I might feel that a certain action is called for on my part toward my friend Inez, an action that would not necessarily be appropriate to other friendships in similar circumstances. The thought here is not "friendship bids me to do x" but "x is what my particular friendship with Inez bids of me." An example might be knowing that I should leave Inez alone during her current troubles but should make sure she knows that my doing so reflects my understanding of what she does and does not want from me. I show my care for her by making sure that she realizes I am available should she feel she wants to call on me, but at the same time that (given our relationship and given who she is) she knows I understand that she would not want my actively offering her comfort.

As mentioned above, people have different understandings of what they take to be involved in friendship per se, just as they do of vocations. So individuals have not only different and unique friendships but also individual (though not necessarily distinct) interpretations of friendship itself, which they do not necessarily expect that others share.

Friendship perhaps lends itself to the distinction between specific relationship and general category for the same reasons that Emmet is reluctant to call friendship a role, namely that it involves too much variability and individuality in comparison with such relationships as doctor-patient or teacher-student. And yet that distinction can be drawn to some (though generally much lesser) extent in vocational relationships as well. As a teacher one can, for example, take on a professional relationship with a student that is somewhat different from that with one's other students – giving extra tutoring, for example, or pursuing a certain topic further than with the rest of one's class. This is especially true of elementary school teaching in which the relationships are much more individualized than, say, in college teaching. The specificity of a particular relationship can generate a set of claims or norms that (to some extent) differ from those of one's other students (though not in a way that involves *violation* of general professional standards and norms), as in the case of friendship.

113

The more particularistic type of appeal to the norms within a specific relationship is a mode of motivation and action that is genuinely morally distinct from appeal to the *type* of relationship in general (friendship or vocational). It is not a mere application to a particular relationship of the norms of friendship in general (except perhaps in the formal sense in which acknowledging the specific understandings and values in a specific relationship is an exemplification of the general principle of acknowledging the individuality or particularity of specific relationships). For one thing, not every such particularistic appeal is governed by a statable principle that it is plausible to think the agent is (even implicitly) drawing on in her action. For another, even when one can find some principle that does seem applicable to an action – for example, be a comforting presence to one's friend – it is not clear that this principle is actually required by the very idea of friendship itself. It seems rather to be implied at best in certain sorts of, or certain understandings of, friendship. Finally, principles that *do* perhaps seem implied in the very concept of friendship and that are pertinent to this situation – such as, support the well-being of one's friend – are pitched at such a level of generality that they clearly underdetermine the specific action appropriate to the situation. Thus even in cases in which there actually is an application relationship between a category principle and a particular friendship, moral attention to the particular friendship will often play a crucial role in the determination of the specific action chosen. (For further argument on the moral work done in applying principles, see Chapter 3, "Moral Perception and Particularity.")

In other circumstances the relationship between the appeal to the category of friendship and the appeal to a particular friendship seems to be that of a minimum standard to what goes beyond that minimum. Thus Da-Wei could well think that the mere idea of friendship tells him not to betray his friend to the government agents, but to know how else he might help his friend, he must appeal to the particularities of the friendship. (Remember, however, that some of his actions are prompted by neither of these motivations but by direct compassion or care for his friend. More generally, as mentioned earlier, the three modes of motivation will often not be readily separable in specific actions or activities.)

The existence of appeal to the norms of particular relationships suggests a fourth notion of impersonality, in which the value to which appeal is made is external to the agent's particular wants and desires in the situation, as in sense (3), yet is internal to a particular relationship of the agent's.

VI

Something like the same breakdown in types of motivations can also be seen in various types of communitarian actions, that is, actions stemming from one's sense of attachment to or implication in a communal entity. Corresponding to spontaneous care for a friend or charge is care for a member of one's group as a member of the group. In some cases such concern can have a morally suspect side to it, as when it is directly preferential (in relation to a nonmember) with no seemingly good reason beyond the group identification. (We seem to accept such direct preferential caring in the case of friends in a way we, or many of us, do not in the case of, say, ethnic-group identification.) In other cases the communal care is not preferential but simply takes a specific form grounded in the shared identification. For example, if the carer and cared-for are both members of a socially vulnerable, disadvantaged, or neglected group, this can be a reason why the carer ought to be more concerned for members of her own group, for they are in special need of it and cannot count on getting that concern from others outside of the group.

In another case of communitarian care (which might overlap with the previous one), care for another individual member involves or implies a concern for the integrity of the group itself, as when a black lending support to a particular black musician is seen both as helping that individual as an individual as well as preserving and advancing a shared heritage. (Some version of this motivation – concern for the preservation of a distinct culture – is available to those outside that cultural group as well. See Chapter 6, "Altruism and the Moral Value of Rescue.") Finally, as in the case of friends, membership in certain groups can imply a trust and confidence in the appropriateness and ability of one helping the other, a trust and confidence that ground the caring response to the other person and make it not a preferential caring (or not a morally suspect one) but simply a specific form of caring.

As with friendship and vocation, there can be an appeal to the communal identification to guide action, and that appeal can take the form of direct appeal either to the communal entity itself or to one's particular relationship to it or particular interpretation of it. Thus as a Jew one can do what one regards as bidden or required of any Jew simply by what it means to be a Jew. Alternatively, one can appeal to the specific relationship one has oneself to Judaism. For example, one might feel that *any* or *every* Jew has a responsibility to do something to keep Jewish culture or heritage alive. But someone else might think that this is required only of herself, given her particular understanding of Judaism or Jewishness, and not necessarily of others who have (what one regards as not illegitimate) alternative relationships to or interpretations of that communal identification. (Of course, many communal identifications contain recognized subdivisions – for example, Reform or Orthodox Jew, black nationalist or integrationist – that mediate between the overall category itself, as Jew or African-American, and the purely individual level of interpretation. There might also be a similar phenomenon within traditions that attach to vocations. For example, the notion of a general practitioner refers not only to a purely medical specialty but to a way of thinking about the practice of medicine itself.) Thus, as in the cases of friendship and vocation, communitarian action can take on a more or less impersonal, as well as a more or less individual and particularistic, character.

It should be noted that the focus of moral concern by members of communal entities is not always internal, toward members of the group. In this way the moral character of (certain) communal identifications is disanalogous to friendship, where to act from friendship is always to act in some way toward the specific friend in question. A good example of a noninternal communal focus is Miep Gies, the Dutch woman who helped to shelter the Frank family (Jewish, German refugees) during the Nazi occupation of the Netherlands. Gies regarded her rescue efforts as very much stemming from her Dutch identity. She thought of her Dutchness as requiring her to reach out to non-Dutch persecuted persons (Gies 1987). This kind of communal identification operates more like a service vocation, in which it is not the practitioners but the charges who are served. It is important to keep these cases in mind, since communitarian identifications are often portrayed as if they were necessarily exclusivist – promoting an inward and (sometimes therefore) parochial focus.

To bring together the discussions of sections 3 to 6, we have the following breakdown of five types of action and motivation distinct from *both* pursuit of personal good *and* the demands of impersonal morality.

1. Direct care or response to an individual by an individual, involving no other specific moral relationship
2. Action from role
3a. Direct caring action on behalf of friend, charge, or fellow (communal) member without (even implicit) appeal to the norms of friendship, vocation, or community
3b. Appeal to the general category of the *type* of relationship (friendship, vocational, communal)
3c. Appeal to a specific relationship (friend, vocational, or communal) with its specific history and character as a norm to guide action, or

116

to an individual interpretation of vocation, communal values, or friendship, to guide action

We have also found three senses or uses of "impersonal" distinct from the view-from-nowhere sense:

1. Independence of personal characteristics (as in a role)
2. Appeal to a value or norm that the agent personally identifies with but that is independent of the agent's desires in the situation (as in vocation)
3. Appeal to values or norms the agent identifies with that are independent of the agent's desires yet are internal to her individual relationship

VII

So a framework for thinking about human motivations as they are relevant to morality (either as being themselves moral or as being separate from morality and potentially in conflict with it) that sees the only alternatives as wholly personal or wholly impersonal will miss a large territory of morally relevant forms of motivation and action.

But the damage that the personal/impersonal framework does to moral theory lies only partly in what it omits. What also tends to happen is that the omitted phenomena are taken up and squeezed into the framework itself, which thus preserves the illusion that personal/impersonal comprises an exhaustive dichotomy of morally relevant standpoints or classes of motives but actually distorts or misportrays the nonpersonal, nonimpersonal phenomena.

Let us look at friendship for an example. Friendship can in a sense be viewed as an example of "the personal." Indeed, friendships and close personal relations often show up on lists illustrating the personal domain in the writings of philosophers working with the personal/impersonal framework (Nagel, Wolf, and Care, for example).

It is actually possible to treat a friend and a friendship (at least for some period of time) primarily from the standpoint of its role in one's own good. This involves, for example, performing those acts of friendship most pleasant and enjoyable to oneself and in any case shunning as much as possible burdensome acts of friendship. It might also involve doing acts aimed at preserving the friendship when it seems to be threatened (e.g., by the friend's recognition that she is not really being valued for her own sake). It would also seem to imply a readiness callously to drop a friend as soon as the friendship stopped providing a balance of good to oneself.

It is evident that a friendship *entirely* in this mode is hardly a friendship at all. And one *primarily* in this mode is clearly a deficient sort of friendship. To treat friendship solely as a personal project, as something contributing to the good of the agent's life, is to distort what friendship is. In a genuine friendship, one must care about and value the friend for her own sake as an independent person separate from oneself, not for the sake of her role in one's own personal projects. And this caring will necessarily involve actions that one will not particularly want to be doing or that are in some way burdensome.

So although the personal-impersonal framework can attempt to encompass friendship, it succeeds only at the cost of robbing friendship of its true character and value.

Paradoxically perhaps, treating friendship only in terms of its good to oneself, only as personal project, actually prevents it from being the deep good to persons that friendship can be. Unless one fully appreciates and responds to the reality of the other person in her own right, to her particular needs, to her way of looking at things, and to her individuality more generally, one's relationship cannot have the depth of real friendship. But without that depth the friendship cannot constitute the deep good to the self that friendship can constitute. Thus, unless friendship is *not* seen on the model of the personal good, it cannot constitute the genuine good to the individual that philosophers (including some of those working within the personal-impersonal framework) have rightly wanted to recognize. (Illusory and superficial friendships can still provide certain kinds of goods – for example, companionship, admiration, connections, the ability to think of oneself as having good friends – though some of these depend on one's deceiving oneself and others are goods not specific to friendship.) The point here is like the paradox of hedonism noted frequently throughout the history of ethics, for example by Aristotle: Pleasure may be most successfully attained by those not seeking it, and the explicit search for pleasure may hinder its attainment. The difficulty of finding a non-paradoxical language in which to state the paradox of friendship contributes, I think, to the hold that the personal-impersonal framework can have on our moral thinking.

Similar points can be made about vocations and communities. Being less private in their nature than personal relationships, they might be less likely to be construed on the model of a personal good. Nevertheless, like friendships, they can comprise profound goods in a person's life. Indeed, in the way I have defined "vocation" (and have assumed in my discussion of community), it is necessarily an important source of meaning and value in the life of the one who has the vocation. And it is a value that can conflict with a moral demand issuing from a more impersonal perspective.

Nevertheless, the distinctive values of vocation and community are lost once one treats them purely on the model of personal goods. That is, if one treats one's vocations and communities only as sources of good or meaning to oneself, one loses the essential point that vocations and communities present a set of values independent of the self, appreciation of which *as* independent of the self is required for the true meaning of vocation and community. If I attempt to view and treat my communities solely in light of their good to myself – for example, by putting in only the time necessary to do the minimum to maintain my inclusion in them, by focusing on how they give my life meaning but not really giving of myself to them as independent sources of value in their own right, by treating them as instrumental to my good – then in a sense I do not treat them as *communities*. And, again seemingly paradoxically, I cannot then derive from them the genuine and deeper good that communities (and vocations) can actually provide.

Thus it is certainly true that friendships, vocations, and communities can be important sources of good to the individual. Yet the way they are sources of good cannot be understood from within the personal-impersonal framework. To treat them as if they were personal goods in the sense of the framework is to deprive them – by failing to recognize them as having value in their own right independent of the person in question – of the substance that they must possess to constitute that good to the person.

The personal-impersonal framework can distort the phenomenon of friendship, communities, and vocations in the other direction as well, by treating them as a species of impersonal demand in the view-from-nowhere sense. A central dimension of this is the way in which the claims of other persons (for example, the German Jews for Miep Gies, the illiterate boy for Kohl, the beleaguered community for a member of that community) are pictured within that framework as presenting themselves to the agent as a set of totally impersonal demands. Although I have delineated three senses in which the claims of vocation, relationship, and community do present themselves as "impersonal," none of those involves the total impersonality of the view from nowhere. Indeed, sense (3) requires those claims to be *essentially* bound up with particular meaning-conferring commitments (friendships, vocations, and communities) of the particular individual self.

119

The nonimpersonal aspect of vocation is particularly striking. In fact, it is when an individual begins to experience the demands of her work as being entirely external – and in that sense [sense (2)] impersonal – that we feel she is losing her sense of vocation (though this may be only temporary). She no longer experiences the personal sense of value in her work that one does when one works from a sense of vocation.

VIII

It is in part this totally impersonalist conception of morality, and especially of the ways in which the claims of other persons present themselves to us, that prevents Wolf, Care, and Nagel from giving a serious or adequate hearing to the idealistic, socially engaged, and interpersonally caring individual. Wolf portrays such a character as obsessively dedicated to an impossible and wholly impersonal moral ideal that necessarily cuts the person off from personal and interpersonal satisfactions. The only satisfactions allowed to Wolf's moral saint are those of a pure devotion to morality itself, as in Kant, or of living out a totally impersonal benevolence toward all of humanity.

In contrast to Wolf, Care does want to recommend a life involving a high degree of dedication to the welfare of others. He calls this a life of "service" and sees it as embodied in career choice. It is thus particularly striking how the personal-impersonal framework constrains Care from making his best case for this worthy ideal. By pitting purely personal self-development against a purely impersonal moral mode of life, Care deprives himself of the resources to portray his morally serious ideal as a psychologically compelling and realistic one. Care seems to imply that the individual who would choose the path he recommends is to be sustained in her life of service by little more than a continual focus on the staggering inequities in access to resources for self-realization, on the moral demands that these inequities yield, on her own responsibilities as a member of a world moral community, and on the reflective sense of "reconciliation" with the human condition in one's own time that stems from living out the "shared fate" perspective.

This individual is imagined to be conceiving of herself, by virtue of making this career choice, as greatly curtailing once and for all any hope of her own self-realization. For Care has conceived of self-development as a matter of purely private, "personal" concerns, such as the development of artistic or scientific talent, and it is this that the individual must forsake for the sake of a career of service to others. Care recognizes the psychological difficulties of his position in the preface to his book, where he says that what the argument of his book seems to recommend is a life that is in many ways quite unappealing and risks "important kinds of disappointment, frustration, or lack of fulfilment in our lives" (Care 1987, xiv).

What Care barely explores – and can hardly do so in view of his personal-impersonal framework – is the way that a career of service can itself be a form of something like what could be meant by "self-realization."

Herbert Kohl, for example, in many ways seems to exemplify Care's recommendation of a life of service. He helps to secure the conditions for the self-realization of many (such as the illiterate boy) who might otherwise be greatly hampered in their own life pursuits. Yet Kohl's life does not embody a systematic denial of personal realization. Rather, by drawing on a certain tradition of understanding and interpretation of what it means to be a teacher, and by being able to root that understanding in his personal sense of values, Kohl has secured for himself a kind of self-realization precisely *in* serving others, within the vocation of being a teacher.

In this regard, it is significant that Care portrays the life choice between service and self-realization in terms of a "career." As Care brings out well, much is at stake for the individual in choosing a life work. A choice which does not suit the psychological makeup of the individual can have a seriously deleterious impact on her life. On the other hand, the notion of career speaks to choice of lifework only from the perspective of its impact on the purely individualistic, or personal, aspect of the person's good. When we speak of someone's career, we regard her mode of work primarily in terms of the values of stature, status, personal attainment, and advancement, which accrue to the person as an individual.

By contrast the notion of vocation that, drawing on Kohl's experience, I have explicated here places choice of lifework in the context of its social meaning and implies a meaningfulness and value to the individual that is bound up with the social significance of her particular vocation. In doing so, the notion of vocation allows one to see how there might be an intimate link between the service aspect of some lifework choices and the self-realization aspect. This is not to say that the notion of vocation is more accurate than that of career – both are entirely legitimate perspectives on individual life choice. The point is that the notion of career *taken by itself* (as Care does) meshes with the limited perspective of personal good as something to be contrasted with service to others, as implied by Care's personal-impersonal framework. Yet the perspective of vocations as neither personal nor impersonal allows us to explore how service to others can be an aspect of good to the person.[4]

It might be replied to this argument that Care does not really intend to address the question of what would make a person psychologically able to handle the career choice that Care recommends on purely moral grounds; his prime concern is only to show that morality does indeed recommend this choice. But if one's notion of morality is so severed from a broader notion of choice-worthiness that takes into account the ways in which choice options bear on the identity and sense of personal good of individuals, then the worth of that notion of morality must be at least partly called into question. And my argument has been that by severing personal good so sharply from morality and from the claims of other persons, moral philosophers have helped to deprive us of the resources to address those questions of choice-worthiness and moral psychology.

To summarize, then, I have argued that vast domains of human motivation do not fit into the category of either purely personal good or taking the standpoint of purely impersonal morality. And by showing how these motivations – specifically, vocation, friendship, and community – are bound up with the moral agent's sense of personal value and meaning, I hope I have suggested some directions for a communitarian moral psychology.

REFERENCES

Bellah, R., Madsen, R., Sullivan, W., Swidler, A., and Tipton, F. 1985. *Habits of the Heart: Individualism and Commitment in American Life.* Berkeley: University of California Press.

Care, N. S. 1984. "Career choice." *Ethics* 94:283–302.

1987. *On Sharing Fate.* Philadelphia: Temple University Press.

Churchill, L., 1989. "Reviving a distinctive medical ethic." *Hastings Center Report,* 19, no. 3: 28–34.

Emmet, D. 1966. *Rules, Roles, and Relations.* New York: St. Martin's Press.

Flanagan, O., and Jackson, K. 1987. "Justice, care, and gender: The Kohlberg-Gilligan debate revisited." *Ethics* 97:622–37.

Gies, M., and Gold, A. L. 1987. *Anne Frank Remembered.* New York: Simon and Schuster.

Gilligan, C. 1982. *In a Different Voice: Psychological Theory and Women's Development.* Cambridge, Mass.: Harvard University Press.

Gilligan, C., Ward, J. V., and Taylor, J. M., with Bardige, B., eds. 1988. *Mapping the*

4. The distinction between "career" and "vocation" (or "calling") is made and put to good use by Sullivan (1988) and by Bellah et al. (including Sullivan, 1985), where both are contrasted with "job" (which is akin to what I have called "nonvocational role").

Moral Domain: A Contribution of Women's Thinking to Psychological Theory and Education. Cambridge, Mass.: Harvard University Press.

Kohl, H. 1984. *Growing Minds: On Becoming a Teacher.* New York: Harper and Row.

Nagel, T. 1986. *The View from Nowhere.* New York: Oxford University Press.

Noddings, N. 1984. *Caring: A Feminine Approach to Ethics and Moral Education.* Berkeley: University of California Press.

Rawls, J. 1971. *A Theory of Justice.* Cambridge: Harvard University Press.

Sandel, M. 1982. *Liberalism and the Limits of Justice.* Cambridge: Cambridge University Press.

Sullivan, W. 1988. "Calling or career: The tensions of modern professional life." In A. Flores (ed.), *Professional Ideals.* Belmont, Calif.: Wadsworth.

Wolf, S. 1982. "Moral Saints." *Journal of Philosophy* 79:410–39.

6

Altruism and the moral value of rescue: resisting persecution, racism, and genocide

Samuel and Pearl Oliner's book *The Altruistic Personality* elicits our great admiration and gratitude for the few who risked so much to shelter Jews in Nazi Europe. This work is of the first importance for moral philosophers concerned to understand the highest reaches of moral excellence. No firm line can be drawn between psychology and philosophy in this area. Both attempt to understand what it is to be a person of heroic virtue, such as the individuals studied by the Oliners; and this quest cannot be severed from the attempt to understand how we can *become,* and help others become, morally excellent, or at least morally better. The Oliners suggest that the rescuers they studied had "altruistic personalities" and that by studying their histories we can learn how to promote altruism in others. I will claim that the concept of altruism by itself is insufficient to express the moral accomplishment of these rescuers. I will argue that there are other moral values implicated in such rescue activities that supplement and enrich – but are distinct from – the value of altruism per se. First is the moral value of resistance to evil. Acts of rescue constituted resistance to Nazism, specifically resistance to both persecution and racism, in addition to being acts of altruism. Second is the value of resistance to genocide, which implies a positive value being placed on the existence of the Jewish people as a people (over and above the value embodied in altruism, of saving individual Jews). I will also discuss the issue of risk and sacrifice as a dimension of altruistic action distinct from altruism per se. My argument will attempt to place altruism within the scheme of these other related though distinct values.

The argument has implications for personal and moral development. The psychic structures underlying altruism are not sufficient to generate the range of virtues involved in heroic rescue. Hence a theory of the psychic conditions for and underpinnings of altruism will not give us all of what the Oliners want in a theory of heroic rescue, though their failure to distinguish the different values involved in altruism does not preclude their having successfully identified, in the name of altruism, some of the prerequisites of the other relevant values. But philosophical clarity serves developmental efficacy here. Until we get clear on the values that we

124

want to promote, we cannot proceed clearly to inquire how these are to be developed.

ALTRUISM AS AN AGENT-CENTERED VALUE

"Altruism" as a positive value is necessarily an "agent-centered" value rather than a "consequence-centered" value. To call an act altruistic is to say more than that it produces beneficial consequences for someone; it is to confer praise on the agent of that action. That is, altruism refers necessarily to an agent's motivation.

Social scientists have understandably found this element in the notion of altruism troublesome. For it is notoriously difficult to be certain of people's motivations – hence difficult to study altruism in the way social scientists wish to do so. For this reason social scientific writers on altruism sometimes try to deny, or at least to mute, the agent-centered nature of altruism by defining it without its full motivational reality. Thus, in *The Altruistic Personality* Pearl and Samuel Oliner say, "For the purpose of our study, we prefer the definition [of altruism] which relies on objective measurable criteria," and the Oliners take their definition to avoid reference to "internal psychological states."[1]

The subsequent discussion in the Oliners' book, however, belies this aspiration. The rescuers cited in the book all appear to (and are taken by the Oliners to) have acted from concern for the rescuee or from moral principle. That is, a condition referring to motivation is in fact adopted in the Oliners' working definition of "altruism," and this is in accordance with their implicit recognition that altruism is necessarily an agent-centered concept.

Rescue presents a less problematic case of genuine moral motivation than do other beneficent acts. Rescuers who received monetary reward were not counted (by the Oliners). Most rescuers could not have acted for the egoistic goal of social approval, first because it was too risky to let others know that one was engaged in rescue, and second because in most cases the norms prevailing in their society or community did not approve of such rescue. Furthermore, even if a rescuer were concerned about approval (of the rescuees, or of a few confidants who knew of the rescue), the personal gain in such approval was so obviously outweighed by the risk to life and freedom in engaging in the rescue that a desire for

---

1. Despite this disclaimer, earlier (p. 3) the Oliners make explicit use of a motivational conception of altruism. Altruistic personality is defined as "a relatively enduring predisposition to act selflessly on behalf of others." "Selfless" makes essential reference to motivation, however difficult it might be to discern it in practice.

125

such approval could not intelligibly be regarded as the motive for rescue. I suggest that the move to a behavioral or consequence-centered definition of altruism defeats the purpose of studying altruism in the first place, and hence serious students of altruism like the Oliners will inevitably end up drawing on an agent-centered conception.

ALTRUISM AND RISK

Some psychologists and philosophers oversimplify the nature of altruism and its value by defining it as involving sacrifice, or at least the risk of it. The element of risk is central to the case of rescue and surely does constitute an important part of why rescue activities are admirable. Nevertheless, building self-sacrifice into the very definition of altruism generally (heroic rescue being only one type of altruism) is misleading. For it masks the fact that it can be morally good or admirable to be genuinely concerned about the welfare of others even when there is no risk or loss to the self. The epithets "compassionate," "thoughtful," and "kind" all refer to admirable traits that involve altruism (in the sense of genuine concern for others), yet none of them requires loss or sacrifice to the agent.[2]

What altruism does require for the specific value that it has is an absence of concern for the self — a direct concern only for the other. But absence of concern for the self is not the same thing as sacrifice or risk to the self.[3] In many ordinary circumstances it is possible to be helpful to

2. It might be replied to this that even when there is no other kind of loss, one always loses the time spent in helping the other, and that this inconvenience constitutes a loss to the self. This distinctly economic conception of human nature reflects prior theoretical commitments rather than attention to the phenomena of loss. We do not necessarily experience the time we take to help others as a loss to ourselves. We do not regard as a loss to ourselves every moment in which we fail to pursue gain. See Michael Slote, *Beyond Optimizing: A Study of Rational Choice* (Cambridge: Harvard University Press, 1989), for a compelling argument that it is not always rational to maximize gain to oneself.

3. In her very interesting article, "Altruism vs. Self-Interest: Sometimes a False Dichotomy," *Social Philosophy and Policy,* vol. 10, No. 1 (January 1993), Neera Badhwar argues that rescuers typically did act out of self-interest. Her argument for this point is that the rescuers had a strong sense of individuality and personal efficacy, and that in their rescue efforts they were typically affirming their values, and in that sense affirming themselves. Badhwar is right to argue that some forms of concern to live up to one's existing values are not incompatible with altruism, though some — namely, ones that get in the way of a primary focus on the plight of the other, or that treat the altruistic act as a *means* to realizing one's values — *are* incompatible with it. Having a strong sense of personal efficacy and individuality are not, however, the same as being concerned for one's *interests.* Leaving aside that it may be misleading to speak of affirming one's values as a form of "self-interest," as long as the motivational source of the agent's action

someone out of compassion or sympathy, and yet to lose absolutely nothing (though gain nothing either). Sacrifice and risk are indeed an important part of what gives rescue its value. But the concern for others shown in that rescue is a separately valuable element, which can exist without the risk.

ALTRUISTIC SPECIALIZATION

Although concern for others may be ceteris paribus a good thing (independent of the sacrifice involved), we do not actually *admire* persons or confer positive agent-centered worth on their concerned actions in all contexts. For example, normally we do not admire someone for her concern for family members or friends. Rather, this is simply expected.

Distinctly praiseworthy altruism involves either a degree of concern toward family members or friends that is above and beyond some threshold, or a scope of concern wider than intimates. How wide in scope does altruism have to be before we count it praiseworthy?

Let us take an example here, which will help to illustrate both the value of altruism and the value of rescue: Jacek is deeply devoted to the welfare of his community. He lives in a relatively poor neighborhood and is always helping his neighbors individually, attempting to secure better services for them, organizing them to articulate their needs politically, and the like. Jacek is genuinely compassionate and caring toward his neighbors. He is tireless and selfless, energetic and imaginative in his efforts to help.

Let us note, however, that Jacek's altruism involves a degree of what we might call "moral specialization" (or "altruistic specialization"). His altruism is targeted to a specific group of persons – defined residentially or by a shared condition. To explore the significance of this fact, let us imagine that a political refugee who is of a different race or ethnic group moves into Jacek's community and either by herself or through an intermediary asks Jacek – as a knowledgeable and helpful person in the community – for help and refuge. Let us further imagine the refugee as a Salvadoran, who is in danger of being killed if she returns to El Salvador. [AUTHOR'S NOTE: This was written before the January 1992 peace accords between the FMLN and the ARENA government of El Salvador.] The U.S. government will not grant her political refugee status and she is thus threatened with deportation.

involves concern for the other's well-being, the agent's further knowledge that performing this act constitutes an affirmation of her values in no way detracts from the act's altruistic worth.

127

Suppose that Jacek refuses to be concerned about the Salvadoran refugee. He feels he has enough to do taking care of the people already in his community; they have urgent needs too, and he spends all his time helping them. He has no interest in the refugee.

What do we think of Jacek in light of his response to the refugee? Do we reconsider or withdraw our previous judgment that he is an altruistic person deserving of admiration? Let us be clear that his unwillingness to help the refugee does not call into question the authenticity and sincerity of his altruistic efforts on behalf of his community. It is not like discovering that all along Jacek has been secretly employed by a wealthy benefactor who is paying him to help the community.

It is true that Jacek has all along been altruistically specialized. But we knew this about him from the beginning and it did not affect our initial judgment of his worthiness. In any case most people are in some ways morally specialized. Their moral efforts are targeted primarily to members of specific groups, whether defined in terms of proximity to the agent or as sharing some characteristic. Are we entirely to reevaluate our moral judgments about the admirability of morally specialized altruism?

At the same time, Jacek's response to the Salvadoran refugee does reflect on Jacek's moral character, and casts a new light on his previous altruism on behalf of his community. The appearance of the refugee constitutes a new moral situation for Jacek, in which the moral specializataion becomes a kind of parochialism. Although in usual circumstances Jacek's moral specialization is not inappropriate and does not render his altruism less than admirable, in this new situation his failure to go beyond that specialization does mark a deficiency in his altruism. This is partly because the refugee's life may be in danger; she is in a situation of greater and more urgent need than the members of Jack's neighborhood. But this is not the only reason. Even if her need were at the same level as that of his neighbors, it would still be a deficiency were he to fail to have some concern for her and a willingness to help.

It would, I think, be too harsh to say that Jacek's altruism toward his community is entirely deprived of moral worth in light of his failure to help the refugee. Yet it seems importantly diminished in moral worth. Jacek himself is rightly admired less in regard to his community-focused altruism.

It seems, then, that in some situations mere altruism — understood as concern for others besides oneself (and, let us stipulate, beyond the bound of family and friends) — is not enough. The altruism has to have a certain degree of scope or inclusiveness to warrant full worth and admira-

128

tion. It must at least go beyond a narrow or customary ethnocentrism or other group centeredness to include groups different from oneself.

This analysis is implicit in judgments many of us make about rescue and other altruistic efforts in the context of Nazi occupation. We regard it as a failure of some kind if a Christian was not able to extend help, or at least concern, to Jews, refugees from other countries, and other groups perceived as different from herself. For example, no matter how heroic a Polish Christian was in sheltering members of the Polish underground from the Nazis, if such an individual refused to be concerned about the plight of Jews as well, then something was lacking.

This is not to make a blanket judgment of condemnation of, say, Polish Christians who did not help Jews. The penalty for helping was death to the helpers (visited upon at least two thousand Polish rescuers), and no one is in a position to condemn those who failed to take such risk – especially not those who have never faced anything like such risks themselves. What can be said with more justification, however, is that a person whose refusal to help a Jew stemmed not from fear of the consequences but rather from an inability to extend her altruistic concern beyond national and religious boundaries evidenced a less-than-admirable trait of character. Although perhaps none can in good conscience condemn Polish non-Jews for failing to help Jews, the indifference of so many to the Jews' plight merits criticism.[4]

UNIVERSALISTIC ALTRUISM AS AN IDEAL

In light of reflection on the Nazi context, and on other situations in which the normal moral specializations prove insufficient or inadequate, it might be tempting to define altruism not as concern for others but as concern for others *simply as human beings* – thus building inclusiveness or universality into the concept of altruism itself. For if one is concerned about others simply as human beings, then one does not exclude from one's concern any human being, no matter what her relation to oneself. If it were true of Jacek that he is concerned about members of his community simply as human beings, than he could not fail to be concerned about the Salvadoran refugee. Such a definition of altruism requires that differences of race, religion, ethnicity, national origin, class, and the like not affect one's caring for others – or else this caring is not to count as "altruism." Jacek's failure to care for the Salvadoran refugee shows that he cares for his neighbors not simply as human beings but

4. On this point, see Istvan Deak, "Strategies of Hell," *New York Review of Books,* vol. 39, No. 16:8–14.

rather as persons standing in a certain relation to himself, hence, on this proposed definition, not "altruistically."

The temptation to so define altruism should be resisted. My suggestion would be to retain this universalistic or fully inclusive concept of altruism as an ideal, but to reject it as a definition. Otherwise one has deprived all altruistic specializations of any of the moral value attaching to altruism, and I have argued that this goes too far and is untrue to our reflective moral understanding.

My proposal acknowledges the value perspective informing the Oliners' book – that universalistic altruism is a higher form of altruism than specialized altruism and that the rescuers exhibited such altruism. (To put it another way: The more inclusive the altruism, the more worth it has.) Beyond this, I have argued also that in some circumstances universalistic altruism is not only an ideal, but constitutes a standard against which specialized altruism becomes parochial and loses much (though not all) of its worth.

ALTRUISM AND RESISTANCE TO EVIL

Although universality or inclusiveness must supplement and qualify altruism in order for it to provide an adequate conceptual framework to express the moral accomplishment of rescuers of Jews under Nazi occupation, I want to argue that a full understanding of this accomplishment and its distinct worth requires an appreciation of several other values distinct from – and not merely qualifying – altruism itself. The first of these is the extraordinary riskiness of rescue activities discussed earlier.

I will discuss two further dimensions of rescue of Jews in Nazi Europe – resistance to evil, and preservation of the Jewish people. It is a morally significant feature of rescue in the Nazi context that to save a Jew was to resist evil – the evil of Nazism. This evil, in turn, has at least two distinguishable aspects – persecution and racism. The Jews were a persecuted group, and were persecuted because of their ethnicity or religion (their [alleged] "race").

Resistance to evil is a feature morally distinct from altruism itself. The perspective of altruism sees the persecuted Jew as a person in need, whose life is under threat of death. The motive of altruism is activated in the altruist insofar as she sees the other as a person in need (or, more generally, as a person whom she can benefit).

But to help, or to save the life of, someone who is persecuted is to do more than just to save life, as in a flood or accident. It is to recognize a further evil – the evil of persecution (by which I refer here to state-sponsored persecution) – and to resist that evil by saying that one will not let persecution be successful in the case of this particular individual. This is why the Salvadoran political refugee implicitly presents to Jacek a moral issue over and above the urgency of her individual need. She presents an issue (persecution) that is not present in the neighbors who are the usual subjects of Jacek's helping activities.

If a rescuer acts with the recognition that in helping the persecuted person one does more than save a life but also resists persecution, the notion of altruism alone is insufficient to express her moral accomplishment. Many of the rescuers in *The Altruistic Personality* articulated this dimension of rescue in the Nazi context, by speaking, for example, of the wrongness of punishing the innocent (see Oliner and Oliner, 1988, pp. 166–7). Beyond those who explicitly voice this dimension, many others can be presumed to have seen their rescue activities at least partly in this light. For the fact that Jews were being persecuted was known to virtually everyone in the Nazi-occupied countries, and certainly to all rescuers. Thus rescuers were aware that in saving a Jewish life they were also saving the life of a persecuted person, and so were resisting or in a sense protesting against persecution. They can be presumed to have understood that saving a Jew from the Nazis was in this regard not simply like helping the victims of natural or technological disasters.

The failure to mention the aspect of persecution could stem partly from the fact that the rescuers took its significance for granted. But there may be another reason as well. Although the existence of persecution was evident, it is also a more abstract consideration than the more immediate one of the danger to the particular, individual Jew or Jews who are potential rescuees. It is not surprising that 76 percent of the rescuers focus on the needy condition of the potential rescuee (Oliner and Oliner, 1988, p. 168); this is the most immediate consideration. Yet it is not the only consideration. Upon reflection, a smaller number of persons would no doubt avow that asserting the wrongness of, or resisting, persecution played some role in their motivation.

Moreover, considerations that function as distinct motives to rescue do not exhaust the way that moral (or other) considerations can play a role in an agent's action. A consideration can be a necessary condition of a motive occurring, or of having the motivational force that it does have.

What directly moves a person to act does not exhaust the meaning that the action has for the person. This point is illustrated in the film *Angry Harvest,* which deals with the rescue phenomenon in its Polish setting.[5] A

5. *Angry Harvest* (original German title: *Bittere Ernte*), directed by Agnieszka Holland, 1986.

lonely and sexually frustrated but materially comfortable Polish farmer comes upon a hungry and terrified Jewish woman in his woods; he takes her to his home and shelters her. His motive in initially helping her would naturally be described as compassion. At the same time the farmer might well not have had such a compassionate reaction to a Jewish male. What young females represent to this farmer's complex and unhealthy consciousness (wife, helpless dependent, sexual partner) may not have been a direct motive itself but have nevertheless been a condition of the actual motive of compassion operating. Analogously, it may be that in some rescuers the Jews being victims of persecution played a conditioning role in the strength of the concern that led people to engage in rescue.

Beyond this, the moral meaning that an action has for an individual comprises considerations that play a role (conscious or unconscious) in what the act means to her; and this goes beyond both motivation and necessary conditions for motivation. Some rescuers may have been fully aware that their actions constituted resistance to persecution, and this could have been important to the meaning that this action had for them; yet the consideration may not have played a *motivational* role. In helping a friend, one may be moved directly by his sorry plight. At the same time one may be aware (whether explicitly or not) that in helping him one is also affirming the importance to oneself of this friendship, and one takes for granted that one's friend is aware of this. This latter element, then, is a part of one's self-understanding of one's act even though it has no direct, or perhaps even conditioning role. In the *Angry Harvest* example a possible interpretation is that the farmer is unconsciously aware of the woman as potentially representing the fulfillment of other desires but this plays no role in his motivation, even as a necessary condition (for the compassion). Still, in describing the meaning of the action for the farmer (even though this meaning is partly unconscious) one would have to include the former element.[6]

To say that rescue of the persecuted involves a further moral dimension beyond that of altruism alone is not to say that a persecuted individual's life is worth more than the life of a nonpersecuted person (e.g., of a drowning person, or a victim of natural disaster). It is not to say that the refugee's life has greater worth than the lives of the community residents (in the example of Jacek) or that a Jew's life was more valuable than a German soldier's. The point has nothing to do with the worth of persons,

---

6. For further criticisms of the focus on motivation and motive for being insufficient to capture the full moral meanings of human action, see L. Blum, *Friendship, Altruism, and Morality* (London: Routledge and Kegan Paul, 1980), Chapter 6.

but with the moral character of rescue activities and the range of values instantiated by them.

I say that resistance to the evil of persecution is an element over and above altruism in the rescue of the Jews, and it is an element that need not (though it may) function as a direct motive. But can it also be an actual motivation all its own, operating in some cases in the absence of altruism altogether? The Oliners say that some rescuers were motivated primarily by their hostility toward Nazis. They quote one rescued survivor describing his rescuer's motivation: "He explained to me in very simple words: 'I decided to fight the Germans by saving those persecuted by them. Who were the most persecuted? The Jews' " (Oliner and Oliner, 1988, p. 144).

One must here distinguish the motive of resistance from that of revenge or hatred. Revenge or hatred does not have a moral character, even if one's reason for hating or for wanting revenge stems from the immorality of the object of hatred or intended revenge. By contrast, resistance to evil is a moral motive whose goal is to prevent evil, or at least to take a stand against it – and not merely to vent hatred or revenge.

Keeping this distinction in mind, it seems to me difficult to believe that a person who rescued Jews as a form of resistance to the Nazis was not at least in some small degree motivated by altruism as well. For in recognizing what is evil about Nazism one recognizes the harm it does to human beings, to those whom it persecutes. Care for human beings must be part of the recognition of the evilness of Nazism in the first place. Hence some of the overall motive (of, for example, the Nazi-resisting individual quoted above) in rescuing must surely involve altruistic concern for the potential rescuee.

This is not to deny that resistance to evil can function as a distinct motive or that some people are more dominantly motivated by resistance and others by altruism. Certainly once some underground resistance movements officially adopted the position that rescuing Jews was to be taken on as a resistance activity, some persons whose altruistic motivation by itself was insufficient to get them to engage in rescue began to do so from a motive of resisting evil.

ALTRUISM AND RESISTANCE TO RACISM

So far, I have discussed persecution as one part of the evil that rescue activities resist. But a further distinguishable part of this evil is the racism involved in the Nazis' persecution of Jews. (By "racism" I mean here the victimization of persons because of their [imagined or actual] race, ethnicity, religious affiliation, national heritage, and the like.) Racism is a particularly virulent scourge, beyond that of persecution itself, which can be visited upon someone for nonracist reasons. One can see this in the case of Jacek and the refugee. If Jacek's refusal to help the refugee stems (in part) from racist sentiments, his inaction is more blameworthy than if he fails to help because his moral energies and imagination are too bounded by his neighborhood community. (One can envision the latter situation if one imagines the refugee to be of the same race as Jacek himself.)

That racism adds a dimension of moral turpitude to an action that is also wrong on other grounds is sometimes recognized in the law as well. A racial attack on an individual is treated more harshly than an attack grounded in jealousy or economic gain, even if the harmed individuals are harmed equally in both situations. In the former case the attack can be a civil rights violation in addition to being an assault.[7]

Thus resistance to racism constitutes a further good element of an action that is morally good on other grounds as well, for example, as an act of rescue. A white sheltering a black on the Underground Railroad during the days of slavery (in the United States), a Turk saving an Armenian driven from his home at the time of the Armenian Holocaust,[8] and a Christian sheltering a Jew – all these actions by their very nature resist the evil of racism being perpetrated against the groups in question. They all do more than save an individual, or even a persecuted individual; they assert the fundamental principle of human equality across racial, religious, and national differences. They help to keep the evil of racism from being triumphant.

Again, many of the rescuers interviewed in *The Altruistic Personality* recognized this antiracist dimension of their actions. Yet, as in the case of persecution more generally, the fact that some rescuers did *not* articulate it does not mean that they were unaware of it, or that it failed to play a role in their action. All rescuers were certainly aware that the Jews were being persecuted for their religion or ethnicity (and alleged race), and most (though not necessarily all)[9] of those

---

7. For examples of such "hate crimes" legislation in the United States, see Lawrence Fuchs, *The American Kaleidoscope: Race, Ethnicity, and the Civic Culture* (Hanover: New England University Press, 1990), pp. 392, 564. For a discussion of their rationale, involving the punishing of racial bigotry, see James Jacobs, "The New Wave of American Hate Crime Legislation," *Report from the Institute for Philosophy and Public Policy*, vol. 112, No. 1, Spring/Summer 1992.

8. Turks rescuing Armenians is discussed by Richard Hovanissian in "The Question of Altruism during the Armenian Genocide of 1915," in P. Oliner, S. Oliner, L. Baron, L. Blum, D. Krebs, M. Z. Smolenska, *Embracing the Other: Philosophical, Psychological and Historical Perspectives on Altruism* (New York: New York University Press, 1992).

9. The generalization that most rescuers could have been presumed to have been declaring opposition to racism is true only for the most part; for some rescuers were them-

engaged in rescue can be presumed to have thought such racial persecution wrong.

In looking back at the activities of these rescuers, and in honoring them for their moral accomplishment, I think we implicitly place these acts in a wider framework than that of altruism alone. We see the actions as resisting the evil of Nazism, as asserting the wrongness of persecution and racism. This is part, I think, of what accounts for our generally unqualified admiration for these actions. If the actions were solely ones in which one person risked her life and often those of her loved ones and other members of her household to save the life of another endangered person, it is not clear that many such acts – for example, ones in which several lives were risked to save one Jew – would or should not be regarded as foolhardy rather than as courageous and morally honorable. If I am in a burning building with two of my children and I endanger their lives and mine to attempt to rescue another person in the building, there would at least be disagreement as to how morally admirable such an action is.

And yet we do admire rescuers who endangered their own and their loved ones' lives to rescue Jews. (The Oliners report that 84 percent of the rescuers lived with other persons, 27 percent with children ten years or younger, all of whom were endangered by rescue activities.) I have often been troubled by the easy and seemingly unambivalent admiration that those involved in the study of rescuers (including myself) feel for these rescuers and assume that others will feel as well. I think the reason such admiration is ultimately justified is that the situation of non-Jewish rescuers of Jews (and Turkish and Arabic rescuers of Armenians) is only partly analogous to the burning house situation. The analogy is in the motivation to preserve life and in the risk to one's own life and (sometimes) those of loved ones and other members of one's household. But the disanalogy is that in the rescue context something larger than saving lives is at stake, namely, resistance to a great evil transcending the particular situation. It is, therefore, not merely a matter of one life against another, but, rather, of fundamental human principles and values at stake on top of (though not apart from) the saving of life. The actions of rescue have an historical importance in their role as countering the hegemony of Nazi power and Nazi values.

Perhaps this point deserves some qualification. I think some moral perspectives do encourage admiring actions of rescue involving nothing

selves avowedly anti-Semitic. They did not object to the racial element of persecution per se, but thought the Nazis were wrong to have taken this to the extreme of killing Jews. See Nechama Tec, *When Light Pierced the Darkness: Christian Rescue of Jews in Nazi-occupied Poland,* Chapter 6.

more than the risking of one's own life to save that of another. Ewa Kurek-Lesik cites a moving example of a nun from the Order of the Immaculate Conception describing a meeting called by one of the sisters, Wanda Garczynska, to decide whether to continue sheltering several (possibly many) children and adult Jews. The nun remembers: "She explained that she did not wish to jeopardize the house, the sisters, the community. She knew what could be awaiting us. There was no thought of self. She knew: you should love one another as I have loved you. How? So that He gave His life."[10] The example suggests a Christian Christlike moral outlook in which risking one's own life to save another – independent of whether the threat to that life arises through persecution and/or racism – is itself a high, or even the highest, form of moral endeavor.[11]

I suspect that most admirers do not share the moral standard involved in the literal interpretation of sister Wanda Garczynska's remarks. If this is so, I suggest that their reaction of unqualified admiration for most instances of rescue depends partly on considering resistance to racial persecution an important element of the action.

Our moral reaction to rescuers is necessarily made from the historical vantage point of hindsight. We see, in retrospect, that acts of rescue were part of a resistance to Nazism. We see their significance as the historical one of asserting a different way of living and different values than those of the Nazis – an assertion not made by bystanders (those who did nothing to help), whatever their actual disagreements with the Nazi regime and philosophy. We see individual acts of rescue, whatever their detailed self-understanding, as imbued with this historical significance – a significance not everyone needed to have been explicitly aware of at the time (though some certainly were).

To summarize: Rescuers are altruistic, and this is certainly part of what we admire in their actions. But it is not only altruism – understood as a concern for the need of the other – that confers on rescuers their exceptional place in our moral evaluation. Aside from the obvious risk and sacrifice, there is the dimension of resistance to evil that their actions involve. In this way, the title of the Oliners' book, *The Altruistic Personality,* is in some ways misleading in implying that the notion of altruism itself is sufficient to conceptualize the moral significance of rescue. Rescu-

10. Ewa Kurek-Lesik, "The Role of Polish Nuns in the Rescue of Jews, 1939–1945," in P. Oliner et al., *Embracing the Other.*
11. Even this case may be ambiguous. For Sister Wanda and the other nuns knew that the lives of the Jews were not just endangered but were endangered because of racist persecution. Even though the biblical passage referred to (John 15:13) does not specify this aspect, it may be that the sisters' sense that it would be wrong to give up the endangered Jews was in part influenced by the recognition of this persecution.

ers were also resisters of persecution and racism, and these are distinct elements in our understanding of their moral accomplishment.

From a developmental point of view, the psychic underpinnings of the value of resistance to persecution and to racism are surely at least somewhat distinct from those of altruism. The former are more conceptually complex values, requiring an understanding of human practices not required for altruism, which can exist in rudimentary forms on the basis of little more than individual empathy. They also involve a degree of abstraction not specifically present in altruism but explored in developmental theories (such as Lawrence Kohlberg's) emphasizing the acquisition of general moral principles.

ALTRUISM AND AFFIRMING CULTURES

There is one other element of moral significance, beyond altruism pure and simple, involved (at least potentially) in the rescue situation we are considering – and that is the preservation of the Jewish people as a people. In contrast to resistance to evil, this aspect was (or could be inferred to be) seldom present in the self-understanding (explicit or implicit) of rescuers.

"Preservation of the Jewish people as a people" is one example of a general value, which I will refer to as "affirming cultures." That value is embodied in valuing the existence of any distinct people (though the boundaries of a "people" may be hard to define), with its distinctive culture, values, traditions, and ways of life (such as the Iroquois, Poles, African-Americans, Gypsies, Lithuanians, Armenians, Turks, Germans). Octavio Paz states this value well, in the context of an attack on a certain notion of "progress": "By suppressing differences and peculiarities, by eliminating different civilizations and cultures, progress weakens life and favors death. . . . Every view of the world that becomes extinct, every culture that disappears, diminishes a possibility of life."[12] Thus, for a Turk to help an Armenian, with an understanding that in doing so he was helping to preserve the Armenians as a people, would be to instantiate the same value I am referring to in the case of the Jews.

The Jewish exemplification of this value as applicable in the Nazi context is this: Under the Nazis the Jews as a distinct cultural, ethnic, religious group were threatened with extermination. This was the goal of Nazi policy. In rescuing an individual Jew or Jews, a rescuer did more than save an individual life; she contributed to preserving the Jews as a

12. I am grateful to Jack Shaffer for this quote. Neither he nor I know its original source, but it appears to be from 1987.

people. By helping to keep alive a bearer or possible bearer of the Jewish tradition, she helped to preserve that culture and tradition, with its particular values and ways of life.

In asserting the distinct value of this preservation of a people, I am not asserting that the Jews have a greater worth than other peoples. Because of the Jewish notion of being the "chosen people," and the way this has been used against them even in the present day, it is particularly important to distinguish *greater worth* from *distinct worth*.[13] "Distinct worth" implies a kind of worth that is different from, but neither greater nor lesser than, that of other peoples.[14] The value of preserving Jews is thus one example of a general value – preserving a people and affirming their worth. The salience of this general value in the case of Jews stems, of course, from the fact that the Nazis were declaring Jews to be a people unworthy of existence, and were attempting to realize their view in genocidal action.

The value of affirming cultures or people is recognized in the category of "genocide" as a particularly heinous crime, expressed for example in the 1946 United Nations Convention on the Prevention and Punishment of the Crime of Genocide. The implication is that in wiping out a people one does something more evil than killing an equivalent number of individuals. A people is more than a collection of individual human beings, and there is value in preserving a people that is over and above the value of saving individual lives. (Part of the evil of genocide can be practiced without directly taking lives, e.g., by preventing a people from reproducing, as by sterilization, or by forcible conversion.)

13. In 1984, a group of Carmelite nuns established a convent in a building on the perimeter of the Auschwitz-Birkenau death camp in Poland. Jewish groups protested this site and in 1987 Jewish and Christian groups and individuals from several countries, including the Archbishop of Cracow, signed an accord promising that the convent would be moved by February 1989. When this move did not take place, Jewish groups protested and a few demonstrators climbed the walls of the convent, an action criticized by many other Jews. Jozef Cardinal Glemp, the Roman Catholic Primate of Poland, protested the actions of the demonstrators by saying (among other things), "[D]ear Jews, do not talk with us from the position of a people raised above all others," in an apparent derogatory reference to the "chosen people" notion. See "Poland's Primate Denounces Jews in Dispute on Auschwitz Convent," *New York Times*, August 29, 1989.
14. The Oliners confuse this point in their book. They deny that most rescuers saw Jews as "particularly worthy" (p. 249) or as "exalted or uniquely worthy of help" (p. 154). Their point is that (most) rescuers acted from universal and human values rather than from a special liking for Jews. Notwithstanding this important point, the Oliners imply that the alternatives are limited to (1) seeing the Jews as especially worthy, and (2) seeing them as human beings like oneself, ignoring their religion. But a third possibility is to see the existence of the Jewish people as having a distinct worth – parallel to the worth of the Armenian people, the Polish people, and so on.

Preservation of the Jewish people as a people is related to the value and goal discussed earlier of resisting racism against the Jews. But it is by no means the same thing. The resister of racism declares a human equality and human kinship in the face of its denial. Thus the resister of racism rescues the Jew as a fellow human being (and some rescuers explicitly articulate this dimension: "Jewish people are the same; all people are the same" [Oliner and Oliner, 1988, p. 166]). But she does not necessarily rescue him as a Jew – that is, as the bearer of the specific cultural and religious traditions of Jews. Those traditions are affirmed by the rescuer who sees the Jew as a Jew. The antiracist rescuer, by contrast, does not necessarily assert the worth of Judaism or Jewishness as a specific culture or religion. What she does is to resist its denial as that denial is used to denigrate the Jew as a human being. What she does positively assert is simply the worth of a Jew as a human being.

The difference between the antiracist perspective and the perspective of asserting the specific value of Jewishness or of the Jewish people is evident in the fact that very few rescuers seemed to evince the latter value, but many (at least implicitly) adhered to the former and saw their rescue activities in light of it. Rescuers interviewed for *The Altruistic Personality* who mentioned the Jewishness of Jews generally did so only to assert the wrongness of victimizing Jews, and to say that they, in contrast to the Germans, saw the Jew as a human being. Several expressed this by saying, in essence, "I did not see him as a Jew, but as a human being." (See *Altruistic Personality*, p. 154: "I did not help them because they were Jewish," attributed to several rescuers.)

Polish rescuers, for example, almost never saw the value in Jewishness per se. Anti-Semitism ran so deep in Polish culture that the moral accomplishment of the Polish rescuer was to rise above that anti-Semitism and see the Jew as a fellow human being (Nechama Tec emphasizes this point in her study, *When Light Pierced the Darkness: Christian Rescue of Jews in Nazi-occupied Poland*). Iwona Irwin-Zarecka points out in her book, *Neutralizing Memory: The Jew in Contemporary Poland*, that Poles have almost always regarded the Jew as "other," as a problem, defined from the point of view of (non-Jewish) Polish society. They almost never saw Jews from the point of view of the Jews themselves; hence they were not able to appreciate the value of Jewishness in its own right. This has been true even of Poles who are not anti-Semitic in the sense of having negative, racist attitudes toward Jews. Given this history, the rarity of the Polish rescuer who could see the distinct value of preserving Jews as a people is hardly surprising – although, given the particularly rich form of Jewish life in Poland for so many centuries, it is a deeply painful fact.

The value of preserving a people is not only a value over and above saving the life of individuals, though it is that too. It is also a value connected with the sense of identity of the rescued individual. Even when conversion of Jews was done for pure security reasons and with no sense of spiritual advantage for the Jew of becoming a Christian, it must be recognized that this conversion constituted a violation of the Jew's identity (unless of course she herself chose to be converted for heartfelt religious reasons).[15] Ewa Kurek-Lesik found that some of the nuns rescuing Jewish children appreciated this fact, and did not convert them, although others had no such compunction. Still others presumably held positions in between, recognizing that it might constitute a kind of violation of a Jewish child to baptize and convert her, but feeling that considerations of security (to both the rescuers and rescuees) weighed in favor of doing so.

One group that did have a sense of the value of Jews as a distinct people were members of the Dutch Calvinists discussed in Lawrence Baron's "The Dutchness of Dutch Rescuers: The National Dimension of Altruism."[16] These Calvinists take seriously, as part of their theological outlook, the sacredness of the Old Testament, the Jewish origins of Christianity, and the fact that Jews were regarded as God's chosen people. In saving an individual Jew, a member of this faith saw herself as doing more than saving life – she was also helping preserve a religious group she saw as valuable.

Yet these Dutch Calvinists embody only one form of the recognition of the value of preserving the Jews as a people – and it is a less than ideal one, for it depends on the idea that Jews possess a special value as the "chosen people." This value, therefore, could not be embodied in other peoples. Hence the way the Dutch Calvinists value Jews would not be transferable to other peoples, and would give no grounds for their valuing, for example, a Muslim or a Buddhist. It is not an example of the *general* value of affirming cultures or peoples.

15. The Oliners cite a striking and complex example of this respect for an individual's cultural and religious identity (pp. 69–70). A French Christian woman placed several Jewish children in parochial schools and convents. These children wanted to be part of the Christmas celebrations going on, wanted to take communion and, in some cases, to convert. The woman felt that conversion would be a violation of their identity, although the children themselves were too young to see this and quite understandably wanted to take on and be part of the way of life of those who were being so good to them.

16. Lawrence Baron, "The Dutchness of Dutch Rescuers: The National Dimension of Altruism," in L. Baron et al., *Embracing the Other.*

ALTRUISM AND EXTENSIVITY

The value of affirming particular cultures may seem morally limited in its particularism, and a retreat from a universal moral concern. But, I will argue, affirming culture is much closer to a form of universal moral concern than it may seem.

Let us distinguish two paths to a universal moral concern, that I will call "care" and "principle." A universal moral concern based on *principle* involves the possession of explicitly universalistic principles such as love or beneficence, or affirming the worth of all persons. Universal "care" involves caring about each individual known to oneself. This will have to involve not only individuals whom one encounters personally, but also individuals known to one but not personally encountered. The caring does not involve appeal to principle but does involve caring about each individual independent of the person's racial, ethnic, religious (and other such group) differences from oneself. The distinction between a caring and a principled universalism is well exemplified by two now well-known rescuers of Jews, Magda and Andre Trocmé.[17] Although there are arguably differences in the specific *forms* of moral concern generated by care and principle, each generates a universal moral concern.

Affirming the value of specific peoples can be a further – distinct but not competing – way of generating a near-universal moral concern, or at least a form of moral concern that goes beyond one's own local concerns and attachments. For most persons have a cultural identity that is important to their own individual identity; they are part of some cultural, national, ethnic group.

Hence affirming cultures will encompass most persons within its scope of moral concern. Yet this value should not be seen as an *alternative* to care and principle. That is, affirming the value of peoples – and of an individual's cultural identity – is not a different way of reaching the exact same place (helping someone because she is a human being); it is not analogous to the way that care and principle are different ways of reaching that place. Rather, affirming cultures is a *complement* to both care and principle. Recognizing a person's distinct cultural identity does not distract from caring for her as a human being; but it is not simply a *way* of caring for her as a human being either. One might say that it is a way of caring for her as a specific individual (with her specific cultural identity); this is a kind of enriching of a care for her as

17. For more on the Trocmés and the care-principle distinction, see Chapter 4, "Moral Exemplars," and Phillip Hallie's *Lest Innocent Blood Be Shed* (New York: Harper and Row, 1979).

a human being.[18] One takes her specific individual identity into account in a way that the notion of "caring for someone else as a human being" does not capture.[19]

Thus, although affirming the value of Jews as Jews (Armenians as Armenians, etc.) is in one way more particularistic – in encompassing and valuing a particular cultural/religious/ethnic identity – than a principled obligation to all humankind, it is nevertheless not so much less universalist.

CONCLUSION

I have argued that attention to the moral significance of non-Jewish rescuers of Jews can help to place the concept of "altruism" in its proper value perspective. Altruism is of value in its own right. But several other dimensions – some of which are present in all cases of this rescue, and all of which can be present – are also distinct sources of value. These other

18. Charles Taylor, in "The Politics of Recognition," in Amy Gutmann (ed.), *Multiculturalism and "The Politics of Recognition"* (Princeton University Press, 1992) develops the idea that affirming a person's cultural identity is a way of affirming that person as an individual, and is at the same time distinct from a desire for equality or being treated the same as others.

19. These remarks can be placed in the context of current debates about the "morality of care," a notion developed by Gilligan (1982) and Noddings (1984). The Oliners draw on the notion of "care" to suggest that previous studies of individuals performing morally exemplary acts have overemphasized individual moral autonomy and individually generated rational principle; the Oliners find, by contrast, that a great number of rescuers can be characterized more accurately in terms of an emotion-based responsiveness to other human beings and direct concern for their welfare, that is, "care." I am accepting this perspective, though the Oliners use "care" to include general principles such as helping others in need, whereas I have wanted to restrict "care" to a one-to-one responsiveness in order more clearly to distinguish it from acting on principles of whatever sort. Nevertheless, I agree with the Oliners that genuine activities of rescue can be prompted by either care or principle.

But in this section of the essay, I am arguing that there is a limitation on *both* care and principle when understood as directed toward human beings qua human beings. The limitation is of failing to grasp the particularized identities of persons, one component of which is cultural/ethnic/religious. It is true that Noddings and Gilligan, in contrast to moral theories seen as more abstracted from concrete realities, emphasize that care is for the particular, and particularized, individual, not for "human beings in general" or "the social good." But most literature on the morality of care does not explore the constituents of individual indentity which would need to be taken into account in a true caring toward a particularized individual. In particular, the cultural/ethnic/religious dimension has generally not been explored, and is not explored by Gilligan or Noddings in their best-known works.

The limitation of a pure morality of care can be seen as well, or even better, in relation to the first two values I have discussed – resistance to persecution, and to racism. For even if we understood caring as "caring for each individual" (where that included ethnic/religious identity) rather than the less particularized "caring for someone as a human being," the former notion would still fail to capture the fact that in caring for *this* individual, one resists evil and upholds justice.

sources are sacrifice or risk; universality (extending one's concern to all human beings); resistance to evil in the form of persecution; resistance to evil in the form of racism; and valuing and preserving a people (here, the Jewish people) as a people. The moral accomplishment – and historical moral significance – of these rescuers can only be understood if these factors are taken into account. Altruism alone cannot express that accomplishment and that significance.

REFERENCES

Gilligan, C. 1982. *In a Different Voice.* Cambridge, Mass.: Harvard University Press.
Irwin-Zarecka, I. 1989. *Neutralizing Memory: The Jew in Contemporary Poland.* Oxford: Transaction.
Noddings, N. 1984. *Caring: A Feminine Approach to Ethics and Education.* Berkeley: University of California Press.
Oliner, S., and P. Oliner. 1988. *The Altruistic Personality: Rescuers of Jews in Nazi Europe.* New York: Free Press.
Slote, M. 1987. *Commonsense Morality and Consequentialism.* London: Routledge and Kegan Paul.
1989. *Beyond Optimizing: A Study of Rational Choice.* Cambridge, Mass.: Harvard University Press.
Sorokin, P. [1954] 1967. *The Ways and Power of Love.* Chicago: Henry Regnery.
Tec, N. 1987. *When Light Pierced the Darkness: Christian Rescue of Jews in Nazi-occupied Poland.* New York: Oxford University Press.

7

Virtue and community

The revival of a virtue approach to ethics has been accompanied by a renewed concern with the notion of community and, many assume, a close link between virtue and community. Yet most discussions of virtue proceed without ever mentioning community. The widespread assumption of a link between community and virtue may be due in part to the Aristotelian roots of virtue ethics, and to Alasdair MacIntyre's semi-Aristotelian *After Virtue*, probably the single most influential contemporary work in virtue ethics. Both Aristotle and MacIntyre emphasize the fundamentally social nature of virtue – the way that particular forms of social life are linked with particular virtues.

Another source of the assumption of a close link between community and virtue may be the moral theory or family of theories that proponents of both community and virtue *reject*. These theories emphasize the primacy of the rational, autonomous individual in moral agency and in the normative foundations of political structures. Communitarians depart from these theories both in placing value on communal entities – a value not reducible to the value of rational agency – and (sometimes) in according communal entities a more fundamental place in the formation or constitution of the moral self. Virtue theorists see the foundations of virtue as lying not, or not only, in rational agency but also in habit, emotion, sentiment, perception, and other psychic capacities.

I explore here some of the possible links between virtue and community, with two ends in mind. First, to indicate the multifariousness of such links, and thus to suggest that the ties between community and virtue may be more significant than moral theory has taken into account. Second, I believe that some forms of community can be crucial to the maintenance of a moral psychology of excellence, and that community has often

I wish to thank David Wong for support and extremely helpful comments on several drafts. I thank the participants in the First Annual Riverside Colloquium on the Virtues for helpful comments on my presentation there. Thanks are due especially to Charles Young, whose remarks as commentator on this paper at that Colloquium were particularly thoughtful and helpful.

been a missing desideratum in the discussion of the nature and development of admirable moral character.

In particular, I argue that communities can shape our sense of what we feel morally "pulled" to do and, integral to this, of what is and is not an "undue burden" or "too much to demand." I sometimes use the language of "duty" as a convenient way to refer to this territory of being morally pulled, or feeling some sort of moral requirement to do something. The territory itself, however, includes other moral motives – such as compassion, or the holding of certain principles, that are not coextensive with duty as ordinarily construed.[1] (Thus I assume that a strong sense of "ought" may – though it does not always – accompany actions done from compassion.) I argue for a view I call "limited community relativism" according to which, given two communities A and B, where A has a more demanding notion of moral compulsion and undue burden, it cannot be said that either has a correct or a more correct view of the matter than the other. Yet, at the same time, one *can* say that the community with the more demanding standard of moral compulsion better realizes virtue (at least in some important respects) than does the other community. In making this argument I reject the notion of "supererogation" as helping to provide a general account of moral excellence.

The notion of community is by no means a univocal one, and I shall not attempt a formal definition. We shall see that different notions of community are sometimes employed in different alleged links to virtue. In general, however, by "community" I mean more than the mere possession of a shared characteristic (such as being left-handed, or hailing from Indiana). I require that status as a member of the community be recognized by others within the community (and generally outside as well), and that

1. One may roughly distinguish between two uses of "duty." In one use, it is distinguished from other forms of moral requirement or moral "oughtness" by being its most stringent form. In the second use duty is simply one form of "oughtness" among others, with no implication that it is the most stringent. On the latter view, for example, I may have a duty to show up for my office hours and I may not have a duty to stop and help out in an accident in which people are hurt; there is a stronger oughtness attaching to the latter, however, than to the former action.

I take no stand on this controversy. (For an exchange, that I will refer to later in the chapter, which turns on this dispute, see Patricia Smith, "The Duty to Rescue and the Slippery Slope Problem," *Social Theory and Practice*, vol. 16, no. 1, Spring 1990: 19–42, and the exchange between John Whelan, Jr., and Smith in the Fall 1991 issue (vol. 17, no. 3) of the same journal.) To the extent that I use the notion of "duty," however, I mean it to encompass "oughts" of a fairly strong variety. In other contexts – and in other essays in this volume – I am concerned about the differences between duty and compassion as motives; but in this essay my interest is in a feature related to moral stringency that cuts across that distinction.

this status be significant (to a degree I cannot pin down more precisely) to the individual member's sense of identity. I generally have in mind communities bound together by either lineage or location or both, though this feature is not absolutely essential.

Let me suggest six possible or alleged links between virtue and community that one can find in the virtue literature, especially in MacIntyre's writings:

1. *Learning.* Virtues can be learned and nurtured only within particular forms of social life, including families. They are necessarily social products and could not be generated ab novo from individual reason or reflection.

2. *Sustaining.* A second, stronger, claim is that virtues can be sustained only in communities. MacIntyre says, "I need those around me to reinforce my moral strengths and assist in remedying my moral weaknesses. It is in general only within a community that individuals become capable of morality and are sustained in their morality."[2] This claim is stronger than the first, for it is consistent with (1) that even if their original source and formation lie in communities, virtues, once originally acquired, are able to be sustained solely through individual effort, and in the absence of the social support to which MacIntyre refers.

3. *Agency-constituting.* A somewhat more radical link is sometimes suggested by MacIntyre — that our very moral identity, hence our moral agency itself as that which realizes virtue, is at least in part constituted by the communities of which we are members. (A similar idea is suggested in Michael Sandel's *Liberalism and the Limits of Justice.*) This point is distinct from the previous one, which takes the character of an individual's moral agency as a given and then claims that community is (part of) what supports it in realizing virtue. Here the character of an individual's moral agency is itself partly constituted by community. Hence the "virtue-sustaining" connection in (2) is consistent with a radically individualistic conception of moral agency; but the "agency-constituting" claim in (3) is not.

4. *Content-providing.* A different sort of link is that forms of communal life fill in the detailed prescriptions that turn abstract principles into a lived morality. That is, our communities tell us how to apply our general moral principles to the world; without them we would not know what our principles bid of us in the particular contexts of social life in which we operate. Alasdair MacIntyre says, "The moralities of different societies may agree in having a precept enjoining that a child should honor his or

2. MacIntyre, "Is Patriotism a Virtue?" (The Lindley Lecture, 1984), University of Kansas, p. 10.

her parents, but what it is to honor . . . will vary greatly between different social orders" ("Patriotism," p. 9).

Only by living within a complex form of communal life can we learn these particularities, not only cognitively as one can learn the rules of another culture or community from reading a book, but also in the lived ways that require forms of perception and consciousness, morally relevant situation-descriptions, habits of action, salience of certain considerations, and the like.[3] Note, however, that the content provided need not be monolithic; the community's morality may involve internal variation and conflict, and can leave some room as well for individual interpretation.

This connection is distinct from the "sustaining" connection. For the latter is consistent with our knowing fully what a virtue bids of us independently of the community, but the community provides psychological support for acting on it. The "content-conferring" connection denies the possibility of having genuine knowledge apart from one's community of what the virtue consists in in the first place.

5. *Worth-conferring.* Another link is that some qualities are constituted as virtues only within particular communities. One could not see the quality as virtuous – or even really understand what the quality was – except by being part of the community in question. This point is analogous to MacIntyre's idea that "practices" such as chess or portrait painting have standards of excellence internal to themselves which can be understood – and seen as excellences – only by someone initiated into the practice (*After Virtue,* pp. 175 ff.). MacIntyre does not make this claim about virtues themselves, even though he sees virtues as involving producing goods internal to those practices, and as involving living up to the internal standards of the practice. (Moreover, a practice is distinct from a community.) Nevertheless, an analogous idea can be gleaned from his earlier example (4) of communal forms of "honoring" (e.g., one's parents). One can imagine that a certain activity or quality of character within a given community would count as honoring only within that community, and would not be a virtue outside it.

It is not clear if this point is distinct from (4, "content-providing") or merely operates at a different level of description. The point about content-providing assumes that a given quality is named as a virtue but that it is only within a community that one knows what that virtue actually comes to in a lived context. The worth-conferring point seems also to presuppose that there is *some* level of description of the activity or quality on which it can be seen to be a virtue; this is not incompatible

3. On this point, see Robert Fullinwider, "Moral Conventions and Moral Lessons," *Social Theory and Practice,* vol. 15, no. 3, Fall 1989: 321–38.

with, and seems even to presuppose, the point of (5), that some qualities cannot be recognized to be virtues except within communities.

6. *Virtues sustaining community.* Some virtues – such as trust, civility, tolerance – are particularly well suited to sustaining communal life in general.[4] And other virtues may sustain the particular forms of particular communities. Such virtues may or may not be communally "worth-conferred" in sense (5). This point is entirely consistent with (2), that communities sustain individuals in the practice of (at least some) virtues (including, but not limited to) the same virtues that sustain community.

I mention these possible links between virtue and community without attempting to assess how extensive such links are, or are being claimed to be. The "learning" link (1) seems plausible for all virtue. But obviously not *all* virtues are internal to communities in sense (5), nor do all virtues sustain community in sense (6). MacIntyre acknowledges ("Patriotism," p. 10) that some rare individuals can sustain their own individual virtue without the support of a community in sense (2). Still, without defending this proposition, I will proceed on the assumption that with the possible exception of (3, agency-constituting), *all* of these links hold in cases of *some* virtues, and that this fact is significant for understanding the moral psychology of virtue. Yet much writing on virtue proceeds as if these links did not hold, or were of no particular significance. One gets the impression in much virtue writing that the social dimension of virtue – expressed in a sustaining, content-providing, or worth-conferring role – is of little consequence.[5] Perhaps in this literature this social dimension is not actually denied; and there may be a bow in its direction. Yet – in strong contrast to MacIntyre's work – the impression is given that the virtues and a life of virtue can be understood apart from particular forms of social life.

I want now to explore in some detail one particularly striking example of virtue tied to a community – in several of the senses above. Before doing so I must distinguish between two ways that virtue is understood in moral theory and everyday life. In one sense the word "virtue" refers to a

4. Edmund Pincoffs refers to virtues that sustain associational life as "meliorative" virtues. *Quandaries and Virtues: Against Reductionism in Ethics* (Lawrence: University of Kansas, 1986), pp. 86 ff.
5. Examples of influential writing on the virtues that generally lack this explicitly social/ community dimension are James Wallace, *Virtues and Vices* (Ithaca: Cornell University Press, 1978); Philippa Foot, "Virtues and Vices," in *Virtues and Vices* (Berkeley: University of California, 1978); and the collections *Midwest Studies in Philosophy XIII Ethical Theory: Character and Virtue* (1988), and R. Kruschwitz and R. Roberts, *The Virtues: Contemporary Essays on Moral Character* (Belmont, Calif.: Wadsworth, 1987).

quality of character which is especially admirable. It is especially admirable because it issues in actions, and expresses itself in emotional reactions, that go beyond those normally expected of people and for which they are not thought to warrant special esteem. I will call this "noteworthy" virtue.

The second conception of virtue (more common in moral philosophy contexts, as the referent of "virtue theory"), however, is of *any* valuable trait of character – not only noteworthy ones but also ones issuing in actions and feelings that, though morally worthy, are simply what are to be expected of a normal moral agent. The latter are thus not regarded as meriting distinct praise or esteem. Many acts of honesty, compassion, temperance, and other virtues are of this sort. Virtue here is *good* but not (necessarily) especially, or noteworthily, valuable; I will call this "ordinary" virtue (though this conception encompasses noteworthy virtues as well).

One sometimes finds the term "virtue" used in a way that restricts it to noteworthy virtues, but the distinction is best seen as a classification of acts of virtue, and perhaps of persons, rather than of entire specific virtues themselves; some virtuous acts are especially worthy and some are only ordinarily worthy. It may be that acts of some virtues – for example, courage – are generally, or even always, noteworthy. And perhaps others – such as honesty – are generally of the ordinary type. Nevertheless, there are certainly some noteworthy acts of honesty in very adverse circumstances, and perhaps even some minor acts of what is still appropriately called courage that are closer to the ordinary pole of moral worth. In general, I would suggest that every virtue has both noteworthy and ordinary manifestations, depending on circumstances.

Note that the distinction between "ordinary" and "noteworthy" cannot be identified with the distinction between "duty" and what is "beyond duty."[6] Generous acts, for example, always go beyond what the agent owes to the recipient; they are always "beyond duty." Yet many acts of generosity are so minor that they would fall under the "ordinary" rather than the "noteworthy" rubric.

The example linked to community that I shall explore is the oft cited case of the village of Le Chambon, a French Huguenot enclave in Vichy France, which during the Nazi occupation of France sheltered about five thousand refugees (mostly Jewish), a number roughly equal to the population of the village. The aspect of this inspiring and fascinating historical episode that I want to focus on here is the communal nature of the rescue

6. This point was made by Joel Feinberg in "Supererogation and Rules," in Judith Thomson and Gerald Dworkin (eds.), *Ethics* (New York: Harper and Row, 1968).

enterprise – the way the community as a whole affected the decisions of its individual members to help with and contribute to the rescue activities.[7]

Scores of individuals made individual, or family, decisions to help the refugees. Such decisions carried great risks. To aid refugees, and especially Jews, was punishable, sometimes by death (although the punishments were not so severe nor so stringently enforced as in other areas in Europe, such as Poland). Three of the town's leaders were jailed for a time for engaging in these activities.

There were many different forms of participation in the rescue activities. Often a refugee would simply show up at someone's door, and that person would have to decide on the spot whether to help, either by taking the refugee into her own home or trying to find other shelter for her. Obtaining false identity and ration papers, moving refugees, getting food, sometimes smuggling persons out of the village toward Switzerland were also essential tasks. Simply contributing to keeping up the facade that nothing worthy of the Nazis' attention was going on was a task shared by all. The failure of anyone in the village to blow the whistle on the whole operation – by informing the appropriate Vichy or German officials – was a precondition of its remarkable success. Hallie says, "Le Chambon became a village of refuge not by fiat, not by virtue of the decision Trocmé [the town pastor, discussed below] or any other person made, but by virtue of the fact that . . . no Chambonnais ever turned away a refugee, and no Chambonnais ever denounced or betrayed a refugee" (p. 196).

Yet the rescue effort was not a collective enterprise of the town in any explicit sense. Both Hallie and Sauvage claim that people never talked about it openly (Hallie, p. 197). There was no clear and publicly visible form of sanction brought against those who did not participate. An individual could refuse to help without penalty or ostracism. Although help often took the form of responding to a request from another villager – not always directly from a refugee herself – whatever individual disapproval one might experience for declining to help was overwhelmingly outweighed by the risks involved in acceding to the request.

There was one significant public forum in which the rescue effort was referred to, if only obliquely – the sermons of the town's pastor and

7. My sources on Le Chambon are Philip Hallie, *Lest Innocent Blood Be Shed: The Story of the Village of Le Chambon and How Goodness Happened There* (New York: Harper and Row, 1979); and Pierre Sauvage's film *Weapons of the Spirit*. Sauvage, an American filmmaker, was born in Le Chambon of refugee parents during this period. His film involves interviews with several villagers who were involved in one way or another with the rescue activities, including the people who sheltered his parents and him. Le Chambon is discussed in two other essays in this volume: Chapter 4, "Moral Exemplars," and Chapter 6, "Altruism and the Moral Value of Rescue."

spiritual leader, André Trocmé. Trocmé was a central organizer of part of the rescue effort. In his sermons he called people to the true teachings of Christianity as he understood them – to love one's neighbor, to cherish human life, not to consort with evil, to be nonviolent. Though only indirectly, he made it clear that he took the providing of refuge as instantiating these teachings.

That Trocmé's moral leadership and organizational efforts (and those of his wife, Magda) were essential in the scope of the success of Le Chambon's rescue activities is undeniable.[8] Some see this fact as detracting from the individual virtue of the villagers. Perhaps in some cases people helped simply because they believed the pastor would want them to do so, or took it on his authority that engaging in rescuing activities was the right thing to do. But moral leadership in general, and that of the Trocmés in particular, need not be understood in this way. We can rather envision it as helping people to see for themselves that rescuing was the right thing to do, or as helping to elicit other moral motives (such as compassion) that would motivate rescue activities. It is plausible to see the authority of the French (collaborationist) government, as well as a reasonable fear for oneself and one's family, as a force that might naturally block the operation of a clear-eyed focus on the plight of the refugees and on the values and motives (concern for human life, a sense of Christian – or nonChristian – duty, a concern not to cooperate with evil, an eschewing of violence) that would lead to the villagers' helping to alleviate that plight. The Trocmés' moral leadership can be seen in part as helping the villagers to stay in tune with those values and to sustain a clear-eyed focus on that plight in the face of those contrary factors.

In fact, it is impossible to explain the widespread collective participation in rescue without attributing to most of the individual villagers compassion and a firm conviction as to the sanctity of human life. Hallie says that key decisions regarding rescue were made "in kitchens" (p. 8), and Sauvage also emphasizes (even more so than Hallie) the grass-roots nature of the rescue enterprise. One thing that moral leadership (in contrast to demagoguery, manipulation, mere charisma) does is precisely to help people find their better motives in the face of obscuring forces. Hallie's account makes it clear that this form of moral leadership was Andre Trocmé's particular gift. (Magda Trocmé's role in this moral leadership was much less prominent than her husband's in that she neither preached nor had an explicit role in the religious organizing of the community. Nevertheless, from Hallie's and Sauvage's accounts, her

8. Chapter 4, "Moral Exemplars," further explores the moral psychology of both André and Magda Trocmé as moral exemplars.

full participation in the rescue activities as the pastor's wife made her a figure who counted for moral leadership in the community.) This form of moral leadership is clearly entirely consistent with – and in fact requires – motives that were truly the villagers' own, not simply compliance with authority.

This is not to deny, however, the complexity of the motivation that led to *sustaining* the rescue efforts. It seems plausible to believe, for example, that for some, and perhaps many, of the villagers, participation was not initiated with a full commitment to the enterprise. Some were "put on the spot" and had to decide in a brief span of time whether to help. Perhaps they were moved by a moral motive at the moment, but that motive was not necessarily (yet) deeply rooted. (On the other hand, there were no doubt many for whom participation was wholehearted from the very beginning.) It may not have been until later, partly through getting to know the rescuees as particular persons, that nobler motives became more fully integrated into their overall moral commitment.[9]

Le Chambon is thus a striking case of a "community of virtue." By "virtue" I refer here to virtuous conduct, with virtuous motive, carried out over a substantial enough period of time to ensure that that motive be a reasonably stable one – not just an impulse of compassion, or a momentary call to conscience. I thus do not include here a person who from a good impulse offers to help but soon after regrets her decision, and perhaps tries (successfully or not) to extricate herself from the rescue activity she has undertaken. The rescue efforts at Le Chambon required much more than an initial compassionate response. Sustained follow-through was necessary, and most individuals engaged in some form of direct participation for months or even years. The tremendous dangers involved plus the absence of mechanisms of direct social pressure toward virtue imply that the individual decisions to help the rescue effort can plausibly be inferred to be virtuous ones. Sauvage's and Hallie's interviews of the villagers confirm this impression.

Note, however, that to speak of the Chambonnais as exhibiting virtue is not (necessarily) to say that they possessed deeply rooted virtues, in the sense of traits of character that would exhibit themselves in almost any circumstances. There is a situational character to the virtue involved here (still distinct from fleeting and superficial motives). It is not that the

9. The point being made here is entirely consistent with ambivalence on the part of (some of) the villagers, even those fully committed to the rescue activities. That is, even the fully committed may have had worries and concerns about their activities. We need not think of each villager as "pure of heart" in the sense of lacking any contrary motivations; virtue requires only that the moral commitment consistently dominate those contrary motivations.

fleeing refugees had the good fortune to discover a town peopled by saints, or moral exemplars.[10]

Note that to attribute virtue to the Chambonnais is not to attribute every sort of virtue to them. In "Weapons of the Spirit," Sauvage reports an interview with a deeply religious fundamentalist Christian (most of the villagers were not fundamentalists) who brings this out. This woman's religion allowed her to see absolutely clearly the evil of the Nazi social order, and to recognize the Jew as a fellow creature, whose life was as valuable as her own. And yet in other contexts this woman may well have evinced rigid, narrow-minded, and even (what many would regard as) immoral sentiments and conduct. The great virtue of the Chambonnais in risking so much to save lives was still in many ways a quite specialized sort of virtue, one which would not directly or necessarily carry over into many other life situations requiring other sorts of virtues.

What relations between community and virtue do we see here? The community certainly played a crucial sustaining role in the villagers' virtue. On the most basic level, knowing that one's neighbors are doing something especially difficult but worthwhile makes it easier for oneself to do the same. This must be part of what MacIntyre means by saying "I need those around me to reinforce my moral strengths and assist in remedying my moral weaknesses" ("Patriotism," p. 10). Note, however, that this is not simply conformity – engaging in action only because one's neighbors are doing so, in order not to be left out. This assumes no, or very weak, independent motivation to engage in rescue, a motivation then supplied by the lure of doing what others are doing; MacIntyre's statement assumes that the villagers already and independently saw the worth in these activities of rescue. Knowing that their neighbors were engaging in them helped legitimize and strengthen their already present motivations.[11]

One reason, therefore, not to place much weight on moral conformity in the villagers' motivation is that there is too much evidence that they independently grasped the moral worth of the acts of rescue

10. Also, I do not, of course, mean to suggest that the behavior of the Chambonnais during the war had nothing to do with their characters. Their characters must have been such as to contain the capability for the relatively stable virtuous motives operative during the Occupation.

11. Neither were the villagers' actions simply a matter of emulation of those one respects and admires (though, like conformity, one can assume that this may have played some role in some villagers' motivation). For emulation is something like seeing the acts emulated as good in part because one regards the emulated person as good; although it may imply a striving to see the acts as in themselves good, it also implies that the agent is not yet convinced of the worth of the actions in their own right.

in a way denied by this form of motivation. A second reason is the aforementioned lack of visibility of the rescue effort, the fact that it was seldom publicly discussed or referred to, that one was not always entirely certain which of one's neighbors was currently doing what for the effort.

The sustaining relationship here has two components: (1) how the community helped the villagers individually to have a firm conviction of the value of the rescue effort in the first place, and (2) the knowledge that (some) others were taking part helped to reinforce the continual translation of that conviction into action.

One significant piece of this sustaining structure concerned the Chambonnais' intense awareness of themselves as a religious minority (Protestants in a Catholic country), with a history of religious persecution and of resistance to that persecution. Sauvage's film depicts a moving ritual – apparently regularly performed – of a large gathering of Chambonnais singing a song of historical resistance to religious persecution. This self-conception can be seen as part of the village's moral tradition.

How did this tradition and historical memory operate to sustain the rescue activities? It is important to understand this, partly because of the role of tradition in discussions of community, and partly because to some the appeal to tradition may, like the invocation of moral leadership and neighbor influence, seem to run counter to the secure attribution of morally good motives to individuals. There seem to be two dimensions here to the role of tradition in moral motivation. One was to make salient, familiar, and "owned" the motive of resisting an evil perpetrated by the state and state authorities. That form of motive directly linked resistance to their own persecution as Protestants in a Catholic-dominated society with the persecution of Jews by the collaborationist French state. The readiness to resist state-sponsored evil was made salient through historical tradition and memory, reinforced by ritual.

A second, more indirect, way that the self-conception and historical memory of the villagers as a religious minority may have helped the rescue effort was to remove one important obstacle in the way of fully experiencing the Jews and other refugees as fellow human beings. That obstacle was the view propounded by Pétain's national government of the Jews as an alien, essentially evil, force (Hallie, p. 39). In laws restricting the participation of Jews in French life, in national propaganda (chilling footage of which appears in Sauvage's film), and (ultimately) in cooperating with the Nazis' "final solution," the French government aimed to make it easy for ordinary citizens to see the Jew as "other," even as subhuman, to confuse and undermine natural human sympathy for the

154

persecuted, and to couch this immorality in terms of an ostensibly worthy larger, patriotic goal.

The Chambonnais were particularly well equipped to resist this state-sponsored moral obfuscation. Their tradition of resistance to persecution made them generally skeptical of the state. In this regard their moral traditions operated not so much to provide a direct motive to rescue but to remove an obstacle to a clear grasp of the shared humanity of all persons.[12]

This last point suggests a useful framing of the way the Chambon community helped sustain its inhabitants' virtue – by helping construct and shape their "moral reality." The community's moral traditions and the moral atmosphere there during the Occupation kept the reality of the plight of the refugees in the forefront of people's minds; they reinforced for the villagers the salience of their danger and suffering. Note that this is very different from claiming that because the villagers had a certain tradition, they thereby incurred an obligation to help refugees that was not incurred by villagers without this tradition. The present discussion still concerns the way the traditions sustain virtue, not how they create moral obligations not applicable to others. This issue will be discussed further later, but the position being taken here does not absolve from obligation those whose practices involve a more minimal level of moral behavior on the grounds that they are not part of a tradition that sustains a higher level of moral behavior.

Besides the "sustaining" relation, a second relation between community and virtue in the Chambonnais is "content-conferring." Let us say that prior to the Occupation, many of the villagers, like Christians elsewhere, professed belief in precepts such as loving one's neighbor, cherishing human life, and resisting evil. Let us further imagine that they not only professed these principles, but actually believed them. Such principles underdetermine action. They require the conferring of more determinate content, which can be provided by the actual practices of a community. Contemplated in abstraction from concrete life situations, one would be

12. The notion of an "obstacle" to moral perception and moral motivation is discussed in Chapter 3, "Moral Perception and Particularity." The notion is taken from Iris Murdoch, *The Sovereignty of Good* (London: Routledge and Kegan Paul, 1970).

It should also be noted that the Chambonnais had taken in refugees from the Spanish Civil War, and in summers had taken children from the city (in a program partly funded by the French Government). These experiences no doubt helped accustom the Chambonnais to dealing with outsiders and thus contributed to withstanding further the racist and national chauvinist atmosphere of the Nazi era. And the villagers' willingness to take in these outsiders in the first place must have itself been a product of that moral tradition which led to the refugee rescue endeavors. (For these facts about the Chambonnais, I am indebted to Mr. Francis Rochat of Yverdon, Switzerland.)

unlikely to get universal agreement that adherence to these principles or values would require one to risk one's own freedom or even life in order to contribute to (but by no means guarantee) saving the lives of others also at risk. Yet living in Le Chambon in the period in question influenced large numbers of people to come to believe that engaging in activities involving such risks was precisely the practical content of the values of loving one's neighbor, cherishing life, and resisting evil.

This content-conferring function may not be sharply distinct from the virtue-sustaining one. In some situations coming to believe that act A is required by a commitment to value V may not be readily distinguishable from being given support for the motivation to perform act A, though these are theoretically distinct.

Note that the virtue of the villagers was internal to the community in regard to both the virtue-sustaining and the content-conferring connections, in that the virtue of the villagers existed and took the character it did only because of the community of which they were a part. But their virtue was not internal in the worth-conferring sense discussed earlier. The worth of the virtue displayed was not supplied or accounted for by, or only within, the community itself. The value of the virtues of compassion, courageous commitment to the value of human life, and the like is seen from outside the community. This is related to the good produced by those virtues – the saving of endangered people – being very much an external good, that is, a good for *non*members of the community. It is a universal good of which anyone (inside or outside the community) can see the value.[13]

13. When MacIntyre talks about "external goods" he generally means competitive goods such as money, power, and status. (See *After Virtue,* pp. 177, 181, and elsewhere.) This conception is part of what allows MacIntyre generally to portray goods internal to practices as somehow more worthy than goods external to them, though MacIntyre does not entirely devalue these competitive goods. That MacIntyre neglects "positive" external goods (like saving the lives of people not in the community), the virtues which produce them, and the communities in which they are promoted seems to me part of what underpins his pessimism, his sense of extreme moral fragmentation, and his notion that moral renewal can come only through relatively self-contained communities unconnected to a larger social order and to each other. (See, e.g., p. 245.) These views are not so pronounced in MacIntyre's later writings; and in a talk entitled "Problems of the Virtues: Friends and Strangers," delivered at Boston College in April 1992, MacIntyre argued that charity toward outsiders is a condition of adequate virtue inside a community.

Many entities with communal features can only be understood as, at least in part, serving ends that are external to them. Educational or medical communities are examples of this. Medical communities have in some sense their own internal standards, authorities, traditions, initiation rites, and the like. Yet one cannot understand the point of a medical community without seeing it as serving its clients and the society as a whole – as serving "health," a good external to the medical community as

Yet the MacIntyrian idea that a quality constituting virtue to members of a community is nevertheless not seen as a virtue by those outside the community contains an idea of insider/outsider moral asymmetry suggestive for the case of Le Chambon. When (separately) Philip Hallie and Pierre Sauvage went back to interview the Chambonnais several decades after the events in question took place, they found that the rescuers did not regard themselves as having done anything worthy of special attention or praise. They were uncomfortable with Hallie's and Sauvage's questions as to why they acted as they did, rightly taking it to imply something in special need of explanation, or of special noteworthiness. The Chambonnais did not see their actions and practices as virtuous in the noteworthy sense. When pressed to say why they helped the refugees, they said such things as "It was simply what one had to do" or "She [a refugee] was standing at my door; how could I fail to help?"[14]

From the outside, however, we *do* see the Chambonnais as having been virtuous in the noteworthy — and not only the ordinary — sense. There could hardly be a clearer example of collective virtue in the noteworthy sense. The Chambonnais did what few Europeans did or felt called upon to do. The fact that the Chambonnais themselves did not see it that way is significant, and perhaps is part of how we are to understand the potential virtue-sustaining function of community.[15] Part of the state of mind enabling the villagers to carry on these rescue activities day after day must have been precisely that they did come to regard these activities as something like normal, unremarkable acts — acts that could simply be expected. To see them as worthy of special praise is to emphasize them as something not expected of anyone. The psychology here seems to go something like this: Everything else being equal, we feel a stronger moral pull to do something we regard as "what can readily be expected" than to do what we regard as "beyond what can ordinarily be expected."

Community, then, can support noteworthy virtue by helping its mem-

---

defined solely by its practices. So standards for judging a medical community and what counts as its virtues must come at least partly from how well it does in fact produce this external good.

14. See, for example, Hallie, p. 154. This point is made more fully in Sauvage's film.
15. I am not claiming that one must have a supporting community in order to engage in noteworthy virtue; the numerous examples of rescuers during the Holocaust who were relatively isolated from their communities, depending on the help only of their families and in some cases working independently even of them (or not having families) testifies to the contrary. It is fair to say, however, that such virtuous activities are much more likely in the context of supporting communities than in the absence of them. This echoes MacIntyre's point, "Of course lonely moral heroism is sometimes required and sometimes achieved. But we must not treat this exceptional type of case as if it were typical" ("Patriotism," p. 10).

bers experience as ordinary and "to be expected" behavior that for others goes beyond the expected.[16] A major factor making a course of action too much to expect or demand is that it is unduly burdensome. In one way or another, the notion of "undue burden" is typically built into accounts of duty. Acts that unduly burden people might be good but cannot be expected as duty. Thus Sidgwick: The duty of beneficence is "the positive duty to render, when occasion offers, such services as either require no sacrifice on our part or at least very much less in importance than the service rendered." Rawls: "Supererogatory acts are not required, though normally they would be were it not for the loss or risk involved for the agent himself."[17]

What people regard as an "undue burden," however, and hence as "what can reasonably be expected," is quite variable and can be deeply affected by their communities. Let us illustrate this with an example in which much less is at stake than in the Le Chambon case. A faculty member switches jobs from one college to another. At her former college, Professor Martinez's department made minimal demands on her. Departmental meetings were infrequent and responsibilities few, beyond teaching one's classes. In her new department, however, the demands are substantially greater. Meetings are more frequent; there are more departmental responsibilities on top of teaching – discussions of pedagogy, reval-

16. The potentially powerful effect of community can be seen as much with regard to vice as virtue. There can be communities of vice as well as virtue, where the community helps to shape a sense of moral reality toward, say, corruption, rather than compassion. The narcotics squad of the New York City Police department as portrayed in the film and book *Prince of the City* illustrates this. (Robert Daley, *Prince of the City* [Boston: Houghton-Mifflin, 1978]; *Prince of the City,* Orion Pictures [1981].) Being a member of those units helped to shape a sense that corruption was an everyday, expected thing – not that it was morally right or distinctly morally permissible, but just that it was an appropriate mode of operation.

17. Henry Sidgwick, *The Methods of Ethics,* 7th edition (Chicago: University of Chicago Press, 1962), p. 253. John Rawls, *The Theory of Justice* (Cambridge, Mass.: Belknap, 1971), p. 117. Compare p. 439, where "reasonable self-interest" is the operative excusing condition from what would otherwise be a duty. Note a not insignificant difference between two construals of both these formulations. The first is that one should offer aid to others when the cost to oneself is negligible or minimal. The second, more demanding view (that is, demanding more in the way of duty), is that the cost to oneself be minimal, in proportion to the good being rendered to the other person. The latter construal would require more sacrifice as a matter of duty than the former, in cases where the good to be promoted (or evil to be prevented) is very great. Both Sidgwick's and Rawls's formulations are somewhat ambiguous on this issue. Even with the more demanding construal, however, the Chambonnais' actions might well not fall under the rubric of duty, since (as will be discussed) many individuals in their rescue efforts risked imprisonment and perhaps death for the sake of the likelihood (but not certainty) of saving life. It is not clear that this could be construed as minimal even on the proportionality view.

uations of programs, expectations of being informed regarding various campus concerns that impinge on students' lives, greater involvement in advising, and the like.

At first Professor Martinez experiences this increased load as unduly burdensome, and more than it is reasonable to expect of a faculty member. It certainly would have been so regarded in her previous department. In time, however, several factors change her outlook and her experience of burdensomeness. She comes to believe that matters not insignificant slipped through the cracks in her former position, and that in her new department the program is improved and the students are better served because of the increased amount of work she and her colleagues do. Her teaching is improved because of improvements in the program and her greater understanding of issues affecting the students. Professor Martinez not only comes to perceive this superiority in her current department but to care about and positively value it as well. She comes to care that students in her department are better served, that tasks are responsibly carried out, that difficult issues are faced and dealt with in a collegial manner.[18]

In time, Professor Martinez comes to experience the departmental work load at her current institution as no longer unduly burdensome. It is not that she resignedly accepts the load as part of her new job responsibilities, hence something she sees herself as obliged to bear. That would be one possible reaction to the new situation, but is not the one I am envisioning. She actually *experiences* the activities once felt as burdensome as no longer so (or as distinctly less so).

An important part of what enables Professor Martinez *not* to see her work load as unduly burdensome is that her colleagues appear not to regard it so. (To say this is not, however, to say that they, and she, never resent the demands of their department, but only that, overall, they do not experience them as undue.) Their already existing sense of the naturalness and to-be-expectedness of the work load, their belief in the values of the program and sense of responsibility toward it, helps to construct a collective reality for Professor Martinez (and for themselves) within which the value of the program is made salient – with the attendant impact on the experience of the work load as perhaps demanding (and

18. Note that this description does not require saying that overall, or in all respects, Professor Martinez's second institution is superior to the first. They may be different kinds of institutions, in which the first makes more minimal teaching and programmatic demands on its faculty in the service of support for scholarship. (I owe this point to David Wong.) The point is only that Professor Martinez's perception of a superiority in some significant respect is tied to her changed sense of "undue burden."

certainly more demanding than in her previous department) but not "unduly burdensome," not "beyond what can reasonably be expected."

Both this and the Le Chambon case illustrate how communities can powerfully shape members' sense of undue burden, and hence of what they regard as "reasonable to expect." Communities thus shape members' ability to sustain a level of virtuous conduct beyond what in some other contexts would be regarded as (though perhaps good and admirable) too much to be demanded. In doing so they illustrate both the "content-determining" and the "virtue-supporting" functions of community. This "insider-outsider" asymmetry is an important element in understanding the person whose noteworthy virtue is grounded in community.

I want to argue now that insider-outsider asymmetry in the context of the communal nature of some virtue poses a challenge to standard accounts of moral excellence. My claim is that although we can stand outside two communities and say that one exhibits (in some important regard) a higher degree of virtue than another, and although this virtue is tied to what each takes to be something like a moral requirement, nevertheless we cannot necessarily say that one community has a more valid notion of what constitutes duty than the other. In particular, we cannot say of one community with a less demanding standard of "undue burden" that its view is inferior to, or less correct than, that of another with a more demanding standard, even though a result of this difference is that the latter community exemplifies greater virtue than the former. These claims imply that there is an irreducible relativism in assessments of duty and dutifulness absent in the case of virtue.

One can see a minor version of this in the case of Professor Martinez. Her former department had a less demanding conception of "undue burden" and a related less demanding schedule of duties than her current one. Yet I do not think we are in a position to say that one of these departments is "right" about what is an undue burden, or about what is an appropriate level of institutional duty. We are confined to saying that the members of the two departments experience the burdens and duties differently. That is, were department number one to impose the kinds of duties department number two has, members of the former would experience them as unduly burdensome.

On the other hand, this "relativism" between the two departments is essential to a comparative judgment that we are in a position to make, namely, that in some important respects the program of department number two is superior to that of department number one and is so in part because of the shared sense of the appropriateness of the greater burdens in the latter. One might also make the point by saying that the professional virtue of members of the current department is superior to that of members of the former department, at least with regard to the important professional respects involved in the example as described.

To make the case for this limited communal relativism, I must show that three alternative accounts of noteworthy virtue are incorrect: (1) The "maximalist" duty view, (2) the "supererogationist" or "minimalist duty" view, and (3) the "personal calling" view.

The first says that those with noteworthy virtue, and the more demanding sense of undue burden, are correct about what is their duty and what is and is not an undue burden, whereas those with lesser, ordinary virtue and the less demanding sense of undue burden are incorrect. Hence this maximalist view rejects a relativity that abjures saying that one view of duty and undue burden is more correct or valid than the other. Applied to the Professor Martinez example, the "maximalist" claim would be that members of department number one are mistaken to think that they are satisfying their professional duties by adhering to the expected standards of their institution. But since the duties have a coherent professional rationale, and are accepted as such by the members and the institution, it seems incorrect or at best highly misleading to say that they are mistaken about their duties. What seems a more accurate expression of the moral sentiment behind that claim is that it would be better if department number one accepted as duties ones grounded in a more demanding sense of "undue burden" than are their current duties.

In the case of Le Chambon, the maximalist claim would be that the Chambonnais are entirely correct to regard themselves as having the degree of moral compulsion they do – which entails risking their freedom and possibly their lives to try to save the refugees – and that others who might admire these actions but not feel a moral compulsion to perform them (or not so strong a moral compulsion) would be incorrect in their view that there was no such moral quasi requirement.

Such a position would make it close to a general moral requirement to engage in extremely risky activities when doing so would greatly contribute to – but by no means guarantee – the saving of lives. It is striking that no theories of duty with which I am familiar entail such a stringent conception of moral requirement. As mentioned earlier, most contemporary theories build in some notion of undue burden that is a good deal weaker than the maximalist view. The burden or risk is either small or else small in proportion to the good achieved; as argued earlier, at least for many of the villagers it was not clear that the risk was not substantially greater than in either of these formulations.[19]

What is true is that it was a good thing that the Chambonnais experienced the degree and form of moral compulsion they did; as a result they instantiated noteworthy virtue. And we may be able to generalize this result to the idea that, ceteris paribus, communities adhering to higher standards of moral compulsion are to be preferred to those that do not; and it would be better if many of those who adhere to a more minimal standard changed their sense of moral compulsion so that they regarded it is as appropriate that more be demanded of them. But none of this is equivalent to saying that those with the lower standard are mistaken about what is their duty.

This line of argument does not deny that there may be strands in our notion of "duty" or "moral compulsion" that push toward the more maximalist account I am rejecting here. Moreover, even if the maximalist account were accepted, there would still be an important lesson about the connection between community and virtue. For since the maximalist account is so far from the ordinary notion of what is our duty, one will still want to inquire what it is that allows a person to have as his or her sense of duty (or moral compulsion) this maximalist sense. How do people come to have that sense of moral compulsion as part of their moral psychology? The support and content-conferring that community can give to this sense of moral compulsion will be an important part of the answer to that question of moral psychology.

This brings us to the second – minimalist or supererogationist – account of noteworthy virtue. Various somewhat distinct analyses have been offered of supererogatory acts, but I will first consider David Heyd's in his comprehensive work, *Supererogation.*[20] For our purposes, Heyd's analysis is that supererogatory acts are good to do but not bad or blameworthy

---

19. An instructive view is that of Patricia Smith in "The Duty to Rescue and the Slippery Slope Problem." Smith argues that there is a duty to "render minimal aid in an emergency." She does this against the background of the contrary assumption that there is no such duty; thus this is as strong a duty as Smith feels she can provide a case for. She says that "No one is obligated to incur great cost or risk to himself in order to help a random stranger" (p. 25). But this obligation (or something like an obligation) is precisely what the Chambonnais regarded themselves as having. Yet I think Smith is correct to think that her viewpoint would be widely shared, and disagreement would come primarily from those who saw even her minimal duty as questionable.

20. David Heyd, *Supererogation* (Cambridge: Cambridge University Press, 1982). A more recent, usefully comprehensive treatment is Gregory Mellema, *Beyond the Call of Duty: Supererogation, Obligation, and Offense* (Albany: State University of New York Press, 1991).

not to do; in not being wrong not to do, they are "totally optional and voluntary" (Heyd, p. 9). Heyd argues further that thus being optional is part of what gives them their distinct kind of value different from the value of dutiful acts (Heyd, pp. 173 ff).[21] This view is minimalist in that it sets the standard of moral requirement at a moderate level, accepting the maximalist level as distinctly not encompassed by it, yet also as distinctly morally admirable in going beyond it.

Describing noteworthy virtue as "supererogation" in this sense does not capture the way that the (noteworthily) virtuous agent sees her own action. She does not regard her act as morally optional; rather, she feels some sense of moral compulsion to perform it. One sees this in both the duty and the nonduty forms of virtuous action found in the Chambonnais' reasons for action. For some the presence of a refugee, of someone in need, aroused a compassion in which the refugee's plight constituted a direct reason for them to act – a reason possibly involving an "ought" but not a duty. For others, a sense of duty was evoked. But in neither case did the villager see the action as optional in the sense of Heyd's analysis.

It is true, perhaps, that the villagers saw their actions as voluntary, in the sense that no organized social or legal pressure or threat was involved. But that does not distinguish such actions from many compliances with ordinary duties, in which the agent feels a moral compulsion to perform the action, but in which there is no other sort of pressure brought to bear, or even implicit. Thus from the point of view of the agent, voluntariness does not distinguish supererogatory action from ordinary duty. This leaves "morally optional" as the crucial characteristic distinguishing supererogatory from dutiful action in Heyd's analysis; but from the noteworthily virtuous agent's point of view, her choices are not more morally optional than are ordinary duties.

A slightly different formulation is that the supererogatory act is one that is "morally recommended" or "encouraged" – in contrast to what is required by morality as a duty, or as obedience to certain moral rules or principles.[22] Yet it would be misleading to see the noteworthily virtuous person under this rubric. For although the idea of "morally recommended" may go a bit beyond the idea of a purely voluntary or morally optional act (toward some degree of moral pull or compulsion), it does not incorporate the strong moral pull experienced by the noteworthily

21. James Fishkin, *The Limits of Obligation* (New Haven: Yale University Press, 1982) uses a similar concept of "morally discretionary" to define supererogation (p. 5).
22. Heyd uses the concept of "morally encouraged" and Bernard Gert, *Morality: A New Justification of the Moral Rules* (New York: Oxford University Press, 1988), uses that (p. 162) as well as the notion of "morally recommended."

virtuous agent. In the idea of a moral recommendation there is still too much implication that the agent can choose to reject the recommendation without a sense of having morally failed in any substantial sense. But the Chambonnais – and noteworthily virtuous agents more generally – would regard themselves as substantially failing were they not to perform the action.

Another variation on this general approach, developed by Bernard Gert in *Morality* (see footnote 22), is the idea of noteworthy virtue as a *personal moral ideal* – that is, a moral project taken up by an individual and seen as having a moral claim on her only because she has chosen it as her ideal. The agent sees ordinary morality as not making the claim on her that the ideal does, but she chooses to adopt it anyway, and personally commits herself to it. Gert gives as examples devotion to the good of a particular group, such as Blacks or Jews (pp. 163ff.).[23]

The noteworthily virtuous agent's moral psychology is not accurately captured in the notion of personal moral ideals in this sense. For she sees herself not so much as adopting an ideal as feeling compelled to engage in an endeavor. The Chambonnais villager saw herself as responding to a given moral reality – the refugee's need for shelter – not as acting out of a sense of personal value or ideal. As mentioned earlier, the villagers did not in general regard their actions as coming under the rubric of an ideal, if that is taken (as it is normally) as a set of principles higher than the ordinary that one strives consciously to live up to.[24]

In addition, the villagers' virtuous endeavors had a collective character not captured by Gert's idea of an individual moral ideal. The difference is not merely a matter of an enterprise shared with others rather than performed alone. It is also, as we have seen, that the community was essential in shaping the agent's (thus shared) sense of moral reality, and in sustaining her virtue and giving it content, partly through the knowledge that the virtuous activities were also being carried out by others.

I have criticized the "supererogationist" or "minimalist" accounts of

23. Gert ties the distinction between personal ideal and moral requirement to that between positive action to relieve suffering (or other evil) and avoiding the infliction of suffering (or other evil). The point being discussed here does not depend on this link but could allow for a more expansive notion of moral requirement or, correspondingly, a more expansive notion of personal ideal (e.g., including the promoting of the happiness of others).

24. This generalization about the Chambonnais does not, however, hold for André Trocmé, whose involvement (and leadership) in the Chambonnais rescue effort can be thought of as stemming from his personal ideals. Trocmé's moral psychology is discussed in Chapter 4, "Moral Exemplars." Yet his self-understanding of his own ideals does not appear to have involved a personal set of values that he saw as going beyond what ordinary morality requires.

noteworthy virtue on the grounds that the notions of "moral optionality," "moral encouragement," and "personal ideal" fail to capture what the noteworthily virtuous person regards herself as doing. These accounts distort her moral psychology. This is not, however, an attack on the notion of supererogation itself. It might be taken as such, for antisupererogationists sometimes use the argument that no firm line can be drawn between duty and supererogation, and also (somewhat following upon this point) that what people may think of as the higher flights of morality are nevertheless no less actual moral requirements than the more ordinary duties to reject the notion of supererogation entirely. (See Mellema, *Beyond the Call of Duty,* Chapters 3 and 4, for a discussion of various forms of rejection of the concept of supererogation.)

I agree, however, that there are some actions that go beyond what can be reasonably expected, and that these are deserving of special praise. Thus I accord a place to the notion of "supererogation." But limited community relativism implies that no general account can be provided that allows us to sort all actions into these two categories ("duty" and "supererogation") independent of the particular moral communities within which people function (although there might be some actions that are supererogatory on any account and in any community). Even in Le Chambon during the period of rescue, there might well have been actions generally regarded by the villagers as above and beyond what could reasonably be expected, and thus as deserving particular praise, even if their standard of "reasonable expectation" was itself so much more demanding than that of other communities.

Can it be replied that noteworthily virtuous persons are simply mistaken about what there is morally compelling reason to do? Although holding such a view about moral quasi-requirements may contribute to their virtue, their view is incorrect.

There are two versions of this reply. One says that because the noteworthily virtuous person is mistaken about what is morally compulsory, her view of morality is defective and it would be better if she were to come to hold the view that the activities she currently thinks herself quasi-compelled to perform are actually morally optional. Yet it seems plausible to suppose that giving up a sense of moral pull or quasi compulsion would have the effect in many cases of reducing the motivation of agents to engage in the activities in question. And so this view would have the effect of supporting what it acknowledges to be lesser virtue.

A second version of the reply would be that, even if the noteworthily virtuous person were wrong in her moral views, it is still better that she believe them, since they lead her to perform more noteworthily virtuous actions and, more generally, to be a more virtuous person. Accepting the latter empirical claim for a moment, one would then want to explore the moral psychology of this noteworthily virtuous person. And one part of this, accepting the argument up to this point, is that the agent's communities can have a substantial impact – both virtue-supporting and content-determining – in that psychology. This result is the flip side of the maximalist view – that the noteworthily virtuous person is right about what is her duty and those holding the more ordinary view are wrong. In both cases one wants to know how noteworthily virtuous people come to hold the view that they do, as it is admitted to be part of what allows them to be noteworthily virtuous.

Yet the minimalist position simply presupposes – without giving any argument for it – a view that is precisely the one challenged by the limited community relativist. The view is that a purely universal account of duty or moral pull – that is, an account that can specify in a formula applicable to all individuals the conditions under which they have duties, and the conditions under which they are absolved from duty because of undue burden – can be given. Such a presumption is present in most contemporary accounts of duty. It is assumed by Rawls, Heyd, Sidgwick, Gert, and others that the proper form of an account of duty is to be purely universalistic. But this is precisely what the limited community relativist position questions. Why not think that the territory of duty (or moral pull) is much more diverse? Perhaps some of it is universal, but other parts are irreducibly relative to various communities or contexts.

Some such diversity is already acknowledged by widely, though not universally, accepted views of professional ethics, namely, that such duties cannot be derived from, nor are they merely applications of, universal principles of duty. The limited community relativist position extends in two directions that depart from pure universalism. One is to include communities in entities regarding which there is relativity in the kinds of duties that exist. The other is to include not only the kinds of duties, but the boundaries of duties (as expressed by the "undue burden" standard) as a dimension regarding which some relativity exists.

Once the assumption of universality is questioned, the limited community relativist position gains another advantage over the minimalist-supererogationist position (and the maximalist one as well). That is that it does not cast as illusory the moral self-understanding of either the noteworthily virtuous person or the ordinarily virtuous person. The maximalist position sees the ordinarily virtuous person as mistaken about morality; the minimalist position sees the noteworthily virtuous person as mistaken. The limited community relativist sees each as having a valid

166

view of their moral (quasi)requirements. It provides a way in which to see each group's self-understanding as nonillusory. At the same time, it enables us to make the well-supported assessment that one group exhibits greater virtue than the other.

A third – "personal calling" – approach to the psychology of the (noteworthily) virtuous agent is taken by A. I. Melden in his "Saints and Supererogation."[25] Melden shares with Gert and Heyd the notion of a distinct division between actions required by ordinary morality and morally good actions that go beyond it. He differs from them, however, in seeing what he calls "saints" as actually acting from a sense of duty, but one not construed universalistically, as applicable to all. Melden explains this nonuniversalistic sense of duty by saying that the saint sees herself as morally different from others, and thus as being bound to a different set of standards from other persons. She does not follow what she sees as a "personal ideal" in Gert's sense of a project she recognizes as morally optional rather than required.

This account has one advantage over the others, that of validating the noteworthily virtuous person's own view of the matter – her sense of moral compulsion and nonoptionalness – that Gert's, Heyd's, Rawls's, and other standard supererogationist accounts see as in some way mistaken. Moreover, Melden's account of the nature of this sense of moral compulsion may be correct for some noteworthily virtuous persons. His account does not appear to hold, however, for at least most of the Chambonnais portrayed in Hallie's and Sauvage's accounts. The Chambonnais did not see themselves as having a distinct moral calling, as morally distinct from ordinary persons. They did not see themselves as bound to a morality for themselves alone. Although nothing in their lives appears to have compelled them to face up to this question, it seems clear that they would never have positively denied that the ethic that guided their actions was applicable to others in comparable situations. They would not have thought of themselves as much different from other people. They did not think, These rescue activities are the right thing for us, but not the right thing for others. On the contrary, as interviews in Hallie's book and Sauvage's movie make clear, the villagers thought of these activities as obviously the right or unavoidable things to do.[26]

25. A. I. Melden, "Saints and Supererogation," in Ilham Dilman (ed.), *Philosophy and Life: Essays on John Wisdom* (The Hague: Martinus Nijhoff, 1984).
26. Again, Andre Trocmé may be an exception to this. There is some suggestion in Hallie's account that Trocmé may have seen himself as having a personal calling in something like Melden's sense.

Note that it does not follow that the Chambonnais themselves held the first, maximalist, view. They gave no evidence of affirmatively holding the view that the ethic that guided their own actions was an appropriate standard for all persons, everywhere, with the corollary that any failure to live up to that standard would be wrong or blameworthy. It is perfectly consistent to say – and seems in accordance with the portrayal of the Chambonnais in Hallie's and Sauvage's treatments – that the Chambonnais affirmed neither the universality nor the exclusivity (to themselves, as in Melden's view) of their ethic.

It might be thought, however, since most of the Chambonnais avowed a specifically Christian morality, that their morality was a universal one. This is true, insofar as their Christian morality prescribed that the set of persons toward whom a Christian was to act dutifully was all persons, not only members of their community or other Christians. But this is not the sense of universality embodied in the philosophic tradition (which Melden is contrasting with his own view of duties for specific persons or groups) that sees duties as applicable to all agents. This latter notion of duty involves the idea that when one conceives of oneself as having a duty, one sees oneself as doing so because one necessarily accepts such duties as binding on all other agents (relevantly similarly situated). There is no evidence that the Chambonnais looked at their own behavior in this way. In fact, the notion of a specifically Christian morality is precisely that of a morality incumbent on Christians only – with no necessary claim to validity for non-Christians – though toward all persons, Christian or not. In any case, there is no evidence that the Chambonnais subscribed to the view that the morality to which they adhered was distinctly incumbent on all persons (and incumbent on themselves for that reason).

By drawing the sharp line that he does between the ordinarily virtuous person and the saint, Melden blocks recognition of two related points about moral excellence. One is that virtue is affected by community. It can be internal to community in the virtue-sustaining and content-determining senses. Communities can shape agents' sense of what is their duty and what is an undue burden. It is not, or not only, what Melden implies – that some individuals just are saints and everyone else is pretty ordinary and not capable of exceptional virtue.

The second point is that noteworthily virtuous persons set an example of virtue for everyone. What is striking about the Chambonnais is precisely that they are not saints. They are more like ordinary people who acted according to a potentiality for excellence that must exist in more of us than we seem to realize. Like Melden's, the limited community relativist position relativizes duty and undue burden. But unlike his, it allows the thought that if ordinarily virtuous people had been (or could be) part of a community with a sense of moral reality suited to noteworthy virtue, they too might have been (or might become) closer to being noteworthily virtuous.

Limited community relativism provides a better framework than its rivals – maximalism, minimalism (supererogationism), personal ideal – in which to express the philosophically significant and deep connections that can exist between virtue and community. In addition, I suggest, it provides a framework for addressing Iris Murdoch's strictures that have so influenced my own exploration of moral excellence: "Ethics should not be merely an analysis of ordinary mediocre conduct, it should be a hypothesis about good conduct and about how this can be achieved. How can we make ourselves better? is a question moral philosophers should attempt to answer" (*Sovereignty of Good*, p. 78). Yet limited community relativism contributes to an understanding of moral excellence that avoids the excessive individualism of Murdoch's conception, and recognizes the insight that MacIntyre has brought so pointedly to our attention – that virtue is not simply generated by pure unconnected autonomous individuals but in communities of various sorts.[27]

Although limited community relativism brings this inquiry into relation with familiar views of moral requirement, suggesting why those analyses have rendered theoretically invisible the connections between community and virtue, my discussion has addressed Murdoch's concerns even if limited community relativism is rejected. For the virtue-supporting and content-conferring connections between community and virtue that I have highlighted in this essay address the question of what (noteworthily) good conduct is like, and how we can make ourselves better. Perhaps these are the matters ultimately most worthy of the attention of moral philosophers.

27. MacIntyre reemphasizes this point in his review of Murdoch's new book, *Metaphysics as a Guide to Morals* (New York: Viking Penguin, 1993) in *The New York Times Book Review*, January 3, 1993. I regret that Murdoch's book emerged too late for me to take account of it in this essay, or in the other essays in this book.

PART III

The morality of care

8

Compassion

This chapter offers an account of compassion as a moral phenomenon. Compassion is a kind of emotion or emotional attitude; though it differs from paradigmatic emotions such as fear, anger, distress, love, it has, I will argue, an irreducible affective dimension.

Compassion is one among a number of attitudes, emotions, or virtues which can be called "altruistic" in that they involve a regard for the good of other persons. Some others are pity, helpfulness, well-wishing. Such phenomena and the distinctions between them have been given insufficient attention in current moral philosophy. By distinguishing compassion from some of these other altruistic phenomena I want to bring out compassion's particular moral value, as well as some of its limitations.[1]

My context for this inquiry is an interest in developing an alternative to Kantianism, in particular to its minimization of the role of emotion in morality and its exclusive emphasis on duty and rationality. I am influenced here by Schopenhauer's critique of Kant's ethics and by his view of compassion as central to morality.[2] But discussion of the specific views of these two philosophers will be peripheral to my task here.

THE OBJECTS OF COMPASSION

How must a compassionate person view someone in order to have compassion for him?[3] Compassion seems restricted to beings capable of feeling or being harmed. Bypassing the question of compassion for plants, animals, institutions, I will focus on persons as objects of compassion. A person in a negative condition, suffering some harm, difficulty, danger (past, present, or future) is the appropriate object of compassion. But

1. Compassion has a particular cultural history: its sources are Christian, it was further developed by Romanticism, especially by the German Romantics. Though I do not focus on this history explicitly, my emphasis on compassion as a particular moral emotion among others should leave room for the results of such a historical account.
2. Arthur Schopenhauer, *On the Basis of Morality* (New York: Bobbs-Merrill, 1965).
3. In general I will use feminine pronouns to refer to the person having compassion (the "subject") and masculine pronouns to refer to the person for whom she has compassion (the "object").

there are many negative conditions and not all are possible objects of compassion. The inconvenience and irritation of a short detour for a driver on his way to a casual visit are not compassion-grounding conditions.[4] The negative condition must be relatively central to a person's life and well-being, describable as pain, misery, hardship, suffering, affliction, and the like. Although it is the person and not merely the negative condition which is the object of compassion, the focus of compassion is the condition.

Compassion can be part of a complex attitude toward its object; it is possible to have compassion for someone in a difficult or miserable situation without judging his *overall* condition to be difficult or miserable. It is therefore necessary to distinguish the conditions for someone being an appropriate object of compassion from the conditions for compassion being the appropriate dominant response to the person. One might predominantly admire and take pleasure in the happiness of a blind person who has gotten through college, found a rewarding job, made close friends – someone whose life is generally happy and who does not dwell on what he misses by being blind. Nevertheless one can also feel compassion for him because his life is diminished and damaged by his blindness.

It is not necessary that the object of compassion be aware of his condition; he might be deceiving himself with regard to it. Nor, as in the case of the happy blind man, need he think of it as a substantial affliction, even if he is aware of it as a deficiency.

That compassion is limited to grave or serious negative conditions does not exclude other altruistic emotions from being entirely appropriate to less serious states. One can feel sorry for, commiserate with, or feel sympathy for a person's irritation, discomfort, inconvenience, displeasure. Nor are all altruistic attitudes primarily directed to particular persons: They can be directed to classes of persons (the blind) or to general conditions (poverty). In addition, there are altruistic virtues not so clearly involving emotions, which come into play in regard to less serious negative conditions: considerateness, thoughtfulness, helpfulness. It would be considerate or thoughtful to warn an acquaintance of an unexpected detour so that he could avoid needless inconvenience and irritation. (These virtues may take as their object potential positive conditions of the other person; for

4. I am making a conceptual rather than a moral point here. The compassionate person cannot regard the object of her compassion as merely irritated or discomforted; but of course a genuinely compassionate person might mistakenly take an inconvenience to be a serious harm. To say that compassion is appropriate in this context is, then, simply to say that the object actually possesses the compassion-grounding feature which the subject takes him to possess. I do not discuss the further issue of when compassion is *morally* appropriate or inappropriate.

example, letting someone know about an upcoming lecture that he would greatly enjoy but would not be likely otherwise to hear about exemplifies thoughtfulness.) Such virtues as these, while not necessarily involving emotion or feeling, do involve attention to another's situation and a genuine regard for the other's good, even when more self-regarding attitudes are conjointly brought into play.

Not all altruistic emotions are focused on negative states. Someone might take delight in giving pleasure to others. Though this altruistic attitude shares with compassion a regard for the good of others, compassion focuses on pain, suffering, and damage, whereas this other attitude focuses on pleasure. The possession of one altruistic attitude is no assurance of the possession of others. It is quite possible for a compassionate person to be insensitive to the pleasures of others. A focus on misery and suffering in the absence of regard for others' joys and pleasures constitutes a limitation in the moral consciousness of the merely compassionate person.[5]

THE EMOTIONAL ATTITUDE OF COMPASSION

The compassionate person does not merely *believe* that the object suffers some serious harm or injury; such a belief is compatible with indifference, malicious delight in his suffering, or intense intellectual interest, for example of a novelist or psychologist for whom the suffering is primarily material for contemplation or investigation. Even a genuine interest in relieving someone's suffering can stem from meeting an intellectual or professional challenge rather than from compassion.

Compassion is not a simple feeling-state but a complex emotional attitude toward another, characteristically involving imaginative dwelling on the condition of the other person, an active regard for his good, a view of him as a fellow human being, and emotional responses of a certain degree of intensity.

Imaginatively reconstructing someone's condition is distinct from several sorts of identification with the other person. For instance, it does not involve an identity confusion in which the compassionate person fails to distinguish his feelings and situation from the other person's.[6] Such a

---

5. Nietzsche saw this focus on misery and suffering as a kind of morbidity in the compassionate consciousness; this view formed part of his critique of compassion.
6. Philip Mercer, *Sympathy and Ethics* (Oxford: Clarendon Press, 1972), and Max Scheler, *The Nature of Sympathy,* trans. Werner Stark (London: Routledge & Kegan Paul, 1965), pp. 8–51.

175

pathological condition actually precludes genuine compassion because it blurs the distinction between subject and object.

In a second type of identification the subject identifies with the object because of having had an experience similar to his, the memory of which his experience evokes. ("I can identify with what you are going through, since I've suffered from the same problem myself.") Here no identity confusion is involved. Although such identification can promote compassion and imaginative understanding, it is not required for it. For compassion does not require even that its subject have experienced the sort of suffering that occasions it. We can commiserate with someone who has lost a child in a fire, even if we do not have a child or have never lost someone we love. The reason for this is that the imaginative reconstruction involved in compassion consists in imagining what the other person, given his character, beliefs, and values, is undergoing, rather than what we ourselves would feel in his situation. For example, I might regard my son's decision to work for the CIA with distress, whereas someone with different beliefs and values might regard such a decision (on the part of her son) with pride; yet this other person may well be able to understand my reaction and to feel compassion for me in regard to it.

The degree of imaginative reconstruction need not be great. The friend in the previous example might find it difficult to reconstruct for herself the outlook and set of values within which my son's decision is viewed with distress. But to have compassion she must at least dwell in her imagination on the fact that I am distressed. So some imaginative representation is a necessary condition for compassion, though the degree can be minimal. Certainly a detailed and rich understanding of another person's outlook and consciousness, of the sort available only to persons of exceptional powers of imagination, is not required for compassion.

Nevertheless, as a matter of empirical fact, we often do come to understand someone's condition by imagining what our own reactions would be. So expanding our powers of imagination expands our capacity for compassion. And conversely the limits of a person's capacities for imaginative reconstruction set limits on her capacity for compassion. Finding another person's experience opaque may well get in the way of compassion. Persons who are in general quite poor at imagining the experiences of others who are different from themselves, may well be less likely to have compassion for them. Yet this failure of imagination is typically not a purely intellectual or cognitive failure; for it can itself be part of a more general failure to regard the other as fully human, or to take that humanity sufficiently seriously. That a white colonialist in Africa does not imagine to himself the cares and sufferings of the Blacks whom he rules cannot be separated from the fact that he does not see them as fully human.

A second constituent of compassion is concern for or regard for the object's good. It is not enough that we imaginatively reconstruct someone's suffering; for, like belief, such imagining is compatible with malice and mere intellectual curiosity. (In fact it is likely to be a component of them.) In addition we must care about that suffering and desire its alleviation. Suppose a neighbor's house burns down, though no one is hurt. Compassion would involve not only imagining what it is like for the neighbor to be homeless but also concerned responses such as the following: being upset or distressed, regretting the different aspects of his plight (his homelessness, his loss of prized possessions, his terror when inside the burning house, etc.); wishing the tragedy had not happened; giving thought to what might be done to alleviate the neighbor's situation; worrying whether he will be able to find another place to live; hoping that he will obtain a decent settlement from the insurance company; hoping and desiring that, in general, his suffering will be no greater than necessary.

The relation between concern for another person's good and these thoughts, feelings, hopes, and desires is a necessary or conceptual one; compassionate concern would not properly be attributed to someone who lacked them (or at least most of them). This concern is not merely tacked on to the imaginative reconstruction as a totally independent component of compassion. Rather the manner in which we dwell on the other's plight expresses the concern for his good.

These concerned reactions must be directed toward the other's plight and not merely caused by it. The distress that is part of compassion cannot take as its focus the vivid realization that I might be afflicted with a like misfortune; for it would then be self-regarding rather than altruistic.

Compassion also involves viewing the other person and his suffering in a certain way. I can put this by saying that compassion involves a sense of shared humanity, of regarding the other as a fellow human being. This means that the other person's suffering (though not necessarily his particular afflicting condition) is seen as the kind of thing that could happen to anyone, including oneself insofar as one is a human being.[7]

This way of viewing the other person contrasts with the attitude charac-

7. This way of viewing the other's plight differs from a fundamentally self-regarding sentiment in which the person's plight is regarded as a symbol of what could happen to oneself. It is not actually necessary that one believe that the afflicting condition *could* happen to oneself: One might have compassion for someone suffering napalm burns without believing that there is any possibility of oneself being in that condition.

teristic of *pity,* in which one holds oneself apart from the afflicted person and from his suffering, thinking of it as something that defines that person as fundamentally different from oneself. In pity the other person's condition is seen as a *given* (at least within the context in question), whereas in compassion the subject is acutely aware of a gap between that unfortunate condition and a condition consisting in that person's flourishing. That is why pity (unlike compassion) involves a kind of condescension, and why compassion is morally superior to pity.

Because compassion involves a sense of shared humanity, it promotes the *experience* of equality, even when accompanied by an acknowledgment of actual social inequality. Compassion forbids regarding social inequality as establishing human inequality. This is part of the moral force of compassion: By transcending the recognition of social inequality, it promotes the sensed experience of equality in common humanity.

Sometimes the reason we feel pity rather than compassion is that we feel that the object has in some way brought the suffering on himself or deserved it, or in any case that he has allowed himself to be humiliated or degraded by it. But such ways of regarding the object do not necessarily undermine compassion, and they are not incompatible with it. It would be a mistake to see the essential difference between pity and compassion in such differing beliefs about the object's condition. No matter how pitiful or self-degraded one regards another human being, it is possible (and not necessarily unwarranted) to feel compassion and concern for him, simply because he is suffering.

Nietzsche's use of the term *Mitleid* does not distinguish between compassion and pity. Because *Mitleid* is focused on the negative states of others, Nietzsche saw it as life-denying and without positive value. But insofar as compassion involves a genuine concern for the good of others and a "living sense of another's worth,"[8] it is, unlike pity, fundamentally life-affirming and positive.

A fourth aspect of compassion is its strength and duration. If the distress, sorrow, hopes, and desires of an altruistic attitude were merely passing reactions or twinges of feeling, they would be insufficient for the level of concern, the imaginative reconstruction, and the disposition to beneficent action required for compassion. Though there are degrees of compassion, the threshold of emotional strength required of compassion (in contrast with other altruistic attitudes) is relatively high and enduring. Because well-wishing and pity can be more episodic and less action-guiding, they are morally inferior to compassion. (One can, however,

8. Nicolai Hartmann, *Ethics* (London: George Allen and Unwin, 1932), vol. 2, p. 273.

have a *twinge* of compassion; this is a more superficial and episodic version of "having compassion.") As the etymology of the word suggests, compassion involves "feeling with" the other person, sharing his feelings. In one sense, this means that the subject and the object have the same feeling-type: distress, sorrow, desire for relief. But in a more important sense the feelings are not the same; for the relation between their subjects and their objects are different. The focus of my neighbor's distress is *his own* homelessness; the focus of my distress in having compassion for him is *my neighbor's* homelessness (or his distress at his homelessness). This can partly be expressed as a matter of degree. My neighbor suffers; in suffering with him there is a sense in which I suffer too, but my suffering is much less than his.

COMPASSION AND BENEFICENT ACTION

When it is possible for her to relieve another person's suffering without undue demands on her time, energy, and priorities, the compassionate person is disposed to attempt to help. We would hardly attribute compassion to X if she were to saunter by on a spring day and, seeing an elderly man fall on the sidewalk, walk right by, perhaps with a sad shudder of dismay, leaving the old man lying alone.

Characteristically, compassion involves the disposition to perform beneficent actions, and to perform them because the agent has had a certain sort of imaginative reconstruction of someone's condition and has a concern for his good. The steps that the person takes to ameliorate the condition are guided by and prompted by that imaginative reconstruction and concern. So the beneficent action of a compassionate person has a specific sort of causal history, which distinguishes it from an equally beneficent action that might be prompted by other sorts of attitudes and emotions.

We saw that concern exists at different degrees of strength in different altruistic emotions and attitudes. Hence its corresponding disposition to beneficence exists at different levels of strength also. The stronger the disposition the more one is willing to go out of one's way, to act contrary to inclination and interest, in order to help the other person.[9] That com-

9. Aristotle recognizes differences in the strength of the disposition to beneficence in his discussion of *eunoia* ("well-wishing" or "good will" in Thompson's translation). Of persons who have *eunoia* toward others, Aristotle says, "Goodwill [*eunoia*] does not imply friendship; for when they have goodwill people only wish goods to the other, and will not cooperate with him in any action, or go to any trouble for him." Aristotle, *Nicomachean Ethics,* trans. Terence Irwin (Indianapolis: Hackett Press, 1985), book 9, 1167a8–10, p. 248.

passion as a motive can and often does withstand contrary inclination begins to address the Kantian charge that emotions, including compassion, are unreliable as motives to beneficent action.[10] As a motive to beneficence, compassion can have the strength, stability, and reliability that Kant thought only the sense of duty could have. As a trait of character compassion can be as stable and consistent in its prompting of appropriate beneficent action as a conscientious adherence to principles of beneficence.

Though compassion is a type of emotion or emotional attitude, it is not like a Kantian "inclination." Acting from compassion does not typically involve doing what one is in the mood to do, or feels like doing. On the contrary the regard for the other's good which compassion implies means that one's compassionate acts often involve acting very much contrary to one's moods and inclinations. Compassion is fundamentally other-regarding rather than self-regarding; its affective nature in no way detracts from this.

Compassionate action may extinguish or diminish compassion itself, most obviously when its object is relieved of the negative condition by the action. But even merely *engaging* in action may involve a shift in the subject's consciousness from the imaginative reconstruction of the object's condition to a focus on the expected relief of that condition, thereby diminishing the compassion (though not the regard for the other's good and hence not the moral value of the attitude or state of mind).

Compassion, however, is not always linked so directly to the prompting of beneficent actions. For in many situations it is impossible (without extraordinary disruption of one's life and priorities) for the compassionate person herself to improve the sufferer's condition (for instance, when one is concerned for the welfare of distant flood victims). In other situations the beneficence might be inappropriate, as when intervention might jeopardize the sufferer's autonomy. Compassionate concern, in such cases, involves hope and desire for the relief of the condition by those in a position to provide it. It does not involve actively setting oneself in readiness to perform beneficent acts, once one firmly believes such acts to be impossible or inappropriate.

In the cases so far discussed a link exists between compassion and beneficent action, through the desire that action be taken by someone to relieve the sufferer's condition. But compassion is also appropriate in situations in which nothing whatever can be done to alleviate the afflic-

10. For this Kantian view, see Kant, *Fundamental Principles of the Metaphysics of Morals,* trans. Beck (New York: Bobbs-Merrill, 1960), pp. 6, 14, 28; and *Critique of Practical Reason,* trans. Beck (New York: Bobbs-Merrill, 1956), pp. 75, 122.

tion, as for instance when someone is suffering from painful terminal cancer. In such situations compassionate concern involves sorrowing for the person, but not a disposition to help.

Because being compassionate involves actively giving thought to the relief of the sufferer's condition, a compassionate person may discover the possibility of beneficent action when it seemed unclear whether any existed. Compassion often involves resisting regarding situations as absolutely irremediable. On the other hand the compassionate person may for this reason fail to see and hence to face up to the hopelessness of the sufferer's situation.

That compassion is often appropriate when there is little or no scope for the subject's disposition to beneficence indicates that compassion's sole significance does not lie in its role as motive to beneficence. Even when nothing can be done by the compassionate person to improve the sufferer's condition, simply being aware that one is an object or recipient of compassion can be an important human good. The compassionate person's expression of concern and shared sorrow can be valuable to the sufferer for its own sake, independent of its instrumental value in improving his condition. Nor does the good of recognizing oneself to be an object of compassion depend on the compassionate person wanting to convey his attitude, though the recipient can in addition value the intention to communicate.

The compassionate attitude is a good to the recipient, not only because it signifies that the subject would help if she could but because we are glad to receive the concern of others, glad of the sense of equality that it promotes. Yet it is morally good to be compassionate even when — as often happens — the object of compassion is unaware of it. For any concern for the welfare of others, especially when it promotes the sense of equality, is (ceteris paribus) morally good. In this, compassion contrasts with attitudes and feelings such as infatuation or admiration which may convey goods to their recipients but which are without moral value because they do not essentially involve a regard for their recipient's good. The moral significance of compassion is not exhausted by the various types of goods it confers on its recipients.

Compassion can hurt its recipient. It may, for instance, cause him to concentrate too much on his plight, or to think that people around him see him primarily in terms of that plight. But these dangers and burdens of compassion can be mitigated to the extent that a person recognizes that compassion is not the sole or the dominant attitude with which one is regarded.

Compassion can also be misguided, grounded in superficial understanding of a situation. Compassion is not necessarily wise or appropriate. The compassionate person may even end up doing more harm than good. True compassion must be allied with knowledge and understanding if it is to serve adequately as a guide to action: there is nothing inherent in the character of compassion that would prevent – and much that would encourage – its alliance with intelligent reflection. Because compassion involves an active interest in another person's welfare, it is characteristically a spur to a deeper understanding of a situation than rationality alone could ensure. A person who is compassionate by character is in principle committed to a rational and intelligent course of action. Nevertheless, failure to engage in the relevant reflection does not by itself rule out the existence of compassion.

9

Moral development and conceptions of morality

Contemporary moral philosophy has been little concerned with developmental questions. The academic division of labor has consigned such matters to psychologists, who, in turn, have generally seen little need to address normative and philosophical issues. This separation has taken its toll on both disciplines. A responsible and comprehensive understanding of morality requires both disciplines and the few signs of cooperation and crossover are to be warmly welcomed.[1]

By and large, contemporary moral philosophy has not felt pressed to explore what it is like to be a person who lives according to its various normative theories, nor how one gets to be such a person. This neglect of the psychic substratum of morality can be given a philosophical rationale – that philosophy's role is simply to demonstrate the rational soundness of views of morality. On this view philosophical acceptability need have no connection to psychological reality.[2] A further assumption in this direction – made, for example (though not consistently adhered to), by Kant – is that rational acceptability is by itself sufficient to motivate conformity to morality. This view at least has the virtue of recognizing the psychic underpinnings of morality as an issue, but it gives an entirely false picture of those psychic underpinnings. Happily, influential contemporary neo-Kantians such as Marcia Baron,

I thank Owen Flanagan and Jerome Kagan for very helpful comments on a late draft of this essay.

1. Owen Flanagan's *Variety of Moral Personality: Ethics and Psychological Realism* is much the most impressive of recent attempts by philosophers to bridge the gap between psychology and moral philosophy. Robert Crittenden's *Learning to Be Moral: Philosophical Thoughts About Moral Development* is an excellent survey of philosophers' and developmentalists' accounts of moral development, and contains a fine statement of the need for cross-fertilization of these disciplines. Lawrence Kohlberg, whose work will be discussed below, pioneered in recognizing the inextricability of philosophical and psychological understanding of morality.
2. The psychologist of morality Augusto Blasi, in his remarks at the "Emergence of Morality in Young Children" conference at which an earlier version of this essay was presented as a paper, implied that the perspective sketched here is the paradigm "philosophers'" conception of morality. I hope to be indicating here that it is rather only one among several philosophical conceptions, and, though currently dominant, has been much less so in the history of ethical thought.

Barbara Herman, Thomas Hill, Jr., Adrian Piper, and Stephen Darwall[3] have shown a much greater interest in moral psychology, though less in moral development.

Unconcern with psychology is often grounded in a certain metaethical view, currently discarded by many ethical theorists, that the foundation of the "ought" – of what is morally right – can have nothing to do with the "is" of human nature – with how humans behave and feel. In this view the validity of a moral position has absolutely nothing to do with our having prior assurance that our natures allow us to live up to it. Rather, as is true for Kant, it is only because we already accept morality that we know we are able to adhere to it. Or, to put it in its more familiar terms, "ought implies can."

Utilitarianism, despite its status as the chief current rival to Kantianism, is susceptible to much the same characterization. The classical utilitarianism of Bentham and Mill took the view that a single principle ought to guide all our actions – to promote the maximum of happiness among all human beings. Mill (1861) claimed that the motives to conform to the utilitarian principle were nothing more than pleasure and pain, and thus were within the scope of ordinary human motives. The trouble with this view, as has been frequently noted, is that the pleasure-pain motivation on which Mill draws works only for the individual and cannot alone generate a broader application of the utilitarian principle. The latter requires the agent to abstract from her own interests or happiness, and to consider everyone's pleasure or pain equally and impartially. This psychic task is not so different from Kant's projection of a universal and impartial point of view, and the psychological wherewithal and motivation to achieve such a standpoint are not adequately supplied by either view.[4]

A second set of philosophical views does exhibit a concern with the psychological substratum of morality, but is not particularly concerned with its development. Such views try to indicate some adult psychological capacity in which to ground morality but do not inquire into how this adult capacity develops from various childhood capacities. These views generally, though not inevitably, base morality on feeling or emotion, and

3. See, for example, Marcia Baron, "On the Alleged Moral Repugnance of Acting from Duty," *Journal of Philosophy,* vol. 91, no. 4, April, 1984: 197–219; Barbara Herman, *The Practice of Moral Judgment* (Cambridge, Mass.: Harvard University Press, 1993); Thomas Hill, Jr., *Autonomy and Self-Respect* (Cambridge: Cambridge University Press, 1991); Adrian Piper, "Moral Theory and Moral Alienation," *Journal of Philosophy,* vol. 84, no. 2, February 1987: 102–18; Stephen Darwall, *Impartial Reason* (Ithaca: Cornell University Press, 1983).

4. The convergences between Kantianism and utilitarianism, which otherwise differ in many ways, have been especially emphasized by Bernard Williams in his various writings.

within that rubric one can distinguish two types. The first, of whom the British empiricists Adam Smith and David Hume are the most famous exponents, sees sentiments, such as sympathy and benevolence, as forming the basis of moral judgment. For Hume, sympathy (corrected for various kinds of parochialism) provides the standpoint from which human beings judge other human beings as possessing virtue and vice. The second view, best represented by Arthur Schopenhauer (1841), sees our emotional nature (in particular, compassion) as underlying our capacity for moral *motivation* rather than moral *judgment.* For Schopenhauer an emotionally based motivation, rather than the capacity for moral judgment, is central to morality. (For this reason Hume is rightly seen as a forerunner of Kagan's [1984] views, whereas Schopenhauer is closer to the view that I am advocating.) Nevertheless, although both views ground morality in emotion rather than reason, neither one is particularly concerned with the ontogenesis of moral emotions.

Aristotle, a philosopher whose views have become increasingly prominent in contemporary ethics (though still much less so than the Kantian, utilitarian, or contractarian traditions), was concerned with both the nature of virtue and its developmental requisites. He thus provides a model of integration of the psychic and purely philosophical that I wish to recommend. Nevertheless, Aristotle does *not* attempt to identify (as I will try to do) specific capacities of children as developmental forerunners of mature adult morality. (Moreover, Aristotle's conception of morality gives little attention and importance to the particular virtues with which I will be concerned.)

A third category of theories is concerned with the adult capacities in which morality can be grounded, their development, and the specific childhood capacities that are their developmental precursors. Some of the most prominent of these theories are of a neo-Kantian nature, such as those of Rawls (1971) and Kohlberg (1981, 1984). Both attempt to specify the way in which a mature morality grows out of specific childhood capacities, sentiments, or ways of thinking, though Kohlberg, as a developmental psychologist, does this more extensively than Rawls. Both views retain the Kantian emphasis on rationality as the foundation of morality but attempt to discard Kant's nonempirical or "transcendental" perspective. Kohlberg and Rawls describe rationality as a specific empirical human capacity with a developmental history. Thus their view abandons a sharp "is-ought" distinction.

Developmental psychologists, and psychologists more generally, may agree with my criticism of philosophers for neglecting their field. But they have no grounds for self-satisfaction. They may regard philosophers' accounts about the nature of morality as "endlessly and tiresomely debatable" (Crittenden, p. 3), and grounded ultimately in nothing more than previously held views about morality, but their own researches cannot avoid taking some stand on the nature of morality. How else can they identify the phenomena that are to count as moral capacities, moral development, and moral behavior?

In particular, I will argue here that some of the most influential moral developmental theories leave no, or inadequate, room for some important moral virtues and their developmental precursors. The virtues in question are sympathy, compassion, kindness, generosity, helpfulness, considerateness, human concern (for specific individuals). And I will identify a quality in children that I will call *responsiveness* and that I will claim (without directly arguing for it) is a developmental precursor of this set of virtues.

My argument will be that theories of development – especially that of Lawrence Kohlberg, still the most influential single theory in the field, but also (though to a lesser extent) those of Rawls, Richard Shweder, and Jerome Kagan – presuppose either explicitly or implicitly philosophical conceptions of morality that fail to identify or to account for the virtues mentioned above. Those conceptions include some or all of the following elements, and claim that those elements constitute a full account of morality: (1) Morality takes the form of *rules of action.* (2) Those rules are *act-specifying* – they direct us to perform specific acts. (3) Morality involves *conformity to standards.* (4) Morality takes the form of *principles.* (5) The principles must be *universal.* (6) The moral point of view is characterized by *impartiality.*

I begin with a discussion of childhood responsiveness, describing some examples, and then moving to a definition.[5]

Example 1

Sarah, twelve months, is sitting with Clara, fifteen months, on Clara's mother's lap. The girls have grown up together and are very close. Clara is holding a plastic cup, which she drops on the floor. She then cries, and points to the cup. Sarah climbs out of Clara's mother's lap, gets the cup, and gives it to Clara.

5. Example 2 is taken from Hoffman (1976); example 4 is from Ned Mueller's presentation at the Emergence of Morality in Young Children conference. The others are from my own and my wife's observations of our own children, their friend, and their cousin.

186

Example 2

Michael, fifteen months, is struggling with his friend Paul over a toy. Paul starts to cry. Michael appears concerned and lets go of the toy so Paul has it. But Paul continues to cry. Michael pauses, then gives his own teddy bear to Paul; Paul continues crying. Michael pauses again, runs to the next room, gets Paul's security blanket, and gives it to him. Paul stops crying.

Example 3

Sarah, two years three months, is riding in the car with her cousin Ali, who is four. Ali is upset because she does not have her teddy bear, and there is a fairly extended discussion about how the bear is probably in the trunk and can be retrieved when they arrive at the house. About ten minutes pass and, as the car approaches the house, Sarah says to Ali, "Now you can get your bear."

Example 4

Two children, twenty-two months and twenty-four months, are close friends. While playing, one accidentally harms the other who cries. Although the one who harms will not respond to an adult's admonition to apologize, he seems concerned with his action; he offers the other child a toy and attempts to reconnect with and apologize to the other child.

Example 5

Ben, three-and-a-half, is playing on the floor with his sister Sarah, six months. Ben sees a safety pin and takes it to his mother in another room, saying that it would hurt Sarah if she got it.

Example 6

Sarah, three, gives Clara, three, her own Donald Duck hat (to keep "forever"), saying that she has done so because Clara has (recently, but not in the moment) lost her (Boston) Celtics cap.

These examples differ in important ways. Their variety suggests that young children's morally relevant capacities are more complex and varied than one might think. Some involve greater moral or cognitive depth than others. In example 5, Ben is responding not to an actual state of harm or distress but to a potential one (Sarah being hurt by the safety pin). In example 2, Michael seems to be "assessing" what will stop Paul's crying; he makes attempts and cognitively processes Paul's reactions to them. Examples 2 and 4 both involve persistence in action. In examples 3 and 6, Sarah responds not to an immediate state of distress of the other child but draws on her memory and knowledge of the other child's condition. In example 6, Sarah's responsiveness is not to a specific state of distress (manifest or assumed) but rather simply to what she believes Clara wants or would like. Examples 2 and 4 involve the child's responding to a distress which he himself has to some extent brought about; this feature is absent in the others.

The six examples share what I believe to be a nonegoistic sentiment or motivation of one child toward another child. By "responsiveness" I refer to an action expressive of an altruistic motive toward others (invoking here Iris Murdoch's notion of responsiveness to a reality, in particular the reality of other persons). Thus "responsiveness" is not to be taken as meaning merely "reacting to another person," for example, smiling when a parent enters the room; it must also involve some altruistic concern. But there is, no doubt, a connection between responsiveness in the former, broader sense and in the latter, more restricted sense used in this essay. Responsiveness is not simply an intention to aid another, since such an intention can be entirely unaltruistic in its underlying motivation; for example, it can be a bid to gain power over another, to gain approval from others (e.g., parents), or to secure a future benefit. Responsiveness is not limited to concern directed toward a specific negative condition of another. It is not limited to actual felt distress, because the other person can be (as in example 5) at risk or in danger without knowing (hence feeling) this, or can even be in a kind of pain without being aware of the pain.[6] Responsiveness is toward another's condition, rather than specifically toward some particular emotion the other is feeling. Yet the condition need not be a particularly unpleasant one; it can simply be a condition of wanting or being able to be made happier by something, as in example 6 when Sarah gives Clara a Donald Duck cap. It should be noted too that, as defined, "responsiveness" involves taking action to address

6. Adam Smith ([1759] 1948) notes the possibility and even appropriateness of sympathy for a "wretched" but nevertheless joyous person in the process of losing his reason (p. 77). As Hoffman (1982) points out, the ability to respond beyond another's immediate situation to a general condition of the person depends on an advanced level of cognitive development, appreciating the other as a continuous person with a separate identity and history (p. 94), though we can see the rudiments of such a development in some of our examples (3 and 6).

another's condition. It thus involves a kind of initiative and is not merely a passive response.[7]

Responsiveness involves both cognitive and affective dimensions. It involves a cognitive grasp of another's condition. Even the twelve-month-old in example 1 seems to understand that the other child is distressed and that this is because she has lost her cup. At the same time the altruistic aspect of responsiveness involves our emotional natures, in that responsiveness is not a purely rational willing of another person's good.[8] The altruistic motivations involved in responsiveness can be understood only by reference to human emotions, though I will argue below that this does not mean that each instance of responsiveness involves a specific feeling-state. The cognitive and affective dimensions of responsiveness are not rightly understood as merely two separate components – a cognition and a feeling-state – added together; rather they inform one another. I will try to show how this is so, as well as generally to clarify the nature of responsiveness, by discussing some other psychological phenomena that might be confused with responsiveness or that might be involved in responsiveness but are not coextensive with it.

First of all *merely* understanding another's condition is insufficient for responsiveness, since this understanding can be used, for example, to manipulate or ridicule.[9] The *purely* cognitive is not sufficient because it does not ensure the altruistic concern for the other. At the same time I suggest that there is a natural link between knowing another's distress and being concerned or inclined to do something about it, though this inclination can be blocked by contrary inclinations or sentiments. In order for the connection between knowing about and responding to the other *not* to be made, some process must intervene to distance the one person from the other.[10] This view is elaborated by Murdoch (1970),

7. The terminology of "responsiveness" is drawn partly from the work of Gilligan (1982). Whitbeck (1983) points out that Gilligan's terminology "may be misunderstood to suggest response to the exclusion of initiation" (p. 83), though this is not Gilligan's intention. Addressing Whitbeck's point, I wish to forestall such an interpretation by building into the notion of responsiveness the taking of action to address another's condition.

8. Whether the purely rational willing of another's good is possible is a question I will not explore here, though its existence in small children can certainly be doubted. The Kantian tradition in ethics, which will be discussed below, claims that such rational willing is not only possible but is the highest, if not the only, expression of morality. A sophisticated contemporary defense of that position can be found in Nagel (1970), although Nagel has modified his position in subsequent writings (1986). I am defining "responsiveness" in a way that excludes this purely rational willing.

9. A good example of a twenty-month-old child showing a sophisticated understanding of another for the purposes of manipulating her is given in Hoffman (1976), p. 129.

10. An interesting argument for a quasi-necessary link between seeing distress and being responsive to it is made by Ross (1983).

who suggests that to truly know or "see" another person involves having some altruistic sentiment toward that person. Her view depends on construing "knowing" to include allowing the perception of another person's distress to affect oneself, vividly imagining the other's distress, and the like.[11]

Second, experiencing the same feeling as the other person is neither necessary nor sufficient for responsiveness. It is not sufficient, for X could feel a distress caused by Y's distress, and yet X might not have any concern for Y's distress but simply have an impetus to rid himself of his own resultant distress. Hoffman points out that a nonaltruistic identity of feeling may occur in children younger than twelve months whose identities are insufficiently differentiated from others' and who thus experience another's distress as occurring within themselves (1976, p. 131). But as Scheler (1965) notes, this phenomenon – which he calls "emotional infection" – is found in adults as well. Mere identity or similarity of feeling can occur in the absence of the cognitive grasp of the other as well as of the altruistic concern.

In addition, having the same feeling as the other is not necessary for responsiveness. This is partly because in order to be an appropriate target of responsiveness, the other person need not himself have any particular feeling. Even when the other is in a particular feeling-state, it is also perfectly intelligible, as Scheler often emphasizes, that a person be truly concerned about another's pain without having feelings of pain or distress herself.

More generally, although responsiveness is grounded in our emotional natures, its occurrence on a particular occasion does not always involve any particular feeling-state on that occasion. To say, for example, that I care about Joan, or am concerned about her, is not to say that at every moment I am experiencing some particular feeling-state. One can intelligibly say that one is concerned about someone but is not feeling that concern at that particular moment. And yet one cannot have concern for Joan without having some feelings regarding Joan in at least some situations. For example, suppose I am concerned about Joan because she is in danger, and then the danger recedes. For it to have been true of me that I was concerned about Joan, I must have some feeling of joy, relief, or the like, when I learn that she is out of danger (though the feeling need not occur at some particular moment since some people react to emotionally charged information more immediately than others).[12]

11. A similar argument is given by McDowell (1979).
12. The complexities of the cognitive, affective, and motivational aspects of sympathy, concern, care, and the like, are further discussed in Blum (1980), Chapter 2.

It might be thought that although adults can be responsive without having a state of mind corresponding to that of another person, this would be impossible or rare in children. Although greater development of cognitive abilities allows for adult responsiveness to be less dependent than children's on the limits of an individual's own experience, it does not seem a necessary feature of children's concern that the child possess the same feeling-state as the object of her concern. In example 3, for Sarah to be responsive to Ali's distress about her teddy bear, Sarah need not have been in a state of distress herself. It seems more plausible to say that the feeling-state will sometimes be present (perhaps, e.g., in examples, 1, 2, 4, and 5) and sometimes not; but in any case it is not a requirement for the attribution of responsiveness.

Just as I want to avoid an overly cognitive understanding of responsiveness, so, too, I am rejecting an overly affective view. But I do not suggest that having the same feeling as the other has nothing to do with responsiveness. In responding to another's distress one can have a comparable feeling within oneself. Being moved or "touched" by another person's plight are metaphors employed in describing responsiveness that express the sense of a distinct emotional reaction to another's situation. My argument here is addressed to an oversimplified and overly affective emphasis, especially on experiencing the identical feeling of the other person.

It might be argued that in the absence of a specific feeling-state, one cannot be sure why the child is acting in an altruistic manner; hence responsiveness cannot be inferred. It is true that the altruistic motivation is a matter of inference. But what are the alternative explanations? It is not enough to say that the child notes the other child's need and therefore fills the need (by saying where to get the teddy bear, or taking the safety pin away). For it is precisely the intentional helping behavior whose explanation is in question. Could it be "conditioning"? Complex issues surround this notion, but it seems that the situations in which children are responsive to one another are too diverse to be encompassed by any purely behavioral conditioning. If a child has been repeatedly rewarded for giving another child a cookie, it might be plausible to explain his continuing to do so without invoking any altruistic sentiment or motive toward the other child. But such an account would not seem plausible in some of our examples, in which the children may well not have encountered similar circumstances before.

For similar reasons a purely biological or instinctual explanation would seem insufficient to explain particular instances of responsiveness that are dependent on cognitive understandings in relatively new situations. My account of responsiveness, however, is not meant to exclude a biologi-

191

cal or physiological substrate for the capacity for responsiveness; it implies only that an explanation of the exercise of that capacity on any particular occasion requires more than physiology.

Let us focus for a moment on the nature of the cognitive dimension essential for responsiveness – the knowledge of the other person's condition. This knowledge has sometimes been depicted as the subject inferring the other's state of mind from a feeling the subject herself has, or has had, in similar circumstances. Although such inference may play some role in the assessment of another's state of mind, it cannot be the sole cognitive process involved in understanding another. This is partly because concern for another does not always involve the assessment of a particular state of mind at all – hence it is not an inference from the responsive person's own state of mind to the other person's. Second, such inference would not account for understanding states of mind different from those one is experiencing or has experienced oneself. Third, grasping another's condition, in the context of responsiveness, does not require being in any particular feeling-state oneself.

More fundamentally, I suggest a theoretical bias in the premise that our knowledge of others inevitably proceeds from an inference about our own state of mind. This bias, rooted in the empiricist epistemological tradition, presumes a division of self from others, so that one has only indirect means of forging a subsequent cognitive link between self and other. This theoretical assumption has been criticized most powerfully by Wittgenstein (1953), whose view I can only mention, not defend. Wittgenstein sees the commonality between persons sharing a "form of life" as a condition of the possibility of knowledge of others, and indeed a presupposition of any processes of inferences made by one person with regard to another.[13] The notion of the individual subject generating knowledge of others purely out of his own experience – the paradigm for empiricist epistemology – is, Wittgenstein argues, an incoherent one.

The issues raised by Wittgenstein's critique of empiricism go far beyond the scope of this essay, but I suggest that our ability to grasp another's condition is a more fundamental cognitive process that more specialized uses of inference can only build on but not replace. Thus, in example 2, while Michael seems to be engaging in inference regarding

13. The interpretation of Wittgenstein on the matter of knowledge of others is not entirely uncontroversial. For example Wittgenstein is sometimes regarded as a "conventionalist," for whom the "forms of life" in question are simply particular social constructions. I follow Cavell (1979) and others in rejecting this reading of Wittgenstein in favor of one in which the sense of connection between human beings which allows knowledge of one another is, at least partly, more fundamental than any socially relative conventional practices.

how to stop Paul from crying, his understanding that Paul is in distress in the first place does not seem a product of such inference but, rather, a more immediate grasping of Paul's condition. Once one gives up the epistemological commitment to the idea of the individual knower severed from any fundamental connection with others, the phenomena of responsiveness can be seen more clearly as involving an immediate and noninferential grasp of another's condition.[14]

A similar point can be made about the cognitive process of "projection," in which the subject projects himself into the other's situation, imagining what he would feel, and then attributing that feeling to the other person. Although such a process can be involved in some instances of coming to understand another's condition, it could hardly be all of what is involved in such cases. The model is too egocentered and presupposes a too-sharp separation between self and other. It sees others only on the model of one's own self. It thus fails to acknowledge, as Scheler emphasizes, how understanding others means understanding them precisely *as other* than oneself — as having feelings and thoughts that might be different from what oneself would feel in the same situation.

The use of self as the model for knowing the other is overdrawn here in the projection model of understanding. As Noddings (1984) points out, the understanding involved in caring for another person is generally more appropriately seen on a model of *receptivity* than projection.[15] One "takes in" the other person, opening oneself to the other's feelings, allowing oneself to, so to speak, receive the other person in all his or her differences from oneself. This description of the process of knowing the other seems more genuinely oriented fully to the other person than does that of projecting oneself outward into the other's situation and noting what one would oneself feel.

Perhaps more so than the previously discussed "inference" model, the "projection" model fails to apply to many of the cases of childhood responsiveness discussed above. Projection requires a level of cognitive development beyond children's capabilities.[16] It is not that these children fail to understand the other child's condition; rather, their understanding does not take the form of projection.

An excessively sharp distinction between self and other can be seen in some views of the altruistic, as well as cognitive, dimension of responsiveness. The views of Martin Hoffman (a leading researcher of children's

14. For a comparable critique of assumptions of a too-sharp self-other split within epistemological traditions in philosophy, see Scheman (1983).
15. Something like Noddings's point is also made by Scheler (1954), part 1, Chapter 3.
16. See Hoffman (1982), pp. 93 ff.

empathy and moral development) are interesting in this regard, for the overall thrust of his work is to portray empathy and sympathy as fundamental sentiments in the child that form the foundation of later moral behavior. He explicitly rejects an egoistic construal of the child's basic nature. Hoffman (1976, p. 135) asks why children come to have active sympathy toward each other once they are able to distinguish their own identity from that of others. He answers by saying that they discover that the similarities between themselves and others outweigh the differences. This belief in similarity becomes the foundation of the child's ability to sympathize with another person.

Hoffman's framing of the issue presumes that prior to the observation of similarities and differences, the child has a sense of her own identity as fundamentally separate from others. The sympathy would occur only after the perception of similarity with other children. If this were correct the sense of separateness would always lie at a more fundamental level than any sense of likeness to other children. Likeness would be forged only through explicit assessment of similarity, whereas separateness would need no inference but would be assumed. My suggestion is that, on the contrary, the sense of likeness (which I would prefer to call a sense of connection), on which sympathy is founded, is as fundamental to a child's sense of who she is as is the sense of separateness.

Although children certainly perceive similarities and differences with other children, and a perception of differences can undercut a sense of connection and a perception of similarity can spur empathy for the other child, empathy itself cannot be explained in terms of such perception. For children sometimes note differences between themselves and other children without that fact's carrying weight for them in whether or not they are able to empathize with them. For example, they might note that another child has a different color of hair or wears different kinds of clothes. Even differences in skin color do not by themselves lead to a distancing between children, except in contexts where skin color has been communicated to the child (by parents, peers, etc.) as signifying differential value or as requiring distancing. Children's delight in commonalities between themselves and others (having Luke Skywalker dolls, wearing a red shirt, or the like) can involve a greater (though perhaps only momentary) sense of likeness or connection; but I would suggest that the sense of likeness or connection which allows for empathy must lie at a deeper level. The issue here partly involves whether the achievement of identity on the child's part involves a fundamental separateness prior to any sense of relatedness. Perhaps what is needed is a notion of identity formation that builds into it a sense of relatedness to others.[17]

As several recent philosophers have pointed out, the counterposition between "egoism" and "altruism," especially in philosophical discussion, suggests a kind of radical separation between self and others.[18] The notion of altruism, for instance, implies that one's giving to others is entirely cut off from any concern for oneself, or even that it is at the expense of the self. In contrast to altruism, "community" and "friendship," for example, are relations in which concern for others, though not reduced to self-interest, is not separable from concern for self. To be concerned for a friend, or for a community with which one closely identifies and of which one is a member, is to reach out not to someone or something wholly other than oneself but to what shares a part of one's own self and is implicated in one's sense of one's own identity.

I have described responsiveness without speaking much of empathy, a concept psychologists often employ in this context. Perhaps some explanation is appropriate. First, the definition of "empathy" is variable. Sometimes, as in Hoffman (1976, p. 126), it refers to the involuntary experiencing of another's emotional state, or "feeling what the other feels" (1982, p. 86). Jerome Kagan, the eminent developmental psychologist (1984, p. 126), though citing Hoffman, seems to construe empathy as inferring another's experience or state of mind. These two definitions of empathy are not the same, as I have argued above. Hoffman's does not necessarily involve cognition, but only a feeling, whereas Kagan's involves cognition but not necessarily any feeling on the part of the empathizer. Furthermore, I have argued that neither of these phenomena is necessary or sufficient for responsiveness. Neither one builds in the requirement of altruistic concern for the other.

It should be said that both Kagan and Hoffman occasionally use the

17. The general critique given here of Hoffman was suggested by some remarks of Gilligan's in a lecture on Hoffman, and is supported by her general perspective on identity and relatedness. (See especially Gilligan, 1984.) I have also been influenced in my remarks on identity formation by Chodorow (1979). Scheler (1954) also sees "fellow-feeling" (*Mitgefühl*) as fundamental to morality. Yet he too, at least by implication, sometimes portrays an excessively separated moral subject. He is rightly critical of all egoistic conceptions of fellow feeling, emphasizing that the other must be seen separately from oneself, and emphasizing both one's capability of understanding people who are quite different from oneself and the necessity of seeing the other in her own terms rather than one's own; nevertheless, Scheler leaves the achievement of this sort of fellow feeling somewhat of a mystery. He articulates no level of connectedness or likeness between persons which could serve as the foundation for such fellow feeling.
18. On the egoism-altruism counterposition and its limitations, see Norman (1979), MacIntyre (1967), Blum (1980) Chapter 4. See also Gilligan (1984).

term "empathy" in a way that does imply the existence of altruistic concern, although this is not explicit in some of their definitions. In Hoffman's 1982 article, empathy is defined "not as an exact match with another's feelings, but [as] an affective response more appropriate to another's situation than to one's own" (p. 95). If "appropriate" is construed as involving both altruistic concern and a cognitive grasp of the other's situation, this definition comes close to what I have meant by "responsiveness"; and Hoffman does seem to see this latter definition of empathy as more accurate than the one mentioned above (feeling what the other feels).

This lack of clarity regarding the definition of empathy does not preclude the possibility of some clearer definition – delineating its cognitive, affective, and/or altruistic components – that will make empathy a phenomenon related to responsiveness. Nevertheless, responsiveness and empathy may still remain distinct phenomena. For the term "empathy" seems to carry a stronger implication of a distinct affect than does "responsiveness" as I have understood it, although responsiveness too is necessarily grounded in our affective natures.

I have described responsiveness without bringing out its relation to morality. Responsiveness should be seen as a moral phenomenon, and I suggest that responsiveness in children is one developmental forerunner of the adult moral virtues of compassion, kindness, helpfulness, sympathy, and the like, in that these altruistic virtues as well as responsiveness involve altruistic motivation and sentiment toward others. The claim of developmental connection can only be established empirically, but it does involve supplementing one influential view of moral development, namely that moral development consists primarily in the child's moving from a stage of egoism to one of social morality or conformity to social rules. Such a view is shared by theories of moral development as different as Kohlberg's and Richard Shweder's. Shweder, a psychological anthropologist studying morality cross-culturally, criticizes Kohlberg's aspiration to a universal morality and his assumption that the highest stage of morality is characterized by autonomy. (Shweder sees this as a cultural bias in Kohlberg's view.)[19] Shweder sees the content of morality as supplied by the norms of the culture in question, with no higher moral appeal possible, or necessary. Yet despite rejecting Kohlberg's account of

19. See R. Shweder, Manamohan Mahapatra, and Joan Miller, "Culture and Moral Development," in Jerome Kagan and Sharon Lamb (eds.), *The Emergence of Morality in Young Children* (Chicago: University of Chicago Press, 1987), a representative example of Shweder's view.

the later and higher stages of morality, Shweder's view retains Kohlberg's account of the earlier ones – the move from a beginning egoism to a socially based, conventional morality.

In rejecting this account, I am not denying that children are egoistic in some ways, and that some part of moral development consists in the inculcation of socially grounded moral precepts. But I do want to suggest that alongside these egoistic tendencies are capacities for altruism (responsiveness) as well, the development of which constitutes a task distinct from the inculcation of rules and precepts.

The moral significance of responsiveness does not lie in the child's appreciation of moral standards. There is no necessary implication that a child who is responsive to another thinks of helping the other as conformity to a standard of right and wrong, or good or bad, or that she sees herself as in conformity with a standard of behavior that defines what it is to be a good person. All that is necessary is that the child understand the other child's state, believe that the other child will be made better off by her action, and have some altruistic sentiment or motivation toward the other child. Thus the responsive child must believe herself to be responding to an undesirable state of the other child (or at least a state capable of improvement), and must regard her own action as trying to make that state better. But this is not the same as judging that her action is good because of its conformity to a moral standard.

In making these claims, I take issue with some of Jerome Kagan's views on the moral development of children. Kagan has emphasized the emergence of the appreciation of standards in children between the ages of one and two and sees this appreciation as a foundation of the child's morality. He also sees the capacity for empathy as one of the sources of this appreciation of moral standards. Nothing I have said is meant to contradict these views. I suggest only that the moral significance of childhood responsiveness not be seen solely in terms of the generation of moral standards. Responsiveness involves ways of feeling, acting, and understanding that have moral significance and value, even if they do not necessarily presuppose use of moral standards.

Thus, in example 1, Sarah's getting the cup for Clara is an act of moral significance, involving a rudimentary kind of sympathy, thoughtfulness, or kindness that I have called responsiveness. Yet it does not seem plausible (and in any case is not necessary) to see this one-year-old child's action as deriving from an appreciation of a moral standard. This could be true as well of Sarah (at two years, three months) in example 3 saying to Ali that she can now get the teddy bear which she (Ali) had been wanting. By contrast, in example 5, Ben's removing the safety pin from his sister's potential path can be seen partly as a response to a general norm saying that it is right or good to look out for his sister, to prevent her getting hurt; but at the same time it seems equally plausible, and certainly in any case possible, that his action also stems from a simple and direct concern for his sister, independent of the expression or codification of this concern in a principle to which he adheres. My suggestion is that the concern as well as the possession of the standard has moral significance.

What Kagan sees as the development of standards is distinct from what I am calling responsiveness. This is apparent in his emphasis on the power of moral standards to inhibit impulses and actions incompatible with those standards (1984, pp. 131, 143, 152), though for Kagan not all moral standards are related to the inhibition of aggression. But the moral significance of responsiveness does not lie primarily in its power to control the child's impulses. In our examples, the altruistic sentiment is not necessarily being opposed by a hostile, aggressive, or selfish impulse in the responsive children. The moral significance of responsiveness (in both adults and children), I would suggest, lies in the mere self-transcending care and understanding of the other, not in the countering of egoistic impulse.[20]

I do not mean to imply that the development of standards is entirely separate from that of responsiveness. It is certainly plausible to link them, as Kagan does, and to see them developing together. The child not only acts out of concern, but comes to see this as good or even right, to feel shame and guilt when failing to do so, and to judge others for such failure. Nevertheless I suggest that even in adult morality the two processes retain some degree of independence. Our caring for others does not simply flow from our adherence to a principle of caring for others. Our caring is often generated spontaneously and does not necessarily bring with it the thought that it is a morally good thing to care for others. Similarly, one can act from a moral principle that enjoins caring, but without actually caring or being concerned for the person in question.

Although Kagan is correct in positing some emotionally based concern for others (taking this to be essentially what he means by "empathy") as fundamental to moral development, he unnecessarily limits what should be seen as counting for morality when he sees empathy's moral significance almost solely in terms of the generation of moral standards of behavior. This is so even though Kagan distinguishes moral standards for positive prosocial behavior, such as helping and cooperation, from standards for inhibition of aggression. For not all helpfulness and cooperative

---

20. The conception of morality as involving self-transcending but not self-denying care is spelled out more fully in Blum (1980) and Murdoch (1970).

behavior is generated by, or is explained in terms of, moral standards. Some of it, like caring, is a spontaneous and direct response to a particular person or situation.

Shifting now to the level of moral theory, I want to argue that some standard features of many dominant moral theories are inhospitable to – or may even be incapable of expressing – those virtues of mature persons of which responsiveness is a developmental precursor. These are the virtues of care, compassion, concern, kindness, thoughtfulness, and generosity.

The features I have in mind are the following: That morality must involve the forming of rules or principles, and acting according to them; that the principles must be universal, or universalizable; that the rules or principles must specify a particular action (in a given situation) as the right one to perform; that at its most basic level morality always involves a stance of impartiality, requiring the moral agent to stand outside of her particular interests and attachments and regard all people as having equal moral significance. Moral principles thus generated cannot be confined merely to the customs or rules of any particular society. They must at bottom rest on a rational and universal foundation that transcends the agent's own society (or any particular society, for that matter), although particular principles of a particular society able to be validated from the moral point of view are included in the set of morally acceptable action-specifying rules and principles. (The distinction between rules and principles will be discussed below.)

Among the moral developmentalists I have discussed, only Lawrence Kohlberg adheres to the whole of this conception of morality, which, following Stephen Darwall's (1983) terminology, I will call "*impartialism.*" And I will accept both Kohlberg's and Darwall's seeing this tradition as rooted in Kant's moral philosophy, although most of the features mentioned apply to forms of utilitarianism as well. Other developmental theorists, however, subscribe to important elements of it. For example, Shweder, despite rejecting moral universalism and the grounding in impartiality, retains the root idea that morality is expressed in the form of action-specifying rules and principles. And Kagan sees morality as expressed in terms of standards for evaluating acts as good or bad, right or wrong. This is not precisely the same as action-specifying rules and principles, but is close enough for my purposes here.

I shall argue that neither a principle-(or rule-)centered nor the larger impartialist conception leaves room for the care virtues, as I call them. (I shall also, depending on context, refer to "caring for particular persons,"

199

or "care particularity.") These all involve concern for and caring responses to particular other persons. This concern can take place toward persons standing in a particular, richly textured moral relationship to oneself – for example, friend, family member, student, colleague, comrade, patient, doctor. Or it can be directed at a stranger, standing in no such relationship. (There are also categories between these extremes, such as a vague acquaintance or one's insurance agent.)

I want to suggest that, although part of morality unquestionably involves principles and impartiality, some of our actions and virtues do not, and in particular the care virtues do not. The latter require a moral theory that at least supplements principle-centered and impartialist ones.

In particular, I make two claims:

1. Care virtues involve a coherent and intelligible form of moral motivation and moral understanding not founded on moral principle or impartiality. This claim cannot be refuted by showing that the same action that is motivated by care or compassion *could* have been generated and motivated by a moral principle; for this by itself would not preclude the action's having been performed from a motive expressive of care particularity.

This claim does not take issue with the notion that important virtues are expressible through impartiality and principle. It takes issue only with impartialism and principle-based theories' frequent aspiration to take over the entire domain of morality, claiming to have articulated the one and only "moral point of view."

2. In addition, there are some morally good actions for which no explanation for or grounding in principle or impartiality is possible.

These claims have been challenged by principle-centered and impartialist theorists. In other essays in this volume I have replied to some of the arguments that have been given in favor of the view that these theories can accommodate the care virtues.[21] Here I will address some others.

To do so I will give an example of an action expressing a care virtue; the example will provide a point of reference for the subsequent argument that principle-based and impartialist theories cannot account for the care virtues. Jane is at a committee meeting of colleagues at her work, one of whom is a friend. Jane becomes aware of some distress on the friend's part; the turn which the conversation is taking is unnerving him in a way the others seem not to notice. Jane intervenes in the conversation so as to divert it from the subject causing her friend anxiety, while not embarrassing her friend by calling attention to him. Jane intervenes in a way that does not undermine the progress of the meeting, thus taking

21. See especially Chapter 10, "Gilligan and Kohlberg," and Chapter 2, "Iris Murdoch and the Domain of the Moral."

seriously the purpose of the meeting and her responsibility to the group. She continues to participate responsibly in the ongoing task of the group, and she awaits the opportunity to find out later from her friend what disturbed him at the meeting.

The care virtue elements in Jane's action are the concern and sensitivity she shows toward the particular friend, extricating him from an unpleasant and perhaps painful situation, and the responsibility she shows toward the particular group of colleagues.

To encompass this care particularly within principle-based or impartialist views would involve showing that there is some principle, statable in general terms, that applies to the situation at hand and, in doing so, specifies the particular action Jane in fact performs. Note, however, that the bare existence of such a principle would be relevant only to the second of my contentions above, showing that particularistic care is not the only way of arriving at Jane's action. It would not engage the first contention – that there is a form of moral motivation lying outside of principle or impartiality.

I shall consider two ways in which the defender of impartialism might attempt to see Jane's action as essentially principle-centered or impartialist. The first appeals to "role" (or "status") morality. One might say that Jane occupies two roles – friend and colleague. Each of these generates a set of obligations. These obligations, though not universal in the sense of applying equally to all human beings, nevertheless retain a formal universality in applying to anyone occupying that role. Could not Jane's action, then, stem from her dual role obligations, and in that way conform to universal principle and impartiality?

In reply let us note first that a role morality in this sense would not necessarily be impartialist in the full sense I have described. For example, the Brahmans in Bhubaneswar, India, whom Shweder (1987) has studied, possess a role morality that (as Shweder describes it) is formally universalist; that is, obligations or prohibitions involved in a role are thought to apply to anyone occupying that role.[22] But a role morality is *impartialist* (in addition to being formally universalist) only if the roles and their attendant obligations are, or are at least presented as being, justified by

22. Shweder notes that his respondents sometimes qualify the application of the role morality so that it is meant to apply only to Indians and not, say, to Americans; for example, it is forbidden, by this code, for an Indian widow to wear bright clothing, but it is not thought to be wrong for an American widow to do so. But this qualification does not count against the role-universalism of the prohibition, since the respondents give an account of the relevant differences between American and Indian widows which makes the prohibition applicable to the latter but not to the former. The relevant role would then be "Indian widows."

reference to a standpoint which accords no inherent favor to one individual over any other.[23] As Shweder presents the Brahman morality, the ground of obligation lies not in such an impartial perspective but in a view about a "natural order" of the world, divinely created, and involving functional interdependency between inherently unequal statuses and roles; such a perspective itself provides a rationale (within Brahman morality) for why the impartial perspective is *not* an appropriate one.[24]

Thus a role morality may not be (and, I suggest, typically is not) impartialist, though it may be formally universalist. Role morality also fails to conform to an important feature of principle-centeredness — action-specifying principles. Responsibilities attaching to statuses like "friend" or "colleague" cannot be understood solely in terms of principles specifying actions to be performed. Although concepts referring to family position such as "father," "mother," "parent" signify a social role, and involve moral responsibilities, these responsibilities cannot be seen as involving very specific tasks and actions like those involved in more explicitly delineated social role positions such as police officer or accountant in a specific firm. A father has a general responsibility to care for and nurture his children; this is how we understand the moral dimension of fatherhood. But this is not to say that there are specific actions that the role morality of "father" specifies. It does not, for example, tell me to spend the afternoon playing ball with my daughter rather than (what I would prefer doing) taking her to a ball game, though the former action can be seen as part of my fatherly responsibility to nurture my child and help her develop. Hence any specific fatherly action will be underdetermined by the role morality, and its selection will perhaps draw on the father's particularistic caring understanding of his daughter.[25] But to conform to the impartialist picture, the principle

23. One finds something like such an impartialist account of role morality in writers defending a "rule-utilitarian" point of view. For an impartialist attempt to ground friendship as a source of special rolelike obligations, see Telfer 1971.
24. For more on the difference between the universality and impersonality involved in role morality and friendship, and impartiality as conceived in the impartialist view, see Chapter 5, "Vocation, Friendship, and Community." That essay also discusses role morality more generally.
25. My argument here is drawn from Melden (1977). Melden argues that "roles" in families, such as mother and father, are not rigidly understood on the model of roles in institutions defined by constitutive rules. We can apply Melden's point, however, as he himself does not, to some elements of the better-defined social roles as well, such as that of police officer. Some dimensions of a police officer's job, like the parent's responsibility to nurture the child, cannot readily be pinned down to the performance of specific actions — responsibilities connected, for example, with the overarching responsibility to protect the community from harm. Such elements will necessarily involve an irreducible particularity in their application to specific situations.

202

itself must fully (even if only implicitly) specify the action; otherwise something outside of commitment to principle will (also) be operating to bring about the action.

The same point applies to the morality of friendship. It is certainly part of a serious friendship that one recognizes responsibilities. But it is not clear that such responsibility consists in principles that dictate that certain actions be performed. The responsibility is better seen as a kind of attitude toward one's friend, which orients one toward noticing certain things (e.g., that the friend is in distress), giving thought to the friend's interests, being willing to go out of one's way to help the friend, and the like. This sense of responsibility functions as a background attitude which conditions but does not determine the particular actions one performs regarding one's friends. But unless the role directly generates the action in a given situation, the criteria of principle-centered morality are not met. For in order to know how to implement in the particular situation what the role in general bids him (e.g., nurture his child, stand up for his friend), the agent will have to draw on moral capacities beyond the mere ability to consult the principle. The foregoing argument is aimed at supporting claim number 2, that some actions cannot be generated from a principle-based morality alone (much less an impartialist one). But it also supports claim number 1 in that it helps establish how Jane might have acted from some motive other than moral principle, namely, care for her friend or a sense of responsibility toward her colleagues that is not based on a general principle.

A second way in which the role morality fails to conform to the demands of impartialism concerns the centrality of *obligation* or *duty* to many versions of that view. As I have portrayed the situation, Jane's action is undertaken not out of any sense of obligation but rather out of a direct response to (Jane's perception of) her friend's anxiety. Even if the action is seen as reflecting some sense of responsibility toward the friend (and in that sense to stem from Jane's role as friend), this does not mean that Jane need think of it as a morally compulsory action. (This suggests that responsibilities are not the same as obligations.) Direct responsiveness to a friend, or to any other person, need not carry with it a quality of "must" or "have to." In addition, not every admirable act of friendship need be seen as part of the responsibilities of friendship. One may out of love or concern for the friend go out of one's way to help him, beyond what one has a responsibility to do.

This argument establishes two points. First, even if an action is covered by a moral principle, an agent may perform it from another morally good motive besides principle or obligation (here, compassion or friendship);

this supports contention number 1. Second, some actions of friendship inspired by one's conception of one's role lie entirely outside the boundaries of obligation and responsibility, yet are prompted by the same morally good motives of particularistic care as can prompt ones covered by duty or principles of obligation. This supports claim number 2.

A further way in which action prompted by friendship goes beyond role obligation concerns each relation's particularity. A significant dimension of Jane's action is lost if one looks at it simply as the working out of a conflict between two sets of general role responsibilities (friend and colleague). For one's sense of responsibility to one's *particular* friend is not simply (though it is partly) an application of a universal responsibility of a friendship. Each friendship has its own particular character and history, generating particular responsibilities and expectations that cannot be fully captured in any listing of general responsibilities.[26]

To summarize, role morality does not support a reduction of particularity to impartiality or universality. For role morality is not necessarily impartialist, and is not expressed solely in terms of obligations. Some roles, and perhaps all, do not generate principles specifying particular actions; thus many particular actions reflective of roles necessarily involve a particularistic dimension. Finally, the generality of role morality does not account for the full range of moral responsibilities attaching to specific instances of those roles. The generality or universality attaching to roles does play some part in moral action; but some dimension of care particularity remains as an intelligible motivational factor, distinct from principle and impartiality.

Defenders of principle-based or impartialist morality may take a different approach to the attempt to encompass particularistic care or care virtues within their moral framework. Abandoning the appeal to role morality, they could nevertheless posit that for every morally good or right act there is a moral principle – though perhaps a very complex one – stated in general terms, that prescribes that action (in all morally relevantly similar circumstances). In the case of Jane, such a principle would have to be cashed out as one generalizing from the particularities of Jane's relations with her friend and colleagues, and the particular circumstances of her action, to *all* friendships, collegial relations, and situations with those characteristics (in that combination). A principle taking this and all other morally pertinent factors into account would certainly be quite restricted in its application, but could still theoretically be utilized by an

---

26. For further elaboration of the moral significance of the particularity of types of role relationships, see Chapter 5, "Vocation, Friendship, and Community."

agent to determine right action, in the few situations to which the principle applied.

If the principle is meant to be statable and directly action-yielding, it is not clear that its theoretical possibility translates readily into a practical reality. In Jane's situation it would have to include a myriad of factors – the particular history (though stated in general terms) of Jane's relationship with the friend, an assessment of the relevant expectations of the friend and the other colleagues, a general characterization of Jane's complex relationship and responsibilities to the colleagues (particularly with respect to the task at hand), an assessment of the outcomes of various acts Jane might perform in the circumstances, and so on. In addition it would have to assign these factors some weight or priority so that the principle would be able to tote up the various considerations and determine a particular action. It is not clear that there could *be* such a statable principle, or that a realistic attempt at one would not somewhere along the line jettison reliance on the principle alone and implicitly draw on some moral considerations lying outside the general characterizations contained in the principle, yet contained in the situation itself and pertinent to the agent's action. Aside from that point, the principle in question is likely to be so cumbersome that few would be likely even to try to make explicit use of it.

But suppose we grant the possibility that someone could make use of such a cumbersome principle; that adherence to this principle is what motivates the agent to perform the Janelike action. What would make us think that the agent was actually doing so?

Admittedly, showing that the agent consciously and in the moment at hand actually consulted the principle would not be required. For people can act according to a principle without consulting it on each occasion. People often initially adopt principles and then come to act on them so systematically and faithfully that the actions become almost automatic. Yet the principle continues to inform their consciousness of their situation; if it is stated, they would generally agree to the principle, and the principle would continue to be part of an explanation of why they act as they do. Yet this process of internalization generally takes place with regard to fairly simple rules and principles such as "don't lie," "don't steal" – or perhaps slightly more complex principles consisting of those simple ones with a few exceptions built in, or with some rough priority rules concerning which principles carry more weight than others. But that a principle with the complexity of the one envisioned here could have come to be articulated and then internalized seems implausible.

As the analogy with grammatical rules suggests, people operate according to sometimes fairly complex principles they do not consciously consult and of whose existence they may or may not be aware. We say that people follow grammatical rules (and not only speak in accordance with them) because the rules seem to us the best explanation of the speech behavior we observe. But in the case of morality, this analogy does not necessarily point to universal or imperialist principles underlying the actions of the morally good agent. For I am contending, care particularity may well be an essential component in the best explanation of the moral behavior exhibited by the morally good agent. In many situations, care particularity may well be a good deal more plausible as an explanation than that the moral agent has internalized an extremely complicated and narrowly tailored principle and is implicitly making use of such a principle in the situation at hand. The grammar analogy suggests that underlying moral behavior there can be a structure that not only externally describes but actually accounts for that behavior. My contention is that this structure can consist of concern for particular persons, a sense of responsibility to particular friends, a disposition to compassion, and the like, all of which are not simply universal principles of action.[27]

A more sophisticated defense of the impartialist position, which avoids the appeal to explicit complex and cumbersome principles, is given by Kohlberg (1982, pp. 520–1). Kohlberg distinguishes between a "moral rule" and a "moral principle." A moral rule is "a general proscription or prescription of a class of actions: for example: 'Do not kill,' 'Do not steal,' 'Love your neighbor.' " By contrast, a moral principle is a procedure or method, in Rawls's original position or what Kohlberg sometimes calls "ideal role taking" (1981), for making moral decisions. Kohlberg uses this distinction to suggest that although moral rules are not situation-sensitive, moral principles can be. In ideal role taking, for example, the agent arrives at the correct action in a decision situation by imagining himself in the situation of all the persons who would be affected by his action.

Kohlberg's point can be put by saying that a universally valid, impartial decision procedure can generate a decision that takes into account the specificity of a given situation, so that actions such as Jane's can be seen as generated by such a "moral principle."

In discussing this claim, I will leave aside some substantial problems in interpreting the procedure itself – for example, problems in the coordination and agglomeration of the different opinions and feelings generated from the ideal role taking process; problems with a particular agent's subjective distortion in attempting to see the situation from the point of

27. A similar argument against the view that the grammar analogy supports a principle-based conception of morality is made by Williams (1985, p. 97).

view of the other person; and problems about whether the procedure really yields a determinate outcome in many particular situations.

If these problems could be resolved, Kohlberg's approach would avoid some of the difficulties of the complex principle and role approaches. Note, however, that even if the procedure in question were able to generate the action that Jane performs, this would tell only against claim number 2, not against claim number 1. Its mere existence does not show that a given agent – even one who carries out the procedure – is actually making use of it. The agent could just – as I am suggesting is true of Jane – be acting from care, compassion, friendship, and responsibility to particular persons.

In one respect, Kohlberg would not be troubled by this limitation in the principle-based critique of care particularity. For he construes "ideal role taking" and other similar descriptions of what he regards as the highest forms of principled morality to be reflections of the highest forms of moral reasoning. In a sense it would not trouble him if many of the same actions could be arrived at by a different route, such as particularistic care or friendship. He would reject such other routes as morally inferior.[28]

Nevertheless, Kohlberg is not looking for a mere rational reconstruction of mature morality – that is, of a form of reasoning people do not actually make use of, but which a moral theory can tell us is an adequate, or even the best, form of reasoning. Such a task might be sufficient for the moral philosopher or theorist, but not for Kohlberg. He wants to be describing the development of people's *actual moral consciousness,* and to show that it heads in the direction of, and then eventually – in the most morally mature persons – actually achieves, impartialist principled moral reasoning. If it turns out that in actual fact people reach a moral result (a morally right action) approved of by "ideal role taking" yet actually arrived at by some other psychic means – for example, through care particularity – Kohlberg will not be entirely happy with this outcome.

In arguing that moral agents do not, need not, and should not always act from universal principles or decision procedures, I am not implying that each situation is so unique that the moral agent facing a problematic situation has nothing to draw on from previous situations to help her act well. A compassionate or sympathetic attitude, a habit of paying attention to others, a sensitivity to others' needs – these are components of a person's moral makeup that she brings to a situation and yet that cannot be cashed out as universal principles of action. A

28. In Chapter 10, "Gilligan and Kohlberg," I consider Kohlberg's arguments on this score and find them wanting.

person can learn to be more compassionate; this does not mean that she comes to hold new action-specifying principles. What is learned in previous situations is not only which principles to consult in action but, as Murdoch (1970) emphasizes, what to notice, how to care, what to be sensitive to, how to get beyond one's own biases and narrowness of vision.[29]

Someone may reply, "But surely to be compassionate *is* to adhere to a kind of principle." Up to this point I have been construing the word "principle" as involving the prescription of the performance of a certain action in a situation of moral choice; and this is a familiar use within principle-based or impartialist moral theories. However, "principle" is not always used in this way. Take for example the injunction "Be kind and sensitive in dealing with colleagues." This might be taken to be a kind of principle which informs Jane's action. Adverting to it may, for example, help Jane to keep from being inappropriately and counterproductively angry at her colleagues' insensitivity to her friend. But such a principle is nothing like a decision procedure or means by which Jane determines a specific action to perform. Rather it expresses, and perhaps helps Jane to call up in herself, certain sensitivities and attitudes toward others which issue in the particular actions – sensitivities which she must already possess or else adverting to this injunction would have little effect. Principles in this sense, in contrast to their use in the impartialist conception, require other moral sensibilities and capacities for their application, beyond the mere ability to understand the principle and to see that a certain situation falls within its scope. In this broader sense, almost any element in our moral natures could be spoken of as a "principle," but this would not lend support to the standard understanding of a "principle-based" conception of morality.

I have argued that the care virtues cannot be captured within the framework of exclusively principle-based or impartialist morality. Two more differences between care virtues and principle-based virtues are important to note. An agent possessing care virtues need not regard herself as doing what is morally right or good (though she may not regard herself as acting contrary to what is morally right). For example, a person may be kind, or compassionate, without regarding herself as being kind, or compassionate. Compassion is attributed to someone on the basis, roughly, that she has apprehended, and is concerned about, some negative state of the other person. She need not have the further view of herself as doing that which is morally right. By contrast, a person acting

29. See Chapter 3, "Moral Perception and Particularity," for further discussion of non–principle-based moral capacities.

from principle necessarily sees herself as aiming to do what is morally right.[30]

This does not mean that the compassionate, or kind, person does not know what she is doing whereas the principled person does. The compassionate person knows all she needs to know for her act to be compassionate, and for it to have (at least ceteris paribus) moral value, namely, that the other person needs help and that she intends by her own action to provide it. The same absence of the requirement of explicitly moral self-direction characterizes other virtues – generosity, thoughtfulness, courage. It would be conceivable for someone to exemplify at least some of these virtues without even having the concept of the virtues, much less applying it to himself. By contrast, a person who is just, dutiful, or (otherwise) principled sees himself as being so, or at least as striving to be so.

Kagan distinguishes between "subjective" and "objective" frames of explanatory reference. The former is a subject's own subjective experience, the motive for which she takes herself to be acting. The latter is the framework of the external observer, seeing her behavior from the outside and as part of a larger pattern. Kagan accords a kind of validity to both frames. It is worth noting that the difference I have described between care virtues and principle-based virtues is not the same as Kagan's distinction. It is true that the attribution of compassion (a care virtue) and justice (a principle-based virtue) refers to something *within an agent's consciousness* – concern for the particular person in the former case, and adherence to a principle in the latter. But this attribution cannot be understood as a hypothetical construct, making sense of the agent's behavior or motivation from a purely external point of view. Hence it is not "objective." Yet neither is the attribution of virtuous motive – in either case – a purely "subjective" matter, that is, what the agent takes her motive to be. So the attribution of either kind of motive (care or principle) is neither subjective nor objective, in Kagan's sense. The difference between the two ways of being moral is this: The compassionate agent need not be thinking of herself as acting compassionately in order to be doing so, whereas the just agent must see himself as acting justly (as instantiating the virtue of justice) in order to be doing so.

In this regard it is significant that Jane's situation is not one of "moral dilemma" as traditionally conceived – that is, a situation in which an agent is faced with two or more alternatives of action and must decide which is the right action to take. Although Jane sees herself as facing a dilemma, it is understood not in terms of "What is the right thing to do?"

---

30. For further argument on this point, see Chapter 2, "Iris Murdoch and the Domain of the Moral."

but, rather, in terms of "How can I deal with the acute discomfort my friend seems to be in (given the overall situation)?" This means that Jane's goal in the situation is not to figure out the right action but simply to figure out how to help her friend, in the light of the taken-for-granted commitment to her colleagues' task. Thus although Jane's action is morally good, its moral goodness does not involve Jane's consciously striving to perform a morally right act. So, in contrast to impartialist or principle-based concepts such as justice, obligation, and universal principle, the moral value of care particularity does not require the agent to regard herself as seeking to perform a morally right act (though, again, it is a necessary condition for the act's moral value that the agent not regard herself as performing a *morally wrong* act).

Richard Shweder (1987) makes a similar point when he notes that Kohlberg's conception of morality unrealistically requires respondents to be able to articulate concepts with which they operate in order for the possession of those concepts to be attributed to them. Possession precedes articulation. Shweder, however, does not go far enough in recognizing the not necessarily articulated nature of morality. For Shweder retains the notion that morality necessarily takes the form of formally universal precepts and prohibitions. In his view the individual acting in accordance with morality always knows that she is doing so; that is, she is aware of the precept or prohibition *as* a moral one. So although Shweder rightly rejects Kohlberg's overintellectualized conception of moral competence (as well as his impartialism), his own view of morality is still unduly tied to universal principle and the notion of moral self-consciousness that accompanies it.

This point relates directly to my earlier remarks regarding childhood responsiveness because childhood responsiveness is a phenomenon not essentially dependent on the child's use of terms like "right," "wrong," and "should." In this sense it does not necessarily involve the use of explicitly moral terminology, and perhaps is even developmentally prior to the understanding of such concepts (though for my view it is only necessary that it be at least to some extent developmentally independent of it). The two can also come together, and naturally though not inevitably do so, in explicit norms relating to caring for others, not hurting, and so on.

Acceptance of an important element of adult morality not involving the moral agent's explicit use of moral concepts can help us to accept that there can be an important element in children's moral development that has this character also.[31]

31. One must be cautious in attributing full-blown adult moral sentiments and virtues to children. For instance, in discussing our examples of children's responses to the distress of other children, it does not seem accurate to refer to their responsiveness as

A second important difference between care particularity and principle-based morality concerns emotion and sentiment. Principle-based morality is concerned only with moral *action*; but morality is broader than this. It includes the conveying of attitudes, sentiments, emotions to the other person, which inform and are expressed in the actions taken.[32] For example, it is not sufficient that Jane simply perform a certain action – say the action of changing the subject of discussion. She must do this *in a certain way*, which involves a sensitivity to the other parties involved. The subject of discussion could be changed in an inappropriate way that would call attention to Jane's friend's anxiety, but this would be contrary to Jane's aim. Or it could be done in a way that would disrupt the group's work, and this too would be counterproductive, though not necessarily uncaring. Any appropriate action Jane takes in this situation will exhibit an emotionally grounded sensitivity, a compassion, an attentiveness to others. This is not to say that emotional sensitivity is a requirement of all moral action. Emotional sensitivity is simply one instance of the more general category of attitudes, emotions, and sentiments that have at most an entirely subordinate role for impartialism's and principle-based morality's emphasis on action and principle, but which in the care virtues are sometimes essential to an appropriate response to a situation.[33]

In summary, I have argued that care particularity is genuinely distinct from principle and impartiality, whose significance for morality has dominated moral philosophy and moral development theory. No conception of morality can be complete without taking account of care particularity.

"compassion." This seems to require a richer cognitive and emotional structure than can be attributed to very young children. Nevertheless, it seems plausible to see the children's responsiveness as a natural precursor to compassion.

32. An extended argument for this point is given in Blum (1980), Chapter 7.
33. It may be that particular moralities of different cultural groups differ in the extent to which the attitudinal/emotional dimension is significant. Certainly some particular moralities emphasize outward action more than (expressed) inner feeling or attitude. It may be, for example, that the Indian morality which Shweder studied is much more interested in compliance with the rules and precepts than with having the right attitude. It is difficult, however, to imagine a morality with absolutely no concern with the attitudinal dimension. Suppose, for instance, that a society places great emphasis on deference toward authority and has very specific behavioral forms in which this deference is to be shown; it would be hard to imagine that there would not be some ways of engaging in this deferential activity that, while formally meeting the correct standard, were blatantly out of keeping with its spirit; that is, they would be taken as conforming in letter but not in spirit and would thus not be so appropriate and right as if the actions were done with the proper attitude. If this line of thought is correct, then even in the most external conception of moral action, the attitude behind conformity to the rule cannot be entirely irrelevant to proper conduct.

211

"Responsiveness" and its attendant virtues of compassion, care, kindness, thoughtfulness can only be understood as grounded in care particularity. Finally, I have suggested that responsiveness in children has moral significance, a significance which can only be understood in light of a conception of morality that leaves room for the care virtues.

I mentioned earlier that, in face of seeming care particularity, the impartialist could challenge this particularity's distinctness from universality or impartiality; or he could acknowledge the distinctness, but challenge care particularity's alleged moral significance. I close with some brief remarks on the latter issue.

I have argued that compassion, care, kindness, thoughtfulness, and concern for others are all virtues and sentiments that have moral significance, just as do the qualities of justice, dutifulness, adherence to universal principle, and the like. Both the former and the latter qualities are part of most people's ideas of character, of what it is to be a good person. Both sets of qualities seem important for moral education; we want our children to be compassionate as well as just, caring as well as principled. We admire people who are kind and compassionate, as we do those who are principled and impartial.

The impartialist or principle-based theorist being considered here challenges this by denying moral significance to the care virtues. But on what basis is this challenge made? It cannot be on the basis that only that which makes reference to a universal, impartial point of view is rightly called moral. For this is precisely the point which the care virtuist denies, and this denial cannot be met merely by a reassertion of the challenged view.

I suggest that there can be no final resolution of a dispute over the meaning and criteria of the term "moral." To a large extent the dispute is a merely semantic one. But one perspective on that term makes it difficult to allow for care virtues as moral and that is the notion that "the moral" points to a unitary phenomenon. Several philosophers (MacIntyre 1966, 1984; Feinberg 1968) have recently proposed that our conception of the domain of the moral is a product of diverse sources, not unified as a single, internally consistent "moral point of view." In his recent work, Kohlberg, responding to Gilligan's criticisms, has proposed that there are two meanings of the term "moral," one relating to justice and one to care and beneficence.

Acknowledgment of a plurality within the domain of morality accords with allowing theoretical room for the care virtues. For on that view, the moral significance of the principle-based virtues is not denied; it is simply asserted that the care virtues too have a claim on that term, and therefore on the attention of moral philosophers and moral development theorists.

REFERENCES

Blum, L. 1980. *Friendship, Altruism, and Morality.* London: Routledge and Kegan Paul.

Cavell, S. 1979. *The Claim of Reason.* Oxford: Clarendon Press.

Chodorow, N. 1979. *The Reproduction of Mothering.* Berkeley: University of California Press.

Crittenden, Paul. 1990. *Learning to Be Moral: Philosophical Thoughts About Moral Development.* Atlantic Highlands, N.J.: Humanities Press International.

Darwall, S. 1983. *Impartial Reason.* Ithaca, N.Y.: Cornell University Press.

Feinberg, J. 1968. "Supererogation and Rules." In G. Dworkin and J. Thomson eds., *Ethics.* New York: Harper and Row.

Flanagan, Owen. 1991. *Varieties of Moral Personality: Ethics and Psychological Realism.* Cambridge, Mass.: Harvard University Press.

Gilligan, Carol. 1982. *In a Different Voice.* Cambridge, Mass.: Harvard University Press.

1984. "The Conquistador and the Dark Continent: Reflections on the Psychology of Love." *Daedalus* 113:75–95.

Hoffman, M. 1976. "Empathy, Role-taking, Guilt and Development of Altruistic Motives." In T. Lickona, ed., *Moral Development and Behavior.* New York: Holt, Rinehart, and Winston.

1982. "Affect and Moral Development." In D. Cicchetti and P. Hesse, eds., *New Directions for Child Development: Emotional Development,* no. 16. San Francisco: Jossey-Bass.

Kagan, J. 1984. *The Nature of the Child.* New York: Basic Books.

Kant, I. 1959. *Foundations of the Metaphysics of Morals.* Trans. L. W. Beck. New York: Bobbs-Merrill.

Kohlberg, L. 1981. *Essays in Moral Development.* Vol. 1, *The Philosophy of Moral Development.* San Francisco: Harper and Row.

1982. "A Reply to Owen Flanagan and Some Comments on the Puka-Goodpaster Exchange." *Ethics* 92:513–28.

1984. *Essays in Moral Development.* Vol. 2, *The Psychology of Moral Development.* San Francisco: Harper and Row.

MacDowell, J. 1979. "Virtue and Reason." *The Monist* 62 (no. 3): 331–50.

MacIntyre, A. 1966. *A Short History of Ethics.* New York: Macmillan.

1967. "Egoism and Altruism." In P. Edwards, ed., *Encyclopedia of Philosophy,* Vol. 2. New York: Macmillan.

1984. *After Virtue.* 2d. ed. Notre Dame: University of Notre Dame Press.

Melden, A. I. 1977. *Rights and Persons.* Berkeley: University of California Press.

Mill, J. S. [1861] 1979. *Utilitarianism.* Indianapolis, Ind.: Hackett.

Murdoch, I. 1970. *The Sovereignty of Good.* New York: Schocken.

Nagel, T. 1970. *The Possibility of Altruism.* Oxford: Clarendon Press.

1986. *The View from Nowhere.* New York: Oxford University Press.

Noddings, N. 1984. *Caring: A Feminine Approach to Ethics and Moral Education.* Berkeley: University of California Press.

Norman, R. 1979. "Self and Others: The Inadequacy of Utilitarianism." In W. Cooper, K. Nielsen, and S. Patten, eds., *New Essays on John Stuart Mill and Utilitarianism. Canadian Journal of Philosophy,* supplementary volume 5.

Rawls, J. 1971. *A Theory of Justice.* Cambridge, Mass.: Harvard University Press.

Ross, A. 1983. "The Status of Altruism." *Mind* 42:204–18.

Sandel, M. 1982. *Liberalism and the Limits of Justice.* Cambridge: Cambridge University Press.

Scheler, M. 1965. *The Nature of Sympathy.* Trans. Werner Stark. London: Routledge and Kegan Paul.

Scheman, N. 1983. "Individualism and the Objects of Psychology." In S. Harding and M. Hintikka, eds., *Discovering Reality.* Dordrecht: D. Reidel.

Schopenhauer, Arthur. [1841] 1965. *On the Basis of Morality.* Trans. E. F. J. Payne. New York: Bobbs-Merrill.

Sidgwick, H. [1907] 1966. *The Methods of Ethics.* New York: Dover.

Smith, A. [1759] 1970. *The Theory of Moral Sentiments.* In H. Schneider, ed., *Adam Smith's Moral and Political Philosophy.* New York: Harper and Row.

Stocker, M. 1976. "The Schizophrenia of Modern Ethical Theories." *Journal of Philosophy* 73, no. 14, 453–66.

Telfer, E. 1971. "Friendship." *Proceedings of the Aristotelian Society,* supplement.

Whitbeck, C. 1983. "A Different Reality: Feminist Ontology." In C. Gould, ed., *Beyond Domination: New Perspectives on Women and Philosophy.* Totowa, N.J.: Rowman and Allanheld.

Williams, B. 1981. *Moral Luck.* Cambridge: Cambridge University Press.

——— 1985. *Ethics and the Limits of Philosophy.* Cambridge, Mass.: Harvard University Press.

Wittgenstein, L. 1953. *Philosophical Investigations.* New York: Macmillan.

10

Gilligan and Kohlberg: implications for moral theory

Carol Gilligan's body of work in moral development psychology is of the first importance for moral philosophy.[1] At the same time certain philosophical commitments within contemporary ethics constitute obstacles to appreciating this importance. Some of these commitments are shared by Lawrence Kohlberg, whose work provided the context for Gilligan's early (though not current) work. I will discuss some of the implicit and explicit philosophical differences between Gilligan's and Kohlberg's outlooks and will then defend Gilligan's views against criticisms which, drawing on categories of contemporary ethical theory, a Kohlbergian can and does make of them.

Gilligan claims empirical support for the existence of a moral outlook or orientation distinct from one based on impartiality, impersonality, justice, formal rationality, and universal principle. This *impartialist* conception of morality, as I will call it,[2] in addition to characterizing Kohlberg's view of morality, has been the dominant conception of morality in contemporary Anglo-American moral philosophy, forming the core of both a Kantian conception of morality and important strands in utilitarian (and, more generally, consequentialist) thinking as well.

A portion of this chapter was originally delivered as a paper at the twentieth annual Chapel Hill colloquium, University of North Carolina, Chapel Hill, North Carolina, October 1986, as a comment on Carol Gilligan's (and Grant Wiggins's) "The Origins of Morality in Early Childhood Relationships." I wish to thank Owen Flanagan and Marcia Lind for comments on an earlier draft, and the editors of *Ethics* for comments on a later one.

1. See especially Carol Gilligan, "Do the Social Sciences Have an Adequate Theory of Moral Development?" in *Social Science as Moral Inquiry,* ed. N. Haan, R. Bellah, P. Rabinow, and W. Sullivan (New York: Columbia University Press, 1983). *In a Different Voice* (Cambridge, Mass.: Harvard University Press, 1982), "Remapping the Moral Domain: New Images of the Self in Relationship," in *Reconstructing Individualism: Autonomy, Individuality, and the Self in Western Thought,* ed. T. Heller, M. Sosna, and D. Wellbery (Stanford, Calif.: Stanford University Press, 1986), and the paper cited above from the twentieth annual Chapel Hill colloquium, published in *The Emergence of Morality in Young Children,* ed. J. Kagan and S. Lamb (Chicago: University of Chicago Press, 1987). See also Nona Plessner Lyons, "Two Perspectives: On Self, Relationships, and Morality," *Harvard Educational Review* 53 (1983): 125–45.
2. The notion of an "impartialist" outlook is drawn from Stephen Darwall, *Impartial Reason* (Ithaca, N.Y.: Cornell University Press, 1983).

Recently impartialism has come under attack from several quarters. Bernard Williams's well-known critique takes it to task for leaving insufficient room for considerations of personal integrity and, more broadly, for the legitimacy of purely personal concerns.[3] Thomas Nagel, though rejecting Williams's general skepticism regarding impartialist morality's claim on our practical deliberations, follows Williams's criticism of impartialism; Nagel argues that personal as well as impersonal (or impartial) concerns are legitimate as reason-generating considerations.[4]

Gilligan's critique of Kohlberg and of an impartialist conception of morality is not at odds with these criticisms of impartialism, but it is importantly distinct from them. For personal concerns are seen by Nagel and Williams as legitimate not so much from the standpoint of *morality*, but from the broader standpoint of practical reason. By contrast Gilligan argues – drawing on the conceptions of morality held by many of her largely (but by no means exclusively) female respondents – that care and responsibility within personal relationships constitute an important element of morality itself, genuinely distinct from impartiality. For Gilligan each person is embedded within a web of ongoing relationships, and morality importantly if not exclusively consists in attention to, understanding of, and emotional responsiveness toward the individuals with whom one stands in these relationships. (Gilligan means this web to encompass all human beings and not only one's circle of acquaintances. But how this extension to all persons is to be accomplished is not made clear in her writings, and much of Gilligan's empirical work is centered on the domain of personal relations and acquaintances.) Nagel's and Williams's notions of the personal domain do not capture or encompass (though Nagel and Williams sometimes imply that they are meant to) the phenomena of care and responsibility within personal relationships and do not explain why care and responsibility in relationships are distinctively moral phenomena.[5]

Thus Gilligan's critique of Kohlberg raises substantial questions for moral philosophy. If there *is* a "different voice" – a coherent set of moral concerns distinct both from the objective and the subjective, the imper-

3. See B. Williams, "A Critique of Utilitarianism," in *Utilitarianism: For and Against*, ed. B. Williams and J. J. C. Smart (Cambridge: Cambridge University Press, 1973), *Moral Luck* (Cambridge: Cambridge University Press, 1980), and *Ethics and the Limits of Philosophy* (Cambridge, Mass.: Harvard University Press, 1985).
4. Thomas Nagel, *The View from Nowhere* (New York: Oxford University Press, 1986).
5. A detailed argument for this point is given in my "Iris Murdoch and the Domain of the Moral," Chapter 2 in this volume and also printed in *Philosophical Studies* 50 (1986): esp. 357–9.

sonal and the purely personal – then moral theory will need to give some place to these concerns.

Gilligan does not suggest that care and responsibility are to be seen either as *replacing* impartiality as a basis of morality or as encompassing *all* of morality, as if all moral concerns could be translated into ones of care and responsibility. Rather, Gilligan holds that there is an appropriate place for impartiality, universal principle, and the like within morality and that a final mature morality involves a complex interaction and dialogue between the concerns of impartiality and those of personal relationship and care.[6]

KOHLBERG AND GILLIGAN: THE MAJOR DIFFERENCES

One can draw from Gilligan's work seven differences between her view of morality and Kohlberg's impartialist conception. The subsequent discussion will explore the nature and significance of these apparent differences.

1. For Gilligan the moral self is radically situated and particularized. It is "thick" rather than "thin," defined by its historical connections and relationships. The moral agent does not attempt to abstract from this particularized self, to achieve, as Kohlberg advocates, a totally impersonal standpoint defining *the* "moral point of view." For Gilligan, care morality is about the particular agent's caring for and about the particular friend or child with whom she has come to have this particular relationship. Morality is not (only) about how the impersonal "one" is meant to act toward the impersonal "other." In regard to its emphasis on the radically situated

6. This is perhaps a slightly oversimplified picture of Gilligan's views, as there is also some suggestion in her writings that there is a deep flaw present in the impartialist-rationalist approach to morality which is not present in the care-responsibility approach. One possible construal of Gilligan's view in light of this seeming ambiguity is that she rejects any notion of justice as (morally and psychologically) *fundamental* or foundational to other virtues – especially to care, compassion, and the like. And that she rejects a conception of justice which is dependent on purely individualistic assumptions such as are sometimes seen as underlying more "foundational" views of justice. On this reading Gilligan would, e.g., reject any notion of justice generated from something like Rawls's original position (though Rawls has recently argued that this individualistic characterization does not apply to his view; see John Rawls, "Justice as Fairness: Political Not Metaphysical," *Philosophy and Public Affairs* 14 [1985]: 223–51). Yet on this construal of Gilligan's views, she *would* accept a notion of justice which exists as one virtue among others, interacting with and no more fundamental than they. It is not clear how this acceptable, nonfoundational notion of justice is to be characterized in Gilligan's work. In her paper at the Chapel Hill colloquium she suggests that it is to be conceived as something like "protection against oppression." It is not clear whether, or how, this characterization is meant to connect with a nonfoundational notion of "fairness" (such as Michael Walzer describes in *Spheres of Justice* [Oxford: Basil Blackwell, 1983]).

self, Gilligan's view is akin to Alasdair MacIntyre's *After Virtue* and Michael Sandel's *Liberalism and the Limits of Justice.*[7]

2. For Gilligan, not only is the self radically particularized, but so is the other, the person toward whom one is acting and with whom one stands in some relationship. The moral agent must understand the other person as the specific individual that he or she is, not merely as someone instantiating general moral categories such as friend or person in need. Moral action which fails to take account of this particularity is faulty and defective. Although Kohlberg does not and need not deny that there is an irreducible particularity in our affective relationships with others, he sees this particularity only as a matter of personal attitude and affection, not relevant to morality itself. For him, as, implicitly, for a good deal of current moral philosophy, the moral significance of persons as the objects of moral concern is solely as bearers of morally significant but entirely general and repeatable characteristics.

Putting contrasts 1 and 2 together we can say that for Gilligan but not for Kohlberg moral action itself involves an irreducible particularity – a particularity of the agent, the other, and the situation.

3. Gilligan shares with Iris Murdoch (*The Sovereignty of Good*) the view that achieving knowledge of the particular other person toward whom one acts is an often complex and difficult moral task and one which draws on specifically moral capacities.[8] Understanding the needs, interests, and welfare of another person, and understanding the relationship between oneself and that other requires a stance toward that person informed by care, love, empathy, compassion, and emotional sensitivity. It involves, for example, the ability to see the other as different in important ways from oneself, as a being existing in her own right, rather than viewing her through a simple projection of what one would feel if one were in her situation. Kohlberg's view follows a good deal of current moral philosophy in ignoring this dimension of moral understanding, thus implying that knowledge of individual others is a straightforwardly empirical matter requiring no particular moral stance toward the person.

4. Gilligan's view emphasizes the self as, in Michael Sandel's terms, "encumbered." She rejects the contrasting metaphor in Kohlberg, drawn from Kant, in which morality is ultimately a matter of the individual rational being legislating for himself and obeying laws or principles generated solely from within himself (i.e., from within his own reason). Gilligan

---

7. Alasdair MacIntyre, *After Virtue,* 2d ed. (Notre Dame, Ind.: University of Notre Dame Press, 1984); Michael Sandel, *Liberalism and the Limits of Justice* (Cambridge: Cambridge University Press, 1982).
8. Iris Murdoch, *The Sovereignty of Good* (London: Routledge & Kegan Paul, 1970).

portrays the moral agent as approaching the world of action bound by ties and relationships (friend, colleague, parent, child) which confront her as, at least to some extent, givens. These relationships, while subject to change, are not wholly of the agent's own making and thus cannot be pictured on a totally voluntarist or contractual model. In contrast to Kohlberg's conception, the moral agent is not conceived of as radically autonomous (though this is not to deny that there exists a less individualistic, less foundational, and less morality-generating sense of autonomy which does accord with Gilligan's conception of moral agency).

A contrast between Gilligan's and Sandel's conceptions of encumbrance, however, is that for Sandel the self's encumbrances are forms of communal identity, such as being a member of this or that nation, religious or ethnic group, class, neighborhood; whereas for Gilligan the encumbrances are understood more in terms of the concrete persons to whom one stands in specific relationships – being the father of Sarah, the teacher of Maureen, the brother of Jeff, the friend of Alan and Charles. In that way Sandel's "encumbrances" are more abstract than Gilligan's.

5. For Kohlberg the mode of reasoning which generates principles governing right action involves formal rationality alone. Emotions play at most a remotely secondary role in both the derivation and motivation of moral action.[9]

For Gilligan, by contrast, morality necessarily involves an intertwining of emotion, cognition, and action, not readily separable. Knowing what to do involves knowing others and being connected in ways involving both emotion and cognition. Caring action expresses emotion and understanding.

6. For Kohlberg principles of right action are universalistic, applicable to all. Gilligan rejects the notion that an action appropriate to a given individual is necessarily (or needs to be regarded by the agent as) universal, or generalizable to others. And thus she at least implicitly rejects, in favor of a wider notion of "appropriate response," a conception of "right action" that carries this universalistic implication. At the same time

9. In "The Current Formulation of the Theory," in his *Essays on Moral Development* (New York: Harper & Row, 1984), vol. 2, p. 291, Kohlberg says that his view is distinguished from Kant's in including a role for "affect as an integral component of moral judgment of justice reasoning." But Kohlberg's more frequently rationalistic characterizations of his views do not bear out this contention. What is true of Kohlberg, as we will see below, is that he sometimes allows a legitimacy to care (as involving emotion) as a moral phenomenon, though, as we will also see, he is not consistent in this acknowledgment. But even when he acknowledges care, Kohlberg almost always relegates it to a secondary or derivative moral status. In this regard it is not clear that Kohlberg's view is significantly different from Kant's, who, at least in some of his writings (especially the *Doctrine of Virtue*), allowed a secondary place for emotions in morality.

Gilligan's view avoids the individual subjectivism and relativism which is often seen as the only alternative to a view such as Kohlberg's; for Gilligan sees the notions of care and responsibility as providing nonsubjective standards by which appropriateness of response can be appraised in the particular case. These are standards that allow one to say that a certain thing was the appropriate action for a particular individual to take, but not necessarily that it was the "right" action for anyone in that situation.

7. For Gilligan morality is founded in a sense of concrete connection and direct response between persons, a direct sense of connection which exists prior to moral beliefs about what is right or wrong or which principles to accept. Moral action is meant to express and to sustain those connections to particular other people. For Kohlberg the ultimate moral concern is with morality itself – with morally right action and principle; moral responsiveness to others is mediated by adherence to principle.

IMPARTIALIST REJOINDERS TO GILLIGAN

Faced with Gilligan's challenge to have found in her respondents a distinct moral orientation roughly defined by these seven contrasts, let us look at how Kohlberg, and defenders of impartialist morality more generally, do or might respond to this challenge. Eight alternative positions regarding the relation between impartial morality and a morality of care in personal relations suggest themselves.

1. Position 1 denies that the care orientation constitutes a genuinely distinct moral orientation from impartialism. Strictly speaking there is no such thing as a morality of care. Acting from care is actually acting on perhaps complex but nevertheless fully universalizable principles, generated ultimately from an impartial point of view.[10]

2. Position 2 says that, whereas care for others in the context of rela-

10. Kohlberg has himself taken such a position in his article "A Reply to Owen Flanagan," in *Ethics* 92 (1982): 513–28; however, this view appears hardly at all in his most recent writings – *Essays in Moral Development,* vol. 2, *The Psychology of Moral Development* (San Francisco: Harper & Row, 1984) – in which he attempts to answer Gilligan's and others' criticisms. There are several minor variations on the view that care *is* impartiality. One is to say that impartialist philosophies have all along been cognizant of the special moral ties and claims involved in particular personal relationships and have mustered their resources to deal with these. (George Sher's "Other Voices, Other Rooms? Women's Psychology and Moral Theory," in *Women and Moral Theory,* ed. E. Kittay and D. Meyers [Totowa, N.J.: Rowman & Littlefield, 1987], pp. 187–8, is an example.) Another is to acknowledge that, although care is an important aspect of the moral life that has been largely neglected by impartialist theories, care considerations can be fully encompassed by impartialism without disturbance to its theoretical commitments.

tionships may constitute a set of concerns or mode of thought and motivation genuinely distinct from that found in impartialist morality, and these can be deeply important to individuals' lives, nevertheless such concerns are not moral but only personal ones. My caring for my friend David is important to me, but actions which flow directly from it are in that respect without moral significance.

Position 2 treats concerns with relationships as *personal* or *subjective* ones, in Nagel's and Williams's sense. Such a view is implied in Kohlberg's earlier and better-known work,[11] where impartialism was held to define the whole of (at least the highest and most mature form of) morality and to exclude, at least by implication, relational or care considerations. In his most recent work, replying to Gilligan, Kohlberg claims to have abandoned this consignment of care in personal relations to an entirely nonmoral status; but this view nevertheless continues to surface in his writing.[12]

In contrast to positions 1 and 2, the remaining views all accord, or at least allow for, some distinct moral significance to care.

3. Position 3 claims that concerns of care and responsibility in relationships are truly moral (and not merely personal) concerns, and acknowledges them as genuinely distinct from impartiality; but it claims that they are nevertheless secondary to, parasitic on, and/or less significant a part of morality than considerations of impartiality, right, universal principle, and the like. Kohlberg makes three distinct suggestions falling under this rubric. (*a*) Our personal attachments to others intensify our sense of dignity of other persons, a sense of dignity which is ultimately grounded in an impartialist outlook. Thus the husband's love for his wife intensifies and brings home to him more vividly her right to life, shared by all persons. (*b*) In a different vein, Kohlberg says that impartialism defines the central and most significant part of morality – what is obligatory and required – whereas the area of personal relationships is supererogatory, going beyond what is required. The demands of justice must be satisfied, but action on behalf of friends, family, and the like, though good and even perhaps admirable, is not required. Thus care is, so to speak, morally

---

11. For example, Kohlberg, "From 'Is' to 'Ought': How to Commit the Naturalistic Fallacy and Get Away with It in the Study of Moral Development," and other essays in *Essays in Moral Development,* vol. 1, *The Philosophy of Moral Development* (New York: Harper & Row, 1981), and Part 1 of *Essays in Moral Development,* vol. 2, *The Psychology of Moral Development.*
12. See, e.g., in "Synopses and Detailed Replies to Critics" (with C. Levine and A. Hewer), in *The Psychology of Moral Development,* p. 360, where Kohlberg says that many of the judgments in the care orientation are "personal rather than moral in the sense of a formal point of view."

dependent on right and justice, whereas impartiality, right, and justice are not morally dependent on care. (c) The development of care is psychologically dependent on the sense of justice or right, but not vice versa.[13]

Position 3 differs from position 2 in granting some moral status to the concerns of relationship; care for friends is not only personally important but, given that one has satisfied all of one's impersonal demands, can be morally admirable as well.

4. Position 4 says that care is genuinely moral and constitutes a moral orientation distinct from impartiality, but it is an *inferior* form of morality precisely because it is not grounded in universal principle. On the previous view (3), the concerns of a care morality lie outside the scope of impartialist morality and are less significant for that very reason. In 4, by contrast, a care morality and an impartialist one cover, at least to some extent, the same territory; the same actions are prescribed by both. I may help out a friend in need out of direct concern for my friend; this action has some moral value, but the action is also prescribed by some principle, stemming ultimately from an impersonal perspective. And it is better to act from impartial principle than care because, for example, impartial morality ensures consistency and reliability more than care or because impartialism is (thought to be) wider in scope than is care morality (covering impersonal as well as personal situations). So on view 4, acting out of direct care for a friend has some moral value but not as much as if the action stems from a firm and general principle, say, one of aid to friends.

This view might naturally regard the morality of care as a stage along the way to a more mature impartialist morality, and such a construal is suggested in some of Kohlberg's earlier writings, where care responses are treated and scored as "conventional" morality (in contrast to the more developed "postconventional" morality) – as conforming to social expectations of "being good."

Position 4 is importantly different from positions 1 and 2. For position 4, even though all the demands of a care morality can be met by impartialist morality, still a moral agent could in general or in some set of circumstances be animated by care morality entirely independent of impartialist morality. For positions 1 and 2 there is no such thing as a morality of care independent of impartialist morality.

5. Position 5 acknowledges a difference between care and impartiality

13. The first two suggestions (*a* and *b*) are made on p. 229 of Kohlberg's "The Current Statement of the Theory," and the second (care as supererogatory) again on p. 307. The last, (*c*), is articulated by O. Flanagan and K. Jackson in "Justice, Care, and Gender: The Kohlberg-Gilligan Debate Revisited," in *Ethics* 97 (1987): 622–37.

but sees this as a difference in the objects of moral assessment; care morality is concerned with evaluation of persons, motives, and character, whereas impartialist morality concerns the evaluation of acts.[14]

6. In position 6, considerations of an impartialist right set side constraints within which, but only within which, care considerations are allowed to guide our conduct. Considerations of impartiality trump considerations stemming from care; if the former conflict with the latter, it is care which must yield. If out of love for my daughter I want her to be admitted into a certain school, nevertheless, I may not violate just procedures in order to accomplish this. However, once I have satisfied impartialist moral requirements in the situation I am allowed to act from motives of care.

Such a view is found in recent defenses of a neo-Kantian position by Barbara Herman, Onora O'Neill, Stephen Darwall, and Marcia Baron.[15] And these writers generally see this view as implying view 3, that care is a less important element of morality than is impartiality. However, this implication holds only on the further assumption that considerations of impartial "rightness" are present in all situations. But many situations which involve care for friends, family, and the like seem devoid of demands of justice and impartiality altogether. In such situations care is the more significant consideration. And if such situations constitute a substantial part of our lives, then even if impartialist morality were a side constraint on care – even if it were granted that when the two conflict the claims of impartiality always take precedence – it would not follow from this that impartially derived rightness is more significant, important, or fundamental a part of morality than care. For in such situations care will be operating on its own, no considerations of impartiality being present to constrain it.[16]

14.　I owe the delineation of this position to William Lycan (in personal correspondence).

15.　Barbara Herman, "Integrity and Impartiality," *Monist* 66 (1983): 233–50; Onora O'Neill, *Acting on Principle* (New York: Columbia University Press, 1975), and "Kant after Virtue," *Inquiry* 26 (1984): 387–405; Darwall; Marcia Baron, "The Alleged Repugnance of Acting from Duty," *Journal of Philosophy* 81 (1984): 197–220.

16.　It might be replied here that even if impartialist considerations do not actually arise in all situations, nevertheless, one must be concerned about them beyond those situations; for (on view 6) one must be committed beforehand to giving them priority over care considerations and so must be concerned with situations in which such considerations might arise, or in which one is not yet certain whether or not they are present. Hence a concern for "impartial rightness" transcends those situations in which impartialist considerations actually obtain. Yet even if this were so, it would not follow that one must be constantly on the lookout for impartialist strictures. For one would need to be on the lookout only in those situations in which one has a distinct reason to think that impartialist considerations *might* obtain; and many situations involving care considerations will not have this feature. An analogy: that considerations of life and

223

Thus by itself the side-constraint view of the relation between impartiality and care seems to leave open the possibility that a morality of care is a central element in a morally responsible life. In this way, view 6 is weaker as a critique of Gilligan than the previous five views (except perhaps 5), all of which relegate care to an inferior, subsidiary, or nonexistent (moral) role. It is only with the additional, implausible, assumption that impartialist moral considerations apply in all situations that 6 implies 3.

But it might be thought that no defender of a Kantianlike view in ethics would accord such legitimacy and allow such importance to a nonrationalist, non–principle-based dimension of morality as I am construing in position 6. Let us examine this. As an interpretation of Kant, this neo-Kantian, side-constraint view (of O'Neill, Herman, and others) sees the categorical imperative essentially as a tester, rather than a generator, of maxims; the original source of maxims is allowed to lie in desires. This view rejects a traditional understanding of Kant in which moral principles of action are themselves derived from pure reason alone.

Nevertheless, such an interpretation leaves ambiguous the moral status accorded the different desires that serve as the basis of maxims. The categorical imperative can, on this view, declare a desire only to be permissible or impermissible. But if we compare compassion for a friend or care for a child with a desire for an ice cream, or for food if one is hungry, then, even if both are permissible inclinations (in some particular situation), the compassion seems more morally significant in its own right than the desire for ice cream.

If the neo-Kantian admits this difference in the moral status of desires, she is then left with acknowledging a source of moral significance (the value of compassion compared with the desire for ice cream) which is not accounted for by the (neo-)Kantian perspective itself, but only bounded by it; and this is the position 6 discussed here – that care in

death tend to trump or outweigh most other moral considerations does not mean that, in order to avoid causing death, one must in all situations be on the lookout for the possibility that one might be doing so. Rather, one need be concerned about such considerations only in situations in which there is positive reason to think that life and death considerations might be present.

I cannot here consider the further impartialist rejoinder that even when there are no impartialist strictures or considerations anywhere on the horizon, a commitment to heeding them still permeates all situations, and this grounds the claim that the impartialist dimension of morality is more fundamental and significant than care, even in the sphere of personal relations. The conclusion does not seem to me to follow from the premise; the inference seems to go from a hypothetical concern to an actual one. But more needs to be said on this. (See the discussion by Michael Slote, "Morality and the Practical," in his *Common-Sense Morality and Consequentialism* [London: Routledge & Kegan Paul, 1985].)

personal relations does constitute a distinct dimension of morality, along-side, and subject to the constraints of, impartialist considerations of right.

To avoid this slide to position 6, the neo-Kantian can accept a moral distinction between types of permissible desires but attempt to account for this distinction in some kind of Kantian way – for example, by seeing the greater moral value of some desires (e.g., compassion) as a reflection of respect for rational agency, or of treating others as ends in themselves, or something along that line.[17] A different move would be to bite the bullet of denying – as Kant himself seems in some passages to have done (in the notion that "all inclinations are on the same level") – any moral difference between a permissible compassion and a permissible desire to eat ice cream. Whether either of these incompatible positions is itself persuasive is a question that I cannot take up here.

The point of this excursus is to suggest that if one sees the thrust of impartialist morality as setting side constraints on the pursuit of other concerns, such as care in personal relations, it will be difficult to avoid view 6, in which care in personal relationships is accorded some moral significance, and a moral significance which cannot be systematically relegated to a status inferior to that of impartiality.

7. Position 7 claims that, while care considerations are distinct from universal principle and impartiality and while they are genuinely moral, nevertheless their ultimate acceptability or justifiability rests on their being able to be validated or affirmed from an impartial perspective.

This view distinguishes the level of practical deliberation from that of ultimate justification and sees the level of deliberation (in this case, care in personal relationships) as taking a different form from that provided by the standard of justification (that is, impartiality). On view 7, from an impartial and universal standpoint one can see how it is appropriate and good that people sometimes act directly from care rather than from impartialist considerations.

This view is distinct from view 1 in that in the latter care consider-ations are held to be really nothing but considerations of universal princi-ple, perhaps with some nonmoral accoutrements, such as emotions and feelings. Unlike views 1 and 2, view 7 acknowledges that care is (part of) a genuinely distinct form of moral consciousness, stemming from a differ-ent source than does impartialism and not reducible to it. Impartiality gives its stamp of approval to care but does not directly generate it.

View 7 is weaker than view 6 as an assertion of the priority of impartial-ity over care. It does not, for example, claim that impartialist consider-

17. This view is taken by Barbara Herman in "The Practice of Moral Judgment," *Journal of Philosophy* 82 (1985): 458.

ations always trump care ones but allows the possibility that care might in some circumstances legitimately outweigh considerations of impartiality. It allows the possibility that, on the level of deliberation and of the agent's moral consciousness, care might or ought to play as central a role as impartiality. The superiority of impartiality to care is claimed to lie merely in the fact that, even when the claims of care are stronger than those of impartiality, it is ultimately only an impartial perspective which tells us this.

Position 7 sees impartiality as more fundamental to morality than care because it is impartiality that ultimately justifies or legitimizes care. Yet this view seems an extremely weak version of impartialism; for unlike positions 1 through 4 (and perhaps 5 and 6), it is compatible with Gilligan's own claim that the care mode of morality legitimately plays as significant and central a role in the morally mature adult's life as does the impartialist mode. View 7 does not even require the moral agent herself to be an impartialist, as long as the mixture of care and impartialist considerations which animate her life can in fact be approved of from an impartial point of view.[18]

8. A final position bears mentioning because it is prominent in Kohlberg's writings. This is that the final, most mature stage of moral reasoning involves an "integration of justice and care that forms a single moral principle."[19] This formulation taken in its own right — according care and justice equal status — does not really belong in our taxonomy, which is meant to cover only views that make impartiality in some way more fundamental to morality than care.[20] In fact, Kohlberg does not spell out this integration of care and justice, and the general tenor of his work makes it clear that he regards care as very much the junior partner in whatever interplay is meant to obtain between the two moral perspectives. So that, it seems fair to say, Kohlberg's understand-

18. I do not discuss the truth of position 7 in this chapter, as I have attempted to do so in Chapter 2, "Iris Murdoch and the Domain of the Moral," where I argue that it is false. (For more on this, see n. 35 below.)

19. Kohlberg, "Synopses and Detailed Replies to Critics," p. 343.

20. For this reason I have omitted views which defend some role for impartiality merely by claiming that it is *not incompatible* with care in personal relations. (Such a view is suggested, e.g., by Jerome Schneewind in "The Uses of Autonomy in Ethical Theory," in Heller, Sosna, and Wellbery, eds., p. 73, though the argument there is about autonomy rather than impartiality.) For this view does not by itself grant impartiality any more significance than care; it simply says that the claims of impartiality do not get in the way of those of care. Although such views are sometimes presented as if they constitute a defense of Kantian or some other impartialist ethical view, in fact by themselves (e.g., apart from views such as 1 through 7) they do not seem to me to do so.

ing of the position mentioned here actually collapses it into one of the previous ones.[21]

In assessing both Gilligan's claim to have articulated a distinct voice within morality and the impartialist's response to this claim, it is important to know which counterclaim is being advanced. These eight views are by no means merely complementary to each other. The earlier views are much more dismissive of the moral claims of care in personal relationship than are the latter. It is an important confusion in Kohlberg's work that he attempts to occupy at least positions 2, 3, 4, 6, and 8, without seeming to be aware that these are by no means the same, or even compatible, philosophical positions. (On the other hand, there is a noteworthy tentativeness in some of Kohlberg's formulations in the volumes I have drawn on, which suggests that he was not confident that he had yet found an entirely satisfactory response to Gilligan.)

Before taking on some of these impartialist responses, the connections between such an inquiry and the controversy between virtue ethics and Kantian or utilitarian ethics bears some comment. Some of the seven contrasts drawn between Gilligan's and impartialist views characterize as well the contrast between a virtue-based ethic and its rivals; and some of the impartialist counterarguments against these contrasts are ones which are directed against virtue theory. Nevertheless, it should not be thought that all of the concerns of a moral outlook or sensibility grounded in care and relationship can be encompassed within what currently goes by the name of virtue theory. And the converse of this is true also; as Flanagan and Jackson point out,[22] attention to some of the concerns of virtue theory, for example, an exploration of some of the different psychological capacities contributing to a lived morality of care in relationships, would enrich the care approach.

Moreover, although Gilligan herself points to the existence of two distinct moral voices, once having questioned and rejected the notion of a single unitary account of the moral point of view, one might well question further why there need be only two psychologically and philosophically distinct moral voices. Why not three, or five? I would myself suggest that, even taken together, care and impartiality do not encompass all there is to morality. Other moral phenomena – a random selection might include community, honesty, courage, prudence – while perhaps

21. Worthy of further exploration is the fact that, although Gilligan would agree with position 8 in its apparent granting of something like equal status to justice and care, she does not see the relation between the two voices as one of "integration" so much as a full appreciation of the not readily integrated claims of both.

22. Flanagan and Jackson, p. 627.

not constituting full and comprehensive moral orientations, are nevertheless not reducible to (though also not necessarily incompatible with) care and impartiality. A satisfactory picture of moral maturity or moral excellence or virtue will have to go beyond the, admittedly large, territory encompassed by care and impartiality.[23]

THE MORAL VALUE OF CARE:
RESPONSE TO IMPARTIALIST POSITIONS 1 AND 2

The foregoing, largely taxonomic discussion is meant primarily to lay out the conceptual territory in which the various impartialist responses to the claims of care in morality can be evaluated. A full discussion of views 1 through 7 is impossible, and I would like to focus most fully on positions 1 and 2, which most forcefully and conclusively deny that there is anything morally and philosophically distinct in the morality of care. Building on these arguments, I will conclude with briefer discussions of views 3 through 7.

Position 1 denies the contrast, drawn in points 1 and 2, between the particularity involved in Gilligan's perspective and the universalism of Kohlberg's; position 2 asserts that, whatever there is to such a distinction, it is without moral significance. Position 1 claims that, when a moral agent acts from care for another, her action is governed by and generated from universal principle derived from an impartial point of view. This means more than that there merely exists some principle which prescribes the action in question as right; for that is the claim made in position 4 and will be discussed below. The mere existence of a governing principle would be compatible with the agent's action conforming to that principle by sheer accident; she could, for example, perform an action of aiding as prescribed by some duty of beneficence but do so for a wholly self-centered reason. There would be no moral value in such an action. What position 1 requires is that the agent who is acting from (what she regards as) care be actually drawing on, or making at least implicit use of, such an impartialist principle.

Both views 1 and 2 imply that what it is to be a morally responsible person – say, within the domain of personal relations – is captured by the conception of an agent coming to hold, and acting according to, universal principles. Let us approach this claim by considering some principles that might be considered universal and impartial and that might be thought to be applicable in the domain of personal relations, such as "Be loyal to

23. For further argument that Gilligan is wrong to limit the number of "moral voices" to two, see Chapter 11, "Gilligan's 'Two Voices' and the Moral Status of Group Identity."

friends," "Nurture one's children," and "Protect children from harm." Each particular morally right or good act within an agent's role (as friend, as parent) would be (according to this claim) prescribed by some such principle, which applies to anyone occupying the role and which is in that sense universal.[24] Benefiting the particular friend or child will then be an application of universal principle to a specific situation governed by it.

Yet although it may be true that, say, a father will regard himself as accepting general principles of protecting and nurturing his children, it does not follow that applying those universal principles is all that is involved morally in protecting and nurturing his children. What it takes to bring such principles to bear on individual situations involves qualities of character and sensibilities that are themselves moral and that go beyond the straightforward process of consulting a principle and then conforming one's will and action to it. Specifically, knowing that the particular situation the agent is facing calls for the particular principle in question and knowing how to apply the principle in question are capacities that, in the domain of personal relations (and perhaps elsewhere too), are intimately connected with care for individual persons. Such particularized, caring understanding is integral to an adequate meeting of the agent's moral responsibilities and cannot be generated from universal principle alone.

Consider the general principle "Protect one's children from harm." Quite often it is only a parent's concerned and caring understanding of a particular child which tells her that the child's harm is at stake in a given situation and, thus, which tells her that the current situation is one in which the principle "Protect children from harm" is applicable. One adult viewing a scene of children playing in a park may simply not see that one child is being too rough with another and is in danger of harming the other child; whereas another adult, more attentive to the situation, and more sensitive about children's interaction, may see the potential danger and thus the need for intervention and protection. Both adults might hold the principle "Protect children from harm"; yet the second adult but not the first rightly sees the situation at hand as calling for that principle. Gilligan suggests that the sensitivity, caring, and attentiveness that lead the second adult to do so are moral qualities. This is supported by the foregoing argument, that such capacities are essential to the agent's being

24. There is another, somewhat more colloquial, sense of universal which implies independence from particular roles. But for now I will adhere to the more formal, philosophical sense of universal as implying applicability to anyone meeting a certain description (here, occupying a certain role within a personal relationship).

a morally responsible person in the way that the principles in question are meant to articulate.[25]

In addition, care for particular persons often plays a role in knowing *how* to apply a principle to a situation, even once one knows that the situation calls for it. In order to know what it is to nurture, to care, to protect (his children) from harm, a father must take into account the particular children that his children are, the particular relationships that have evolved between himself and them, and the particular understandings and expectations implicit in those relationships. For example, suppose a father has to decide whether and how to deal with a situation in which his daughter has hit her younger brother. He must take into account what various actions, coming from himself in particular, would mean to each of them. Would his intervention serve to undermine (either of) his children's ability to work out problems between themselves? Would punishing his daughter contribute to a pattern of seeming favoritism toward the son which she has complained of recently? How might the self-esteem and moral development of each of the children be affected by the various options of action open to him?

Knowing the answers to these questions requires that the father care about his children in a way that manifests understanding and appreciation of each one as an individual child and human being, and of their relations to each other and to himself. Such a particularized caring knowledge of his children is required in order to recognize how the various courses of action available to the father will bear on their harm in the situation. Merely holding or averring the principles "Protect one's children from harm" or "Nurture one's children" does not by itself tell one what constitutes harm (and thus protection and nurturance) in regard to individual children and in a given situation.

So it is no support to the impartialist view to assert that the role of particularity in moral action lies in the application of general role-principles to the particular case; for, I have argued, that process of application itself draws on moral capacities not accounted for by impartialism alone. Both knowledge of the situation and knowledge of what action the principle itself specifies in the situation are as much part of accomplishing the impartialist's own goal of acting according to the principle as is

25. I do not mean to imply that every situation presents a significant issue of moral sensitivity or perception involved in knowing that a principle applies. If a child reaches to touch a hot stove, no one observing the situation could fail to see that here one needs to keep this from happening. But situations in life often do not come with their moral character so clearly declared to any and all beholders, a fact which is often masked in discussions of examples in philosophy, where the moral character of the situation is already given in the description.

the intellectual task of generating or discovering the principle. Yet they are tasks which cannot be accounted for by an impartialist perspective alone.[26]

I suggest then that both universality and particularistic care play a role in morally responsible action within personal relationships. Remember (see above) that it is no part of Gilligan's view to advocate *replacing* a concern for impartiality with care in personal relationships. If so, then acknowledging some role for universal principle even in the domain of personal relationships does not lead one to positions 1 or 2, which leave no distinct moral role for care in personal relations at all.[27]

Nevertheless, the foregoing argument should not be taken to imply that all morally good action within personal relationships does in fact involve application of universal principle; my argument has been only that even when it does it often requires some care for particular persons as well. But one can certainly imagine individually worthy actions of friendship or parenthood which are animated not by a sense of applying principle but by a direct care for the friend or child. This can even be (though it is not always) true of unreflective and spontaneous impulses of care. But in addition, care which is direct and unmediated by principle need not be unintelligent, impulsive, or unreflective; it can be guided by intelligent attention to the particular friend's or child's good, yet not be derived from universal principles regarding children or friends in general.[28]

If care in personal relations is granted to be of moral significance, both as

26. For more on the nature of moral perception, and a fuller argument that impartialist and principle-based moral theories cannot account for the moral capacity for moral perception, see Chapter 3, "Moral Perception and Particularity." The argument there does not explicitly link up moral perception with care.

27. Note that the argument so far has been couched in terms of "universality." But universality is not the same as impartiality. A morality of personal relationship roles (such as father, friend) is not fully impartialist unless the precepts governing the role morality are derivable from the position of pure impartiality postulated by the impartialist view. For a criticism of this supposition, see Chapter 9, "Moral Development and Conceptions of Morality," where it is argued that even if a role morality, such as that involved in parenthood, is applicable "universally" to all parents, the content of the moral precepts involved in it cannot be derived, even indirectly, from the impartialistic moral standpoint from which, from the point of view of the agent, each individual is to count for one and no more than one. If this is so, the acceptance given in the argument of the present essay to (some role for) universality is not tantamount to an acceptance of the same role for impartiality. But the argument advanced therein to show that universal principle itself cannot cover the whole territory of morality will apply ipso facto to the narrower notion of impartiality. For more on levels and types of impartiality and universality, see Chapter 5, "Vocation, Friendship, and Community: Limitations of the Personal-Impersonal Framework."

28. For a more elaborate argument that care and concern can be intelligent and reflective without involving moral principle, see my *Friendship, Altruism, and Morality* (London: Routledge & Kegan Paul, 1980), esp. Chapter 2.

231

an integral part of what it is for one's life to be informed by certain principles of responsible friendship, parenthood, and the like, as well as in its own right, then we must reject both position 1 — that there is no difference between care and universal, impartial principle — and position 2 — that although there may be a difference, it is of no moral significance.[29]

IS CARE A UNIVERSAL PRINCIPLE?

One can imagine the following response to my argument against positions 1 and 2: "All right. One can acknowledge that specific relationships are central to the moral life of the individual and that, therefore, care for specific persons in its various modes of kindness, friendship, compassion, and the like are important human qualities which have a claim on being considered moral. Furthermore, one can admit that a moral decision procedure characterized by strict impartiality cannot be made to generate all the forms of moral response appropriate to this domain of morality.

"Nevertheless, in acting from love, care, compassion, is the moral agent not acting from some kind of 'principle'? Does not Gilligan want to say that everyone should be kind and caring, responsible to those to whom they are connected? Is she not saying we should all follow the principle,

29. There seems to be a range of different types of moral personalities, a range in which both universal principle and care for particular persons have varying degrees and kinds of involvement and interaction with one another. To some persons, responsible friendship and parenthood comes more naturally than to others; they find it easier to keep attentive to, to remain in touch with the needs of, to consistently care for friends and children. By contrast, others, also responsible as friends and parents, might find it more often necessary self-consciously to remind themselves of the general principles governing friendship and parenthood — to use their principles to get them to do what the others do without an even implicit recourse to principles. Of course, the operation of principle in a person's motivation does not always show itself in explicit consulting of that principle. One might have so internalized a principle that one acts on it almost automatically, without having to call it up in one's mind. Yet, as positions 2, 3, 4, 6, and 7 acknowledge, there is still a difference between acting from an internalized but universal principle and acting purely from care and concern for a specific individual, even if this difference is hard to make out in many specific instances. It is only position 1 which denies such a distinction entirely. That there can be a range of differences among persons in the degree to which universal principles animate their actions does not mean that one can imagine a fully responsible moral agent for whom they play no role at all. It would be difficult to imagine a person fully confronting the complex responsibilities of modern parenthood and friendship without giving some thought to the general responsibilities, formulable as principles of some sort, attaching to the various roles that she inhabits. Yet at the same time it should not be forgotten that some people who are not especially reflective about their general responsibilities seem as if instinctively to know how to act well toward their particular friends, or toward their or others' children, much better in fact than some other people who are nevertheless quite articulate about the appropriate principles of responsible friendship and parenthood.

'Be responsible within one's particular relationships,' or even 'Be sensitive to particulars'? If so, is she not therefore proposing a morality which is meant to be universal, indeed to be based on universal principle?"

This objection is useful in bringing out that in one important sense a morality of care is meant to be a morality for all. It is not a relativistic morality in the sense of applying to some but not others or of being confined to one particular group.[30] However, the objection presents itself as if it were a defense of the strongest impartialist view, namely, position 1 (or perhaps position 2). Yet the notion of "universal principle" in the objection has moved entirely away from the sense in which universal principle is meant to *contrast* with a morality of personal care. It has become a notion which encompasses emotional response and which acknowledges that moral action – acting according to that principle – requires a care for particular persons which cannot be exhaustively codified into universal principles. In that sense it is a notion of "universal principle" which has abandoned rationalism, impartiality, and the sense that adherence to universal principle alone (perhaps together with a strong will) is sufficient to characterize the moral psychology of Kohlberg's maturely moral agent. It acknowledges that other moral capacities, involving perception and sensitivity to particulars and care and concern for individual persons, are equally central to moral agency. Such a view no longer involves a critique of a particularistic morality of care in relationships.

RESPONSE TO IMPARTIALIST VIEWS 3 THROUGH 7

Positions 3 through 7 will be considered more briefly. But first, one more point about position 2. Suppose it were replied to the argument of the previous section that the capacities of care, sensitivity to particular persons, and the like, may be good, and perhaps even necessary for the application of moral principle, but – precisely because they are not themselves a reflection of universal principle, impartiality, rationality, and the like – they are not themselves moral.

30. This does not mean that Gilligan's view of morality is incompatible with all forms of relativism. Gilligan does not, I think, aspire, as Kohlberg does, to a timeless morality valid for all people in all historical times and cultures. It seems to me that Gilligan's view is compatible with the qualified relativism suggested in Williams's *Ethics and the Limits of Philosophy*, Chapter 9 – the view that, e.g., a care morality is appropriate for any culture which is a real historical option for us; but we cannot say that it either is or is not valid for ones which are not. Something like this view is suggested in Gilligan's article with J. Murphy, "Development from Adolescence to Adulthood: The Philosopher and the Dilemma of the Fact," in *Intellectual Development beyond Childhood*, ed. D. Kuhn (San Francisco: Jossey-Bass, Inc., 1979).

Naturally if "moral" is defined in terms of impartiality, then anything outside of impartiality – even what is a necessary condition of it – is excluded. But then no independent argument will have been given as to why such a definition should be accepted.[31]

Let us consider position 3 in light of Kohlberg's suggestion that care in personal relations be seen as "supererogatory" and therefore secondary to or less significant than impartialist morality. "Supererogatory" can mean different things. If supererogatory is taken to imply "having greater merit," then those who exemplify care would have greater merit than those who merely fulfilled obligations. In that case it would be hard to see why that which is supererogatory would have less importance than that which is merely obligatory.

On the other hand, if "supererogation" implies strictly "going beyond (impartial) duty" (with no implication of superior merit), then it seems implausible to see care in personal relations as supererogatory. For there would be no duties of the personal sort which acting from care within personal relations involves doing more of, since duties would all be impartialist. Yet if duties (or obligations) of personal relationship are countenanced, then, leaving aside questions about whether these can in fact be encompassed within an impartialist framework (see note 27), it becomes implausible to regard all forms of care as going beyond these; for one thing, many caring actions can themselves be acts which are in fact obligatory. Out of care I may do something for a friend which I am in fact obliged to do anyway. But also many acts of friendship, familial care, and the like seem outside the territory of obligation altogether, rather than involving more of the fulfillment of obligation.[32]

Finally, if supererogation is taken more generally to refer to that which is (morally) good but not required, with no implication either of superior merit or of going beyond duty, then it seems contentious to relegate that which is supererogatory to a less significant domain of morality than that governed by impartial obligations. That (on this view) impartialist obligations are *requirements* whereas the supererogatory would not be, would

31. For further discussion of the definition of "moral" and the delineation of the domain of the moral, and of the place of care, responsiveness, and compassion in that domain, see Chapter 2, "Iris Murdoch and the Domain of the Moral," and Chapter 9, "Moral Development and Conceptions of Morality." See also the presentation above of position 6, in which the argument presented there has the force of shifting to the defender of Kant the burden of proof of denying moral worth to care and compassion and of restricting moral worth to that which is done from a sense of duty.

32. For an argument that many morally worthy acts of friendship, familial care, and the like, lie outside the structure of obligation or duty altogether, see my *Friendship, Altruism, and Morality,* Chapter 7.

mean only that one needed to satisfy the former first. This is the position taken in 6, and, as argued in the discussion of that view, nothing follows from it about which domain or orientation within morality is the more significant or valuable. For it can plausibly be argued that that which is (morally) good but not required casts a much wider net than the merely obligatory, and is, at least in that regard, a much more significant part of a typical human life.

View 4 says that, although care is distinct from impartiality and does have moral significance, it has less moral value than impartiality, which can also fully encompass all of its demands. The picture here is of a range of morally bidden acts, which are prescribed by both care and impartiality (though impartiality extends beyond this range as well).

First of all, it can be doubted whether all of the actions bidden by care morality can be seen as generated by principles of right or duty; as mentioned above, many caring actions seem outside the obligation structure altogether. But leaving this point aside, actions stemming from principles of right and acts stemming from care are not simply identical acts prompted by different motives. Leaving aside the problems of recognizing the situation as calling for the principle and knowing how to apply it, it is also true, as suggested in the fifth contrast between Gilligan and Kohlberg, that within personal relations actions grounded in principle or duty alone will often not be seen by their recipients as expressing an attitude or emotion thought to be proper to that relationship. Thus although I can, out of adherence to a principle of aiding friends, do something to aid my friend, that action will not have entirely fulfilled what a fuller notion of friendship bids of me, which is to perform the action of aiding as an action expressing my care for my friend.[33] If emotionally expressive action is an integral part of appropriate behavior within personal relationships, then a philosophy grounded in rational principle alone will be importantly deficient in this domain and cannot be seen as superior to one of care.

View 5 regards a morality of care as concerning the evaluation of persons and impartialist morality as involving the evaluation of acts. This seems unsatisfactory in both directions. Most important, care morality is meant to encompass not only inner motives but outward acts, specifically, as argued immediately above, emotion-expressing acts. Care involves a way of responding to other persons and does not merely provide standards for the evaluation of agents. What is true of a morality of care, which view 5 may be pointing to, is that it rejects a sharp distinction

33. See Michael Stocker, "Values and Purposes: The Limits of Teleology and the Ends of Friendship," *Journal of Philosophy* 78 (1981): 747–65.

between act and motive that would allow for a standard of act evaluation wholly separate from one of agent evaluation.[34]

Apart from what has been said in the presentation of those views, positions 6 and 7 raise philosophical issues beyond the scope of this paper.[35] Nevertheless, as we noted in those discussions, neither of these views, as they stand, put forth a strong challenge to Gilligan's views or to a morality of care.

Finally, it might be felt that the impartialist counterpositions discussed in this paper have served to push some of the contrasts 1 through 7, discussed earlier in the paper, into the background. This seems true. At the outset I claimed that Gilligan's work is of the first importance for moral philosophy, and that pursuing its implications for an adequate moral theory will take one into territory not readily encompassed within the categories of contemporary ethics. This essay is meant only as a preliminary to that enterprise, clearing out of the way some of the intellectual obstacles within contemporary ethics to pursuing some of these more radical directions.[36]

34. For a sustained critique of the sharp separation between act and motive presupposed in view 5, see Stephen Hudson, *Human Character and Morality: Reflections from the History of Ideas* (London: Routledge & Kegan Paul, 1986), esp. Chapter 3; and Blum, *Friendship, Altruism, and Morality,* Chapter 7.

35. Some of the issues concerning view 7 are addressed in my "Iris Murdoch and the Domain of the Moral" (see n. 18 above). There it is argued that the reflective point of view outside of the specific individual's caring for his friend, from which it can be seen that the individual's caring action is a good one – or that compassion, concern for specific individuals' welfare, and similar traits and sentiments can be acknowledged as having moral value – cannot be identified with the specific standpoint of "impartiality" found in impartialist moral theories. Such impartiality is, it is argued, only one possible reflective viewpoint. If this is so, then it is no support for position 7 to argue that all rational beings would include principles of care, compassion, and the like, as part of an ultimately acceptable morality, for the standpoint from which these rational beings do so is not necessarily an impartialist one.

36. Since this article was first written, a substantial literature – often inspired by feminist concerns – has developed the idea of morality of care, extending the pioneering work of Nel Noddings, *Caring: A Feminine Approach to Ethics* (Berkeley and Los Angeles: University of California Press, 1984), and Annette Baier in several articles. See collections by Claudia Card (ed.), 1991, *Feminist Ethics,* Lawrence: University of Kansas Press; E. Cole and S. Coultrap-McQuin (eds.), 1992, *Explorations in Feminist Ethics, Theory, and Practice,* Bloomington: Indiana University Press; Eva Feder Kittay and Diana T. Meyers (eds.), 1987, *Women and Moral Theory,* Totowa, N.J.: Rowman & Littlefield; Mary Jeanne Larrabee (ed.), 1993, *An Ethic of Care: Feminist and Interdisciplinary Perspectives,* New York: Routledge.

11

Gilligan's "two voices" and the moral status of group identity

Carol Gilligan's work in moral development has had an extraordinary impact on many academic fields. Her 1982 book *In a Different Voice: Psychological Theory and Women's Development* (henceforth cited as *IDV*) evidently resonated deeply with the experiences, thoughts, and feelings of countless women who have seen in it an articulation – and an implicit validation – of an approach to morality and human relations in which (sometimes for the first time in a piece of academic writing) they can recognize themselves.[1] Feminist philosophers have developed the philosophical aspects of views like Gilligan's far past Gilligan's own (including her post-1982) work; but Gilligan herself remains a crucial reference point and source of inspiration, and it is on her views that I will focus.

Gilligan's work developed against the backdrop of the views of her former teacher and associate Lawrence Kohlberg, perhaps still the single most influential figure in moral-development theory. Kohlberg (1981, 1984) hypothesized a course of development toward moral maturity that he claimed to be common to all cultures. The path leads the individual from egocentrism to a concern with relationships, then, transcending that, to a focus on social rules, and finally to the highest stage (based on Kant's moral theory) of universal moral principles grounded in individual autonomous reason.

Kohlberg's formative research was based on an all-male sample, and Gilligan claimed that partly for this reason Kohlberg devalued, mischaracterized, or entirely failed to see a range of moral qualities such as the following: direct concern for individual human beings and their needs; empathetic attentiveness to others; sensitivity to others; compassion; emotional support and nurturance; sensitivity to particular context and to the

I thank the audiences at presentations of drafts of this chapter at Johns Hopkins University (especially Susan Wolf), and at an NEH Summer Institute ("Principles and Practices") at Santa Cruz in 1992, as well as Mark Tappan and Elizabeth Kiss for very astute comments on a later draft.

1. To some extent Gilligan was just in the right place at the right time. In psychology, Jean Baker Miller was saying similar things in 1976, and Nel Noddings (1984), working from a philosophy of education context, proffered a much more detailed and worked-out account of a "morality of care" at about the same time as Gilligan.

details of individual situations (with an attendant avoidance of appeal to highly general moral principles); concern for the vulnerable; exhibiting and valuing qualities especially appropriate to personal and familial relations; a general placing of value on human relations and their preservation; and in contexts of personal-moral conflict, searching for mediation and conciliation rather than holding fast to principled positions.

In *IDV* Gilligan refers to these qualities taken together as a "voice" – the "care voice" – and she has also called them a moral "perspective," "orientation," and "framework." All these terms imply a pervasive moral outlook rather than merely a set of qualities of character. Gilligan suggests, correctly I believe, that not only Kohlberg but also representatives of other dominant traditions within both psychology and philosophy have failed to give a valued and fully legitimate place to these qualities. (Precursors of parts of the care orientation, however, can be found in the philosophical tradition in Aristotle, Hume, Adam Smith ([1759] 1970), and Schopenhauer ([1841] 1965).) But Gilligan does not herself devalue the moral qualities of justice, impartiality, and concern for rational principle that Kohlberg put at the pinnacle of moral maturity. Rather, following Kohlberg's usage, she calls this the "justice" voice (or orientation) and officially accords it equal status with the care voice.[2] Hence the hypothesis of "two moral orientations."

TWO STRANDS IN GILLIGAN'S THOUGHT

Gilligan is famous not only for the two moral orientations hypothesis but also for claiming a correlation between these orientations and gender. There are two distinct strands in Gilligan's thinking regarding this connection, and these correlate roughly (though by no means absolutely) with the earlier *IDV* and some later writings, such as "Moral Orientation and Moral Development" (in Kittay and Meyers [1987]) (MOMD), and "Adolescent Development Reconsidered" (ADR), "The Origins of Morality in Early Childhood Relationships" (with Grant Wiggins) (OMECR), and "Two Moral Orientations" (with Jane Attanucci) (TMO) in Gilligan, Ward, and Taylor (eds.), *Mapping the Moral Domain* (1988) (*MMD*). (Later I will discuss Gilligan's most recent work as a third strand in her thought.) Philosophers have tended to pay more attention to the first, earlier strand in Gilligan's thinking.

In *IDV* Gilligan's major concern was to validate the care voice both as distinct from justice, and as possessing an integrity and normative legitimacy

2. I say "officially" here because several passages in *IDV* suggest that Gilligan really sees the care voice as superior to the justice voice.

of its own. But she also wanted to claim that the invisibility of this voice in psychological and moral theory was related to its empirical link with women and the absence of women's experience and voices in psychology. However, she claimed only an "in general" – not an absolute – correlation between women and the care voice, and men and the justice voice. She emphasizes: "The different voice I describe is characterized not by gender but by theme. Its association with women is an empirical observation, and it is primarily through women's voices that I trace its development" (p. 2).

In *IDV* Gilligan remains largely agnostic about the psychic roots of care and justice. Partly because no explanation is given of this gender link, and despite the remark just quoted, she leaves the impression that the care voice somehow belongs to women in some fundamental way – though she avoids a strict "essentialism" regarding women's characteristics. While theoretically acknowledged, the idea of a "male career" is left as an anomaly. The impression of a deep, though not absolute, gender link is also supported by the one tentative explanation offered by Gilligan, and that is the work of Nancy Chodorow (1978). Following Chodorow, Gilligan suggests that women's sense of self and gender identity is bound up much more than men's with being in relations with others, the model for this being the mother-daughter bond. By contrast, boys gain their male identity by having to disidentify with their mother, the primary parent in most households, and thus come to associate maleness with independence and lack of attachment. The moral voice of care then builds on the girl's sense of embeddedness in relationships. She feels connected to other people, and out of this grows the moral value of caring for others, sustaining relationships between persons, responding to others in need (*IDV* pp. 8–9; MOMD, p. 28).[3]

Gilligan reports as a "watershed" in her thinking (ADV, p. xxii) Kay Johnston's study in which eleven- and fifteen-year-olds were asked to respond morally to two of Aesop's fables and their responses were scored in terms of care and justice. Johnston then asked the children if they could see another way of looking at the situation, and (sometimes with gentle prodding, sometimes not) almost all the children who picked one mode, she claimed, could readily see the situation in terms of the other.[4]

3. It is worth noting that Chodorow's account, although proffering an explanation of deeply rooted gender differences, also holds the possibility of change in these differences. If men and women shared parenting equally, Chodorow says, the dynamic generating the deep psychological differences would disappear, or be greatly muted. (I am indebted to Elizabeth Kiss for drawing my attention to this point.)

4. Gilligan's account of Johnston's findings is given in MOMD (pp. 26 ff.) and ADR (p. xxii). Johnston's own account is D. Kay Johnston, "Adolescents' Solution to Dilemmas in Fables: Two Moral Orientations – Two Problem-Solving Strategies," in *MMD*.

Gilligan and Johnston drew from this study the idea that every child had access to, or in some sense *possessed, both* moral orientations. This contrasts with the *IDV* account, which implies that every individual has one or the other orientation, but not both.

Gilligan connected this access to two fundamental and universal early childhood, morality-grounding experiences – inequality and powerlessness (in relationship to adults), and attachment – experienced by children of both sexes. The inequality runs the risk of "oppression" and domination at the hands of the adult, and the experience of this risk-bearing inequality underpins the development of a sense of justice as a desire to correct for that inequality and protect against that risk. The experience of attachment runs the risk of abandonment or loss of that attachment, with consequent hurt to the child, and this fear of attachment loss underpins the voice of care, which bids people respond to one another and maintain attachment.[5]

Since children of both sexes undergo both these experiences – attachment and inequality – they both possess the psychic grounding for the moral orientations of justice and care; therefore, children of both sexes can understand and have access to both moral orientations.

In this strand of Gilligan's thought, gender differences regarding morality still remain – differences regarding both the spontaneous or first-chosen moral approach to a given moral situation (as in Johnston's Aesop's fables), and also in the approach preferred by the subject after reflection on the recognized alternatives.[6] In contrast to the earlier strand, however, a psychologically deep foundation for access to both voices is distinctly and explicitly provided to both genders.

GILLIGAN'S BINARY VIEW OF MORALITY

The early and later accounts differ regarding the nature of the gender-moral orientation link and the psychic underpinnings of the two orientations, but they both posit a substantial gender-moral orientation link. Moreover both share a tendency to conceive of morality in "binary" or

5. Gilligan mentions this psychic underpinning in *IDV* (pp. 62 ff.) but does not follow the insight through in the way done in the later writings, and it remains somewhat at odds with the main thrust of *IDV*.
6. A further interesting finding in these experiments is that girls tended spontaneously to select the justice voice even when on reflection they preferred the care voice; whereas boys overwhelmingly both selected and preferred the justice voice. Gilligan reads this result to suggest that the voice of care is suppressed or delegitimized in the dominant culture so that children (and especially girls) tend to lose hold of it as they move into adolescence. See *ADR* (p. xxii) and elsewhere.

dichotomous terms. Just as there are two genders, so there are two moral orientations. I will argue here that this binary conception of morality is a very misleading way to think about morality and the moral life. Moreover, though I will be giving less attention to this point, this dichotomous conception of morality contributes to a misleadingly overstated way of thinking about gender and gender differences. It overemphasizes the differences that do exist between men and women, and potentially contributes both to further divisions between them and to unequal treatment of women.

I will characterize more fully what I mean by Gilligan's "binary" conception of morality. But before doing so, I want to emphasize that this characterization can be attributed to Gilligan only as a distinct tendency (though a pervasive one) in her thought. She never takes an explicit overall stand on the nature of morality itself, such as would allow one unequivocally to attribute these claims to her; moreover, as I will mention, she says some things that suggest she does not hold one element or other of the conception I will spell out. That having been said, I think it impossible to read Gilligan without recognizing the following features implied in her view of morality, and in the writings of many who have been influenced by the idea of the "morality of care." I see four elements in Gilligan's binary conception of morality. Although I discuss only the first two of these, the others are mentioned to round out Gilligan's conception.

1. *Exhaustiveness:* Care and justice exhaust the moral orientations that exist. There are no significant moral considerations not subsumable under care or justice.

This view cannot be attributed unequivocally to Gilligan. In MOMD, for example, she talks about "at least" two moral orientations (pp. 20,26), thus holding out the theoretical possibility of more than these two. But the entire structure of Gilligan's discussion of morality is framed around these two orientations, and as far as I am aware, no recognition of any other concrete possibilities is entertained. The exhaustiveness assumption is supported also by the citing of the two childhood experiences (powerlessness and attachment) as being *the* psychic underpinnings of the two moral orientations. As no other childhood experiences are cited, Gilligan leaves the impression that these two – and the moral orientations growing from them – exhaust the field.

2. *Unitariness:* Each moral approach provides a unitary approach to ethical situations. Each orientation is an indissoluble, self-consistent whole. It is "all of a piece." This claim rejects the possibility that both the care voice and the justice voice might contain disparate elements, ones at least partly distinct from, and even not always entirely consistent with,

241

one another. It implies that each of the elements implies all the others; for example, that attentive concern for individuals implies valuing the sustaining of personal relationships, and vice versa.

Both the unitariness and the exhaustiveness claims are supported by Gilligan's use of the "ambiguous figure" metaphor (in MOMD and OMECR). The "duck-rabbit" figure, familiar from Wittgenstein's *Philosophical Investigations,* can be seen only as a duck *or* a rabbit (but not both). A (not strict, but suggested) implication of this Gestalt metaphor is that the care orientation is a unified whole, as is the justice orientation; each is, as it were, either "a duck" or "a rabbit," rather than a combination of partially disparate elements.

3. *Comprehensiveness:* A somewhat different form of dichotomization is involved in the claim that each of the moral orientations provides an approach capable of addressing any moral problem or situation. There is, as it were, both a care approach and a justice approach to any life situation or moral dilemma one might encounter.[7]

Gilligan seldom explicitly addresses the issue of whether an orientation or approach is normatively adequate or not, so it is possible that to the extent that she inclines toward the comprehensiveness claim, her view is not that either approach is normatively adequate to all situations, but only that each is psychically possible and intellectually coherent.[8]

There is an apparent tension between 1 – exhaustiveness – and 3 – comprehensiveness. For the former implies, to put it in spatial terms, that each voice covers *half* the territory, whereas the latter implies that each covers the entire territory (though yielding different moral results). Nevertheless, evidence of both views can be found in Gilligan, and both support a binary view of morality.

4. *Exclusiveness:* The two approaches are entirely distinct from one another; they are mutually exclusive. There is little sense in Gilligan that care and justice might contain areas of overlap – in terms of the kinds of moral considerations on which they draw, the prescriptions which issue

7. Compare "The tendency for people to organize experiences of conflict and choice largely in terms of justice or of care has been a consistent finding of research on moral orientation" (ADR, p. xviii). Note that Gilligan says "largely" here. This can be taken as a hedge against the comprehensiveness or the exhaustiveness claim; however, no indication is given here, or elsewhere, that some other moral element might be necessary to round out the justice (or care) approach, or that there is a specific kind of situation that simply cannot be approached in a "care" or a "justice" way. So, again, one cannot unequivocally attribute the "comprehensiveness" claim to Gilligan, but her work certainly tends strongly in that direction.

8. Flanagan, *Varieties of Moral Personality,* has a very good discussion of Gilligan's claims of normative adequacy, exhaustiveness, and comprehensiveness. (See Chapters 9 and 10.)

from them, or the psychic states informing them. At best they are seen as complementary, and although this is not spelled out clearly, the implication is of two entirely disparate items complementing one another. This point is not strictly asserted, but the general counterposing of the two and the ambiguous figure metaphor discussed above strongly suggest this view.

Gilligan presents her view of the two moral orientations as a purely empirical finding, as if she had been open to the possibility of a plurality of voices but her data revealed only these two. Without going back over the actual protocols, the purely empirical dimension of this matter cannot be definitively established. But I venture the hypothesis that the two-gender framework provided a partly controlling (and, I will argue, distorting) lens through which the data themselves were viewed. Just as the two genders are, in a manner of speaking, "exhaustive," "exclusive," and "unitary," so are the two moral orientations.[9]

I shall question Gilligan's binary view of morality, focusing on *exhaustiveness* and *unitariness*. Before doing so, however, I want to note what kind of criticism I will *not* be making of Gilligan's work. This criticism is the most common one made in mainstream moral philosophy, and it consists in saying one of two things: (1) There is nothing theoretically interesting in the "care orientation." It is all already encompassed within the familiar deontological and consequentialist traditions. (2) The care virtues are a genuine part of morality, yet are deficient to the extent that they are not regulated and deeply informed by standard and familiar conceptions of universal and rational moral principles.

I have replied to these criticisms elsewhere[10] and will just reiterate here that in my view the care qualities mentioned above and elicited in Gilligan's research and conception of morality are absolutely central to the moral life. Nor can they be either fully accounted for, nor shown to be inadequate, by standard deontological or consequentialist conceptions of morality. On these points Gilligan is entirely correct; my own criticism of Gilligan lies elsewhere.

9. One might note a similar dichotomization within ethical theory, between the "right" and the "good," categories also seen as exhaustive, exclusive, and in some sense unitary. (Many philosophers dispute this division, however, just as I am doing with Gilligan's view.) Gilligan was certainly not influenced by this particular philosophic tradition; but Kohlberg himself was, in his response to Gilligan's criticisms. One of his responses was to say that the domain of morality that Gilligan tapped into could be thought of as "the good" or "individual conceptions of the good life," in contrast to his own account of morality which concerned the domain of right or justice (Kohlberg, 1984).

10. See Chapters 1, 2, 3, 9, and (especially) 10 in this volume.

EXHAUSTIVENESS

I begin my discussion of exhaustiveness by focusing on an area of moral life not readily placed in either the *care* or the *justice* orientation – thus calling into question whether care and justice exhaust the moral domain. I will call this territory "morally significant group identities." It is a heterogeneous category – in many ways it should not be thought of as a natural kind – encompassing items such as one's profession, one's (work) institution, one's gender, one's race, one's ethnic identity, one's religious group (not simply one's religion per se – the group element is essential), one's political group, one's family, one's nation. Though in different ways, any of these is capable of orienting a given agent "in moral space," to use Charles Taylor's metaphor.[11] The group identity can orient an agent with regard to a significant area or dimension of her life, defining obligations, standards, ideals, commitments, and concerns. Only group identities that do this will be called "morally significant group identities" (MSGI). No single one of these is necessarily an MSGI for a given individual; different ones will be so for different individuals.

I do, however, limit MSGIs to those that provide *conscious* moral orientation. For example, it could well be argued that for some men, their gender identity deeply affects their moral being – for example, a male professor who is sexist and fails to take his female students as seriously as he does his male ones. But, unless he consciously "owns" this attitude and affirms it (an unlikely prospect at most universities in the United States), his gender will not count as a morally significant group identity for him.

MSGIs are not, however, limited to positive group identities, ones that the agent is glad she possesses. For some Germans, for example, after World War II, being German was a source of deep shame; many no doubt wished they were not German (though such a wish is not entailed by the shame). It may, however, be an MSGI if the person in question made use of her German identity to orient her values and aspirations – for example, by attempting to "live down" that identity, or (a more positive example) by attempting to get German society to face up to its Nazi legacy.[12]

MSGIs provide moral orientation in different ways; some general ways

11. Charles Taylor, *Sources of the Self,* Chapter 2.
12. One might think that, even though not all MSGIs need be "positive," all the examples I have given involve a morally positive use of one's MSGI. But clearly MSGIs need not be positive in this sense either. Membership in a white-supremacist group can be an example of an MSGI, an entirely negative one from a moral point of view. Though it is beyond my scope to do so here, obviously one needs to evaluate both (particular) MSGIs and the uses to which they are put.

can be mentioned to bring out the contrast with "justice" and "care." One is through the idea of *role obligations*, which apply most clearly in professional and institutional settings. Something like this conception can apply as well to race, however, as in the African-American conception of a "race man" – a person seen as discharging what are taken to be his or her special obligations to the African-American community.

Another form, related to but distinct from role obligations, are what might be called *role ideals.* For example, as a faculty member at a given institution I may feel drawn to organizing an effort to make the climate of my institution more hospitable to racial minorities (persons of color) than it currently is, although I am not and do not regard myself as under any actual obligation to do so. This effort will stem from the way I conceive of my professional role, or my place in my institution, and it illustrates the idea of a role ideal.[13] There may be other forms of these ideals – race, gender, nation, neighborhood – and I refer to this category generally as "group ideals."[14]

There are further ways of acting out of one's group identity which are neither obligations nor attempts to realize ideals. Suppose I wish to bring philosophy to high school students, simply because I think it would be a good thing for high school students to study philosophy, and not because I want to further the cause of philosophy itself, nor out of my ideal of what a philosopher is. I have nevertheless acted in some sense "out of" my identity as a philosopher and teacher.[15] Another example would be avoiding doing what one regards as shameful as a member of one's group; or when one tries to repair damage done by other members of one's group (where one does not see this either as obligation or ideal).[16]

A final mode of group moral consciousness that I will mention is the familiar special concern for members of one's group – for their welfare, for securing their rights, and the like – simply because they are members of the group. Presumably such a mode of concern is not morally trou-

13. The idea of a professional ideal and its distinction from role obligations is discussed more fully in Chapter 5, "Vocation, Friendship, and Community."
14. The terminology of "ideals" may be slightly misleading, however, if it is taken to imply that the agent with the ideal necessarily sees the efforts taken in its name as especially worthy, or distinctly above and beyond the call of duty. As I argue in Chapter 7, "Virtue and Community," persons who act from what others would regard as "ideals" or "supererogation" often see themselves as acting from something closer to ordinary duty.
15. I owe this example to Susan Wolf, though I believe she meant it to make a different point.
16. See Michael Stocker's excellent discussion in "Values and Purposes" or the "out of" and how philosophers have given insufficient intention to this form of action.

bling if it does not infringe on the rights of others, or does not stem from vicious attitudes toward other groups, and so forth. (Discussion about how this mode relates to care, to which it seems similar, will come later.)[17]

MODES OF GROUP-BASED ACTION

I am concerned here with the way *individuals* act with regard to their group – that is, their *collective* – identities. There are (at least) three distinct modes of action in this respect. One is of an individual acting alone ("individualistic" mode), but *on behalf of* or, more generally, *out of her sense of,* the group in question. (This can be in any of the above four categories – obligations, group ideals, special concern, other "out of's.") For example a woman might write to her state representative supporting a "freedom of reproductive choice" bill pending before the legislature, and think of herself as doing so very much *as a woman.* She sees herself not only as expressing the opinion of a constituent, but specifically a female constituent.

A second mode – that might be called "putatively collective" – would be exemplified by someone who writes the letter to her state representative but with the sense of being part of a larger group of women who she imagines are doing the same thing, writing to their own state representatives or more generally supporting efforts for freedom of reproductive choice elsewhere. She acts individually (as in the first mode), not coordinating her efforts with other members of her group (here, women) yet with a sense of participating in a collective effort.

The third mode – "organizedly collective" – involves coordinating one's efforts with those of other members of one's group to realize a collective end, taking action in concert with others. (One might write to one's state representative as part of a general letter-writing campaign.)

All three of these modes are distinct from acting purely "as an individual" (the preferred mode in much moral philosophy), yet they differ in degree of collectivity involved in the individual's agency. (The individualistic is the least collective and the organizedly collective is the most.) I elaborate these distinctions partly because action from group identities is

17. For a good discussion of the ways in which our social memberships provide moral orientation, see David Wong (1988), though I think Wong comes down too hard on the notion of action as being the cash value of this notion of orientation. I would want to allow a notion of orientation as "providing meaning" which would allow greater room for attitudes, emotions, and concerns not necessarily, or anyway fully, translatable into action.

often portrayed solely in the "organizedly collective" mode. To do so is to overcollectivize the way that MSGIs typically function in our lives.[18]

COMMUNITARIANISM

My remarks have an evident bearing on the "communitarianism" debate, and I want to bring this out more explicitly before moving on to the way the MSGIs provide moral orientation differently than either "care" or "justice." I take the notion of morally significant group identity to be a commentary on Michael Sandel's (1982) notion of "encumbered identity" and Philip Selznick's (1992) (perhaps more aptly named but conceptually almost identical) "implicated identity." Both are meant to illustrate the point that our group memberships can in some sense constitute our moral identities. That this is a possibility – that our agency is not always exercised "purely as individuals" (i.e., in abstraction from our group memberships) – might be thought of as the "identity" strand in communitarianism. It must be distinguished from a "social or political" strand in which communitarian values (such as civic responsibility, civic participation, a sense of community with other members of various groups, including one's polity) are taken as worthy ends to be promoted by the society.[19]

In my notion of MSGIs as part of the "identity" strand, the notion of "orienting" the moral agent carries less of an implication of permanence and involuntariness than does Sandel's. For example, I want to allow that a person's profession can provide a pervasive moral orientation for an individual; it can shape the ways she looks at the world, what she values and cares about, what she sees herself drawn to do. Yet professional identity is in some important sense voluntary (which does not mean that leaving a profession is entirely voluntary), and, more to the point here, it is an identity that one can shed. But even if one comes to shed it, it might still be the case that when one did possess that identity, one was deeply shaped by it, and it constituted one's moral self. I want to allow, that is, for some notion of a constitutive element of the self that lasts for only a certain period of one's life (though I think it has to be a fairly substantial period in order to count).

Given the structure of contemporary debate, it may not be easy to see how distinct the group identity orientation is from the care orientation.

18. For example, when Sandel talks about a wider sense of agency than the individual, I think he is often taken to mean only the most collective form of the three modes mentioned (when he is not taken to mean something so mysterious as to be unintelligible). But I think he could well mean any of the three.
19. See Charles Taylor's (1989) very illuminating discussion of this distinction (which he calls "ontological" and "advocacy"). (Compare discussion of this matter in Chapter 1.)

Both are alternatives to the *universalism* of the Kantian and consequentialist traditions. In both the care and the group identity orientations, the moral pull operating on the agent lies not in universal considerations applicable to all agents, but rather in some more particular aspect of a given moral agent's identity – either a particular caring relationship with a particular individual, or a particular group identity. In this sense both are particularistic rather than universalistic.

At the same time both the group identity and the care orientations are *relational* rather than *individualistic*. The agent sees herself *essentially* relationally, rather then *essentially* individualistically. The moral pull operates through the agent's relationships rather than through appeal simply to moral principle generated through the autonomous individual's reason.[20]

Yet the two orientations – care and group identity – are nevertheless importantly distinct. The notion of "relationality" in the care orientation is very much individual-to-individual. This is obviously so in personal relationships. If one also allows the care orientation application beyond the personal domain to strangers, the strangers are still encountered individually by the agent. If I can be spoken of as caring about a stranger, it is still a stranger with whom I come into some kind of contact.[21] Seyla Benhabib's (1992) notion of the "concrete other" (counterposed to the "generalized other") as the object of care is a useful way of capturing this feature of care morality.

One can also "care" about groups, institutions, and even morality itself, but the specific force of individual-to-individual care is lost if one lumps

20. This is not, however, to reject the notion of "autonomy" entirely as applicable to relationality. There can also be an autonomy that operates within relationships of caring, one that allows for (mutual) dependence.
21. Although this interpretation of the care orientation expands it beyond the personal domain, it does not take it as far as "caring at a distance," that is, caring toward persons one does not encounter. I do think this points to one of the limitations of the care ethic, though that fact is problematic only if one has a prior commitment to the idea that "care" must be a comprehensive morality. Without defending this here, I think that notions of justice and duty, along with various MSGI concepts such as "fellow citizen," are better suited than "care" to generating moral concern for nonencountered strangers.

This having been acknowledged, I do not think the elements of care morality are entirely useless in the nonencountered strangers domain. There is something to the idea of particularizing a nonencountered object of concern, as a way of eliciting an empathy and engaging moral imagination directed toward that person's plight. For example, there simply is a difference between "a starving Somalian child [this was written in 1992]" and "Ali Hassan, a 12-year-old child, living in [a named village], whose mother, brother, and sister [names given] live with him, and who is starving." I think it is some kind of insight of the care orientation itself that the latter more readily (though not always, or inevitably) taps into our moral concern than does the former.

all these concerns as part of a morality of care. And I think this restriction to individuals is implicit in Gilligan and other care theorists (such as Noddings). For example, if as a member of a particular college, I am moved to try to improve the curriculum in that college, my focus is not on particular individuals as it is in the "care" situation, though of course I hope and assume that individual students will benefit from the changes. Rather the focus is on the more abstract entities of the college and the curriculum, although it would be natural to say that my action stems from my "caring" about the college.

An example that well illustrates the differences between care, group moral identity (even when involving a kind of caring), and justice is the following: Suppose someone visits a racial slur on Kevin, a member of my racial group. In morally responding to this event, I might do so from one (or a mixture of) three motives: (1) I might be concerned about Kevin and the effect of the action on him. I attend to him and his needs, perhaps helping him to talk through what he feels about being the target of the slur, and what he or we together might do about it to help him feel good about his response to what happened. This is the (individual) care mode. (2) My concern might be that a member of my race has been the target of a racial slur. Thus my moral concern here is not individual-to-individual (or friend-to-friend) but member-of-group toward individual-as-member-of-group. It can also be toward the group itself. That is, I can focus not only on how Kevin (as a member of the group) is harmed by the slur, but how all persons of group X are harmed. In either case my concern is grounded in my being a member of the same group as the person targeted by the remark. This is the group identity mode. (3) My concern might be with the injustice of anyone's being a target of a racial slur. Here my concern has nothing to do with my membership in any particular group. It is simply as a human being that I see the injustice in the situation and want to do something about it. This is the justice mode. The justice motivation does not require concern about Kevin as an individual. Though such concern might in a sense seem natural, one of Gilligan's insights is that a concern for violations of moral principles can get dislodged from concern for particular persons and their needs. This is not necessarily a problem for justice as a moral concept in its own right, but only with a view that sees it as covering the entirety of the moral territory, thus depriving it of the "concrete other" focus supplied by care, and available as a corrective for this potential problem about justice.[22]

22. Note that the more abstracted form that the object of moral concern can take in MSGIs cannot be unequivocally identified with Benhabib's concept of the "generalized other." The latter is the appropriate object of justice-based concern; Benhabib

Thus, although both care and group identity are distinct from the universalism and individualism of at least Kohlberg's Kantian version of the "justice" orientation, and they are both in important senses "relational" and "particularistic," they are nevertheless distinct from one another. Care remains focused on the concrete and particular other person. MSGIs do not necessarily take such a focus, but can take more abstract entities as their objects of concern. Moreover, they draw on group aspects of our own moral identities in a way that care does not. Thus I would regard someone who saw herself as a caring professional (e.g., teacher, doctor, or nurse) as fusing two analytically distinct moral orientations or virtues – that of a (particular kind of) professional, and that of care. Even if it turns out that the most adequate ideal of the professional involves the idea of caring, I will want to argue that this ideal is still a combining of the two moral orientations, and that the form of care in any given profession is shaped by the nature of that particular profession.[23]

GENDER AS A MORALLY SIGNIFICANT GROUP IDENTITY

A particularly striking area in which the difference between a care orientation and a group identity orientation manifests itself is that of gender. For all that Gilligan finds and emphasizes gender differences in moral orientation, she does not link the care orientation to, or otherwise note, the moral agent's explicit awareness of her own gender as a feature of her own moral consciousness. Gilligan seldom looks at the ways that women act with a consciousness of themselves as women.

says the generalized other is the bearer of rights and duties (p. 158), and is thus universalistic in a way that MSGIs are not. Yet the object of MSGI-based concern does meet another of Benhabib's criteria of the generalized other, and that is that the person's concrete and particularized identity is abstracted from; this is so, for example, in the second situation above, where it is not Kevin-in-his-particularity that concerns me, but Kevin-as-member-of-my-group.

23. For an argument that each profession has its own form of caring, see Chapter 5, "Vocation, Friendship, and Community."

The issue of morally significant group identities is obviously much vaster than I can take on in this context, where only certain aspects – particularly constrastive with individual care, and with justice – are salient. But I want to mention at least three other points: (1) MSGIs are not generally simply given externally (to their possessors) as strict role obligations are. What it means to be an X (woman, doctor, teacher, faculty member at institution Y) is partly a matter of individual construal and interpretation. (2) Most persons have more than one MSGI, and how to handle the different moral pulls of these multiple identities is an important moral matter; moreover, each MSGI will affect the way in which one possesses any given other one, a point made well by Spelman (1988). (3) As mentioned earlier, MSGIs are not a natural kind, and they make moral claims on us in very different ways, even apart from the points in (1) and (2).

Such actions could be taken in the individual, putatively collective, or organizedly collective ways discussed earlier. These modes do not find expression in Gilligan's work.

Let us explore this in a specific case. A woman acts in either a putatively or an organizedly collective mode in pursuit of justice for women. I pick such a case to obviate for the moment the worry that I have not established the group identity voice as morally worthy. I avoid that concern here by making the example one of seeking justice (specifically, for women). This case is thus distinct from the mere pursuit of benefit for one's own group, which on some views would be morally suspect.[24]

This orientation is not the pure voice of justice, since it is as a woman that the woman in question is concerned for justice for women, although it presupposes some recognition of the worth of justice in its own right. And it is certainly not the voice of individual care. It is a third form of moral consciousness, informed by gender yet not accounted for by Gilligan's theory. And this is so even if the individual caring woman is herself an adherent of Gilligan's doctrine and thinks of her caring as somehow being more "female" than "male."

The lack of focus on gender as a dimension of explicit moral agency is related, in Gilligan, to another absence pointed out by several feminists—a neglect of structural inequality between men and women, and how the development of what Gilligan sees as women's moral consciousness may be bound up in various ways with the systematic injustices suffered by women in our society. Although it is true that Gilligan does stress the suppression of women's voices both in society and in social science, and sees this suppression as a matter of power, not merely of socialization, what she does not focus on is the complex and systemic suppression of women's opportunities and attainments, for example, in work, political and economic life, and civil society in general. She seldom concerns herself with the structural inequality of domestic life (such as discussed in Okin 1990), though she (rightly) treats domestic life as an important moral domain. It is as if Gilligan's main concern in her writings is with women as bearers of their voices

24. How about the case where the member of group X is concerned about justice (and not merely benefit) for her group, but is concerned for justice only for her group and for no other? As long as the person recognizes other groups' claims of justice (though not caring about them), there is no problem in her focusing her concern on her own group; and to do so must be adjudged a morally good thing insofar as it is the seeking of justice. (Again, a case can be made that this is true of simply seeking the welfare of one's own group as well; but I am taking the less problematic case.) Nevertheless it would be better if she were to have concerns for justice beyond her own group.

and their experiences, and not so much with women as full striving agents in the worlds of work and the home.[25]

Feminists and others have put forward several distinct criticisms of Gilligan for failing to take sufficient account of these structural inequities and their possible link to the care orientation.[26] I will not discuss these criticisms here, but want to suggest that the relative absence of focus on structural inequity is connected to Gilligan's failure to theorize women as acting in the group identity modes – as a woman and with women to protest, resist, or try to change those structures that keep women subordinate and unequal.

Note that the distinction between the care voice and the group identity orientation does provide the resources to defend Gilligan against one criticism made of her, like the first one mentioned in footnote 26, that is, that she has mischaracterized the voice she hears in women, that it is the voice of solidarity of the oppressed in general, not specifically that of women. It is the voice one would hear in any oppressed group – of group solidarity and mutual interdependence such as one finds in African-Americans.[27]

Group solidarity is not the same as individual care. The former partakes of a group consciousness that the latter does not, though both are relational and provide an alternative to justice by itself. Group solidarity does not guarantee the individual attentive care involved in the care orientation; just as care does not yield the sense of collectivity involved in group solidarity. Hence it is misleading to identify Gilligan's "care" voice with the voice of group solidarity among the oppressed.

Gilligan's general failure to investigate group gender identity as a dimension of explicit moral consciousness is partly corrected in her most

25. A striking illustration of the failure to see structural inequality as a moral problem in its own right is on page 16 of *IDV*, where Gilligan does refer to women's "social subordination," but does not treat that social subordination as of concern in its own right. (Nor does she see it as a possible causal source of the "care voice.")
26. For criticism of the lack of attention to structural inequality, see Linda Kerber (1986), Houston (1987), Epstein (1988). Specific criticisms of the morality of care as being linked to this inequality are the following: (1) "Care" is simply the voice of the weak and subordinate, specifically of those who serve men; valorizing it as Gilligan does reinforces women's subordination (Card 1990). Care has no value in its own right. (2) Care may be in itself (ceteris paribus) a good thing, but it still plays into women's subordination. (3) Care is a good thing but male-dominated institutions keep it from being realized (Grimshaw 1986). (4) Current forms of caring are tainted by their roots in female subordination and passivity, but a good form of caring can disengage itself from these distorting roots.
27. Something like this argument is given in Puka (1990) (reprinted in Larrabee 1993) and Harding (1987).

recent work on the consciousness of adolescent and preadolescent girls, seen in her Tanner Lecture of 1990, "Joining the Resistance: Psychology, Politics, Girls, and Women." Broadly, the argument of this work is that preadolescent girls are immersed in a world of relationships, that they seek to preserve these relationships, and that they are aware of the world as generally negating that value, and more generally as devaluing women and their values. Gilligan sees preadolescent girls as able – based on this knowledge – to protest against and in various ways to resist this sexism and other forms of unjust authority. When girls reach adolescence – with the intense onset of the power of cultural messages about what girls "are supposed to be like" – they tend to lose this ability to resist; they lose confidence in their values. Gilligan puts this point by saying that the girls forget what they know and turn their resistance inward to themselves. Gilligan urges adult women, and especially mothers, to help girls to hold onto their knowledge and to use it to promote social change.

Gilligan means this new work to be more explicitly political than her earlier work, in the sense of contributing to a psychology of resistance to injustice. Especially with regard to adult women, there is an injunction to act *as women* and with a sense of acting on behalf of females (especially girls). So there is some recognition of the gender group identity feature, especially in its individual and putatively collective modes, as applied to the women, though this does not take the form of organizedly collective action, nor is its target the manifold inequalities suffered by females in the wider world.

This degree of group identification does not apply to the girls themselves however. Although the girls sometimes resist what amounts to sexism, Gilligan does not find or highlight in these girls a consciousness of themselves as doing so or as sharing a common condition of inequality with other girls.

For example, Gilligan cites a powerful passage from Anne Frank's diary.[28] This passage had been excised by the editors of the diaries (including her father) for the first – that is, the worldwide–best-seller – version of the diaries. It was excised on the grounds that it might offend the sensibilities of some readers. In this passage, Anne Frank protests the inferior treatment of women throughout history, and includes in her protest a recognition of the ways in which what she sees as "men's values" – for example, military and physically heroic values – have served

28. Anne Frank was a German-Jewish girl who, with her family, was sheltered by Dutch friends in Amsterdam until the very end of World War II, when they were betrayed; Anne was ultimately killed in a concentration camp. Her diary remains one of the most influential and moving documents of the Holocaust.

to keep unrecognized and unsung women's accomplishments of daily courage and endurance of pain in service to humanity.[29]

I am not second-guessing Gilligan's findings, but I find it interesting that despite unearthing Anne Frank as a budding feminist – even one with "different voice" tendencies – Gilligan does not pick up on or develop the aspect of women's moral consciousness that consists of treating that identity as a source of moral orientation toward collective action (individualistic, putative, and organized) to correct the many injustices toward women.

The argument up to this point has been directed against the "exhaustiveness" dimension in Gilligan's thought – the idea that care and justice together exhaust the moral domain. I have argued against this by suggesting that morally significant group identities provide (different kinds of) moral orientations, that cannot be subsumed under either care or justice.

I shall elaborate on the consequences of this argument further, but I want to take up another issue first. I have tried to show the analytic distinctness of MSGIs from the care perspective. But I do not want to be taken as implying that MSGIs should operate in isolation from individual care, or – a related point – that all MSGIs (in all their different modes) are in perfectly good moral order as they stand.[30] Caring for individuals needs to temper a distinct tendency in many of the MSGIs to focus on the alleged welfare of fairly abstract entities, with the resulting danger that the concrete needs of individuals will be overlooked, as mentioned earlier.

This danger is entirely familiar in the case of many MSGIs. A concern for one's nation can cause one to lose touch with the welfare of its particular citizens (leaving aside here that it may also block concern for the citizens of other nations) and can readily take the form of jingoism, militarism, blind loyalty to the head of state, and the like. Even "family" – despite its status as the paradigm for intimate and car-

29. Gilligan (1990), p. 517, citing *The Diary of Anne Frank*, The Critical Edition (New York: Doubleday, 1989), p. 678.
30. Gilligan has herself sometimes been accused of a similar failing with regard to care – that she implies that care morality is "all right as it is," and (a further but related claim) that it is so because this is how women look at morality. This criticism is not entirely without foundation but it is largely unfair in that Gilligan recognizes defective or lesser forms of "care morality," just as Kohlberg recognizes defective or lesser forms of justice morality. However, in one sense Kohlberg's account rests on a firmer normative foundation than Gilligan's, in that he attempted to give an avowedly normative underpinning to his view of higher and lower moral stages, and specifically to his claim that stage 6 represented the highest development of moral maturity, whereas Gilligan does not do the same for care morality.

ing relationships – can become a distorting abstraction, where one serves a certain image rather than the needs of the actual members of one's family.[31] A concern for one's profession and its deserved recognition can also become disengaged from the well-being of the individuals served by that profession, and from the well-being of the professionals themselves.

The same process can take place regarding race, gender, and ethnicity. A concern with the group can become too easily separated from concern with individual women, Jews, Latinos. The group concern can take on a life of its own too far removed from individual persons.[32] It is a permanent value of caring as attentive concern for individual persons to temper and correct for these deleterious tendencies in some MSGIs.[33]

31. This distortion of "family" is found in the views of what was called the "Christian Profamily" movement (Vice President Dan Quayle being its most prominent spokesperson in the late 1980s and early 1990s). A particular image of the family is used as a club against any families that do not fit the image, and the focus on genuinely caring relationships between particular individuals in a family is almost entirely lost. This tendency is delightfully, though somewhat gruesomely, lampooned in the film *The Stepfather* (director: Joseph Ruben, 1988), in which the protagonist, seeking his image of a satisfactory family, marries women with children and then murders them when they do not live up to this image. (See feminist film critic Kathy Maio's appreciative review of this film in her *Feminist in the Dark.*)

32. Note that the converse of this – focus on individual well-being can make one lose sight of the requirements of collective well-being – also holds, but that is not the point I am making here. Moreover, certain moral distortions of group consciousness are best corrected not by care but by justice; but that is not my point here either.

33. Elizabeth Kiss has objected to this argument that concern for more concrete personal relations can also suffer from this abstractness; one can serve a certain image of what the other person is, rather than her actual needs or interests. I accept this objection but would only point out that such a deficiency in a personal relationship is a distortion of caring (for an individual) itself. The danger of abstractness in acting for the good of various MSGIs (professional, national, institutional) is not contrary to acting from the MSGI itself. Thus, "If you really cared about your country, you would care about the welfare of each individual in it" is less compelling than "If you really cared about me, you would not keep seeing me through that false image you have of me." This is why the individual care perspective provides entirely internal resources for correcting these problems, whereas (many) MSGIs must look at least partly outside themselves for such correction.

This is not to deny, however, that justice can also be employed as a corrective for various distortions of care – for various forms of mistreatment in personal relations, for example. This is a point often made by feminist philosophers, proffered as a critique of "care morality." (See Okin 1990 and Friedman 1993 [collecting previously published essays] for especially forceful and influential versions of this perspective.) Yet it is worth remembering that some failures of fairness or justice in personal relations are also failures of care, and that an appeal to caring can sometimes be a more effective way to influence the violator of justice. (The converse is true as well.) In any case, the objection does not clearly hold against Gilligan herself, who also cites justice (in the form of rights) as a corrective for some of the problems in caring. (See, e.g., *IDV,* p. 149.)

OTHER MORAL ORIENTATIONS?

Recognizing morally significant group identities as providing moral orientations that cannot be fully encompassed by either care or justice is sufficient to throw the "exhaustiveness" assumption into question. This is all the more true if these MSGIs are acknowledged to comprise a significant dimension of many people's moral lives. But there are other moral considerations that do not seem to fit readily into either "care" or "justice." Flanagan mentions moderation, courage, and integrity in this regard.[34] It could perhaps be claimed that these are "second-order" virtues, presupposing first-order ones like care or justice. For example, courage would consist in pursuing valuable ends against obstacles or risks to oneself, but the valuable ends could be either justicelike or carelike. Similarly integrity – as in holding on to one's own values in the face of pressures to compromise them – can be grounded in either care values or justice values.

Yet even if this analysis of these virtues is correct, there is an important difference between saying that a given value presupposes some other value (which could be care or justice), and saying that it can be fully understood in terms of that value. The former abandons the exhaustiveness claim, whereas the latter does not. The former acknowledges as a distinct moral consideration the fact that some actions are cowardly or involve compromising one's integrity.

In addition, there seem to be other values that are as first-order as care and justice – honesty, for example. Being honest is not simply a way of being just or fair, nor is it merely a way of caring about another individual. If I am honest to Jim only because I care about him, then I have failed to grasp the full significance of honesty, which is a good for its own sake. Honesty is bound up with how we deal with other people and is a dimension of good human relations. It is not simply recognizing the validity of a moral principle – such as justice – and adhering to it. (This means that honesty is not simply the "duty to tell the truth," if there is such a duty.)

None of the virtues mentioned here – honesty, integrity, courage – is a "moral orientation" or "moral perspective" in the way in which Gilligan conceives of care and justice. None of them are comprehensive enough to constitute an entire way of looking at a situation. But this fact does not support the exhaustiveness claim. For if significant moral considerations lie outside the two frameworks, this simply shows that thinking of moral-

---

34. Flanagan (1991), pp. 209ff.

ity in terms of frameworks or orientations is only part of its story. And in fact there is a danger that thinking in these terms will tend to mask (or misleadingly incorporate) moral considerations that do not fit into the frameworks.

Note, however, that abandoning the exhaustiveness claim still leaves a weaker but quite significant claim about care and justice as moral orientations. It could be said – and this may be the best way to interpret Gilligan's view – that both care and justice are dimensions of any actual moral situation involving action that will affect other persons. That is, they are both always relevant, although other considerations may be relevant as well. Thus, it could be argued, in a situation in which honesty is a pertinent consideration, fully resolving the situation may require caring attentiveness to the parties involved, as well as a sensitivity to justice-fairness issues. In a sense I have suggested such a hypothesis in my discussion of MSGIs and caring – that caring must always be present to inform action out of one's MSGI. (And the same could perhaps be said for justice.)[35]

Once the exhaustiveness claim is abandoned, there may be nothing to be gained by insisting that care and justice are everywhere applicable. It may be enough to insist that they are pervasive moral considerations that are frequently relevant, if perhaps not the most salient consideration in every given situation.

Abandoning the exhaustiveness claim throws into question Gilligan's suggestion that two childhood experiences – inequality-powerlessness and attachment – are the psychic foundation of all adult morality. (She does not assert this claim explicitly; rather it is a by-product of the claim that these experiences underlie justice and care, and that justice and care together exhaust the moral domain.) As Flanagan (1991) suggests, why can not another childhood experience – the development of a sense of continuous self stretching into the future – be a psychic grounding for certain intrapsychic moral concerns (wholeness, integrity, moral equilibrium).

35. May Sarton's novel *The Small Room* illustrates the general point here. The story takes place at a small college and revolves around a brilliant student who is caught plagiarizing. Issues of fairness (in following rules impartially) are presupposed, though not generally highlighted, in the book. And also involved are issues of the student's dishonesty and violation of the faculty and the college community's trust. But the thrust of the book is that these issues can only be put in their proper context by a caring attentiveness to the principals involved, especially to the student herself but also to other students, and to certain faculty members particularly close to the situation. The value of this novel for our purposes is in suggesting that in real-life situations in which moral action is being pursued within a complex context of persons and relationships, the virtue of care is likely to be essential to an adequate response to the situation.

257

Beyond this, why need all adult moral virtues or approaches have a distinct psychic grounding experience in early childhood? It may be that certain morally significant group identities, for example, require a certain level of maturity to develop a sense of the requisite loyalty and identification. I do not mean to suggest, however, that any particular MSGI – or even group identities in general – follows a developmental pattern comparable to the one claimed by Kohlberg to exist for justice, and by Gilligan in *IDV* to exist for care. (Gilligan tends to abandon this "stage" model of development in her subsequent writings.) Kohlberg claims that everyone develops a sense of justice and does so through the same invariant sequence of stages; Gilligan suggests something like this regarding care morality (though generally limited to women) in *IDV*. But I am not suggesting either (1) that everyone does develop MSGIs as part of their moral orientation, (2) that when they do, they go through a distinct developmental path to arrive at that group moral orientation, or (3) that anything like an ideal form of group moral consciousness can be identified as an end point of development (whether stagelike or not), or as capturing moral maturity. There is too much variety in the category MSGI, as well as room within each MSGI for plausible but different construals.

Accepting that group identity comprises an important moral dimension or voice – and that there are other moral considerations as well – distinct from both justice and care has implications for the connection between gender and voice. For one thing, proliferating moral considerations beyond care and justice helps to break the hold of the binary view of morality that so naturally feeds into our binary view of gender. It disinclines us to see a correlation between moral orientation and gender. In doing so, it helps to undercut the strong sense of moral difference between the sexes that one gets (though ambivalently) in Gilligan's care-justice framework.

Note, however, that the existence of moral considerations outside care and justice does not by itself have any bearing on the question of whether care and justice are themselves gender-linked in any significant way. This is a complex empirical question which I do not address here.[36] However, the significance of such a link is diminished if one acknowledges important moral considerations outside care and justice. For, even if there were such a link, it would not imply that the genders are as different from one another as they would be if there were not also acknowledged to be

36. On the matter of empirical differences, see the articles by Walker, Baumrind, Brabeck, Greeno and Maccoby, and Gilligan in Larrabee (1993); and the excellent discussion by Flanagan (1991) in Chapters 9–11.

significant dimensions of the moral life in which no gender differences exist.

UNITARINESS

Let us now turn to the idea that the care orientation is an internal unity. As mentioned earlier, this view is not so much explicitly claimed by Gilligan as implied by the constant use of "*the* care orientation" (voice, framework, perspective) as if that referred to one self-consistent and internally uniform item.

My argument will be that there are several forms of significant internal variety within what Gilligan refers to as "the care orientation." Although these may not strictly preclude our ever talking about "the care orientation" per se (indeed, I myself have done so throughout this essay), it must at least caution us about how this usage may be misleading.

We can distinguish two implied "unitarinesses" in the unity claimed for the care orientation, which I will call "person consistency" and "virtue consistency." Restricting caring for our purposes to individual persons as I have done here, "person consistency" is the claim that if a person can be spoken of as possessing the care orientation, then her caring will be directed toward all persons toward whom that caring would be appropriate. Caring is indivisible – one either possesses it toward persons in general, or one does not.

"Virtue consistency" is the assumption that all the virtues that constitute the care orientation have a unity – that there are neither significant differences nor possible tensions between them. Another way to put this is that "care" refers to something like a single virtue or single moral capacity.

Against person consistency, I will point to two kinds of distinctions among persons as objects of care, across which distinctions care often fails to travel. The first is the distinction between persons in personal relationships with the agent ("relatees"), and persons not in such relationships, but encountered personally by the agent ("encountered strangers"). One can care in Gilligan's sense about persons in either of these groups. One can respond with compassion and attentive concern to an encountered stranger. Yet it is clear that some people are much more caring or better at caring for relatees than for encountered strangers. Their emotional attachments to relatees drive their carings, and they are much less moved in a caring direction by persons whom they do not know. The converse is true as well. Some persons are better at a kind of caring for persons they are not personally close to than persons they are.

The messiness of personal relations – the difficulty of avoiding enmesh-ment in one's needs and desires regarding the relatee – may contribute to the blocking or distorting of caring in the personal domain.[37]

I think this point can be extended to nonencountered strangers as a third category. That is, I think (as Gilligan suggests and Noddings tends to disavow) there is a coherent notion of "caring" applicable to persons one never meets but only hears about. This is so even though (as argued earlier) the notion of universal duty or individual dignity may be more effective than "care morality" in eliciting moral concern for the unen-countered stranger. This caring for unencountered strangers would have to particularize the unencountered stranger – providing detail about the person and her situation – so as to make the moral transaction more analogous to the encountered stranger (see footnote 21).

Granting this possibility for the moment, one can recognize that some persons are better at caring about nonencountered persons than they are about either encountered strangers or relatees, and vice versa.

In any case, we have here an illustration of "person inconsistency" with respect to caring, suggesting that caring for these different categories draws on at least somewhat distinct psychic-moral sensibilities, forms of moral understanding, and the like. This is by no means to deny that some, even many, people are caring toward both (or all three) categories, and it may be that we could not properly say that someone was a caring person unless she were like this. But it does suggest a flaw in the "unitariness" assumption regarding the care orientation.

A second distinct way of categorizing the objects of care, cutting across the dimension of emotional distance just discussed, but similarly illustrat-ing person inconsistency, concerns social divisions such as those of race, social status, and ethnicity. E. V. Spelman (1991) makes the point that advocates of a morality of care have generally neglected the ways in which racial differences have been barriers to women's caring. She cites an excellent study by Judith Rollins (1985) exploring how (mostly) white employers can be very caring to others in their own social realm but decidedly insensitive and deficient in caring toward their (mostly) black domestic workers. The barriers in this case appear to be related to both race and class or status.

Alexis de Tocqueville makes a similar point regarding social inferiors (of the same race) in his *Democracy in America.* He discusses an aristo-

---

37. This is a point made frequently by Iris Murdoch in her essays and novels. She describes eloquently the difficulties of genuine caring toward relatees, and sometimes portrays characters who are much better at caring for encountered strangers. Compare, for example, the character of Tallis Browne in *A Fairly Honourable Defeat.*

cratic woman (Madame de Sévigné) who is kind and generous to her social equals but entirely callous and unfeeling toward the sufferings of her social inferiors (though the callousness is tempered in the case of her own servants).[38]

Here too we see a person inconsistency — a failure of care to span all its appropriate objects among both encountered and unencountered others.[39] One may be less inclined here than in the previous case of emotional distance to speak of semidistinct types of caring for persons of different races or social status; for the precise point seems to be that we do not want those divisions to affect the availability or character of our caring. Even if this is correct, the different sorts of barriers or obstacles to caring do constitute a refutation of the "unitariness" hypothesis, which should as it were guarantee care to all its appropriate (types of) objects. But the point is in any case somewhat overstated. There may be some social differences that warrant partly distinct types of caring. The recent turn toward multiculturalism should sensitize us to the ways in which particular racial and ethnic groups do not want to be treated and cared about in the same way as other such groups.[40]

In partial defense of Gilligan on the issue of caring across various social divides, she has recognized general differences between persons as a point of moral significance. Especially in OMECR, Gilligan explicitly builds an appreciation of difference into the care voice. She says, for example, that to care for someone involves seeing the world from her distinct point of view, being alive to the possibility of its divergence from

---

38. Compare "She [Madame de Sévigné] had no clear notion of suffering in someone who was not a person of quality." Book 3, Chapter 1 ("How Customs are Softened as Social Conditions Become More Equal"), p. 175.

39. One common criticism of Gilligan's work is its general limitation to white, middle-class women, and its often implicit use of this group as a paradigm for the category "woman." It is true that Gilligan has a tendency, especially in her early book *IDV*, to draw only on fairly advantaged white women, though the subject group in her abortion study discussed in Chapter 3 contained somewhat greater economic and racial diversity. (Gilligan does frequently refer to her subjects as "advantaged," and thus shows an awareness of the limitations of her sample. Her research team's later work has branched out more, to inner-city girls, white and nonwhite, and to nonwhite girls at elite private schools.)

I want to note here that the criticism I have drawn from Spelman and de Tocqueville regarding racial and class differences is distinct from (though related to) the one just mentioned. My point concerns not so much the representation of nonwhite voices in the subjects studied — and the related lack of representation at the level of theory of those women and their experiences — as Gilligan's failure to see how class, race, and other divisions might impact on caring itself.

40. For more on this point see my "Antiracism, Multiculturalism, and Interracial Community: Three Educational Values for a Multicultural Society," Office of Graduate Studies and Research, University of Massachusetts, Boston, November, 1991.

one's own. This important insight provides some of the resources needed to take on the systematic differences of race, ethnicity, power, gender, and the like; however, Gilligan does not herself take this insight in those directions.[41]

DIVERSITY IN CARE VIRTUE

Gilligan implies a unity to the care orientation that suggests a "unity of the care virtues." Like the claim of person consistency, this view is incorrect. There are important differences and sometimes tensions between some of the qualities counted by Gilligan as part of the care orientation.

First, there is an important difference between the idea of care as sustaining connection or preserving relationships, in the sense of preserving people's already existing relationships, and that of care as attentive concern to individual need. This is partly because attentiveness to an individual's needs may reveal that certain relationships of which she is a part are actually damaging to her, and that sustaining them will be harmful to her.

Perhaps it could be replied to this that Gilligan never meant "preserve relationships" to mean "preserve *all* relationships" but only, say, *healthy* relationships. Indeed, in *IDV,* Gilligan sees the preservation of a relationship at all costs as an inferior form of caring – a stage to be transcended on the way to one that ensures that the carer is also cared for in the relationship. But this modification does not collapse the distinction between the value of preserving relationships and that of attentive care for needs, although it may lessen the in-practice tension between them. For the value Gilligan places on the sustaining of existing relationships is important in its own right. It is distinct from attentiveness to individual needs (a value some have tended to collapse into a rights mode – the right to have certain needs met)[42] and is a value largely absent in the Western tradition of moral philosophy.

Because it is a distinct value, even if it applies only to relationships that pass a moral test of acceptability, it might on some occasions conflict with attentive care for individual need. Although the conflict between rela-

---

41. In Chapter 5, "Vocation, Friendship, and Community," I argue that different forms of caring are appropriate to different professions (nursing, athletic coaching, law, teaching). This could be a source of both virtue inconsistency (different forms of moral understanding and moral sensibility appropriate to different professional contexts) and person inconsistency (persons served by different professions appropriately cared for differently).

42. See, e.g., Kymlicka 1990, pp. 275 ff.

tional and individual goods can be exaggerated (and often is by anticommunitarians), it cannot be entirely eradicated.

Perhaps another reply to this point is that attentiveness to individual need itself involves a kind of "relationship" – between the carer and the caree. Certainly Gilligan conceives of it this way, and I think there is some value in framing the point in these relational terms. But then one will still want to distinguish between already existing relations and those that simply consist of caring attentiveness to another.

A second tension within the "care orientation" has been mentioned – that between the personal relation and the universalistic strands in care morality. As argued earlier, a person possessing care virtues in the personal domain does not necessarily do so with regard to all people universally. A valuing of caring in personal relations does not guarantee, and can divert energy from, a valuing of caring toward all human beings; and the converse is true as well.

A third, perhaps minor, internal difference has to do with what one might call the consequentialist and agent-centered strands in Gilligan's thought. (By the agent-centered strand I mean not the legitimizing of agent-centered prerogatives as part of morality itself but, rather, the focus on a person's existing relationships, perhaps including those with encountered strangers, as the context of moral action and assessment.) The consequentialist strand is found in statements like the injunction to "prevent harm," and in the famous discussion of Jake and Amy in *IDV* (Chapter 2 and elsewhere). That discussion can be read to imply that Jake is concerned about the agent-focused question of what is the right thing for Heinz to do, whereas Amy is concerned about the consequentialist "best outcome" of the situation. There is some implication, in that discussion and elsewhere, that Amy's mode is superior: Jake gets hung up on what is the right principle of action for an agent whose role in the situation is given, but Amy is concerned with bringing about the best resolution to the situation overall.

To the extent that such a form of consequentialism is present in Gilligan's thought, it is definitely in tension with a more dominant theme of starting with the relationships in which one finds oneself, and making moral judgments from that agent- (or relation-)centered vantage point. I think ultimately, however, it is incorrect to attribute this philosophically familiar form of consequentialism to Gilligan; her use of such language is not meant to carry that particular baggage.[43]

43. There may, however, be a modified form of the tension present – between an injunction to "preserve (healthy) relationships" and an agent-centered focus on the particular relationships of the agent in question. The former may, for example, enjoin an

In these different ways, the "care orientation" is not so unified a moral approach as Gilligan implies. Persons can instantiate one part of the set of values but neglect some of the others. The bearing of this on the question of gender differences is similar to that implied in the exhaustiveness discussion. If there is less unity to the care voice (and similar arguments could be made for the justice voice), there is less temptation to talk in terms of a single voice's being more characteristic of one of the two genders. The picture is, rather, of a loose family of virtues. If some of them have a significant correlation to gender, it does not follow that all of them do. The binary and dichotomous conception of morality would be jettisoned, and with it the temptation to speak simplistically about the relations of the two genders to two moral orientations.

I have argued that Carol Gilligan's conception of morality is misleadingly binary. She tends to treat "care" and "justice" as exclusive and internally unified moral approaches or voices. Against the former, I have argued that there are other moral considerations not encompassable within either care or justice. I have focused especially on "morally significant group identities" (MSGIs) such as profession, gender, ethnicity, and institutional identification, and have argued that these provide moral orientations and forms of moral understanding and reflection that are distinct from both individual care and universal principles of justice.

The differences are especially evident in the case of group or role obligations and ideals. The moral orientation provided by role, institutional, or group ideals is not the same as that provided by caring for individuals, although part of the ideal itself may involve caring for persons (e.g., if the professional ideal of a nurse involves caring for patients). It is not the same as justice, even when the content of the obligation is securing justice for one's group.

Acting from responsibility or obligation to a group is not the same as acting from a sense of justice involving universal principles governing behavior of all persons toward all other persons. It is more particular than justice, yet is focused on entities that transcend the individual; hence it is distinct from individual care.

The differences among MSGIs, care, and justice may seem less obvious in the case of other modes of MSGI, such as caring for the group or caring

abstract policy that has the consequence of promoting the preserving of many (good) relationships, but at the expense of the agent's own relationships. This territory has been much mined by philosophers (Railton, Scheffler, Nagel) but is not really pertinent to Gilligan, who would not countenance this dilemma because she would not have a commitment to the consequentialist form of "preserving relationships."

264

for individuals because they are members of the group. It is certainly possible to care for a group – for one's college, one's profession, (the group of) women, Asian-Americans – but I have argued that this form of care is significantly distinct from individual care, and that it is the latter that has played the central role in the development of the "morality of care," in Gilligan's work in particular.

Because my main purpose has been to show the falseness of the "exhaustiveness" view of care and justice, I have not been much concerned with how the different forms of moral consciousness are related. As just mentioned, the different modes can inform one another. They are not rightly thought of as applying to different domains of life (public, private, professional, etc.). Every domain will require all the different modes. Moreover, care, justice, and some MSGIs articulate with one another. A person acting from a professional ideal should still do so in a caring way and with a concern for justice (at least to the extent of not violating justice). A person acting justly often needs to do so caringly, and a caring person needs to be so with a concern for justice. Sometimes, as mentioned, the connections are even more intimate, as when either justice or caring is itself the content of the MSGI's ideal, or even obligation.

I have also argued against the "unitariness" hypothesis by showing that caring is not an internally unified voice. It contains semidistinct moral capacities and virtues, and some of these can be in tension with others. No doubt, a similar argument can be given about justice – citing, for example, a tension between "negative" and "positive" rights, or between individual rights and a consequentialist dimension of justice (though a purely libertarian conception of justice will deny the second of each of these features and this will obviate the tension).

I hope my argument here will contribute to throwing into question the conceptual scheme that has fostered asserting a strong link between gender and moral approach while that argument at the same time allows for the continual provision of insights by those who are scrutinizing women's experience for dimensions of the moral life neglected in most traditional approaches to ethics.

REFERENCES

Aristotle. 1985. *Nicomachean Ethics.* Translated by Terence Irwin. Indianapolis, Ind.: Hackett Publishing Company.
Benhabib, Seyla. 1992. "The Generalized and the Concrete Other: The Kohlberg-Gilligan Controversy and Moral Theory." In *Situating the Self: Gender, Com-*

munity and Postmodernism in Contemporary Ethics, Cambridge, Mass.: Polity Press, pp. 148–77.

Blum, Lawrence A. 1991. "Antiracism, Multiculturalism, and Interracial Community: Three Educational Values for a Multicultural Society." Office of Graduate Studies and Research, University of Massachusetts, Boston, pp. 1–21.

Card, Claudia. 1990. "Gender and Moral Luck." In *Identity, Character, and Morality: Essays in Moral Psychology,* ed. Owen Flanagan, Jr., and Amelie Rorty. Cambridge, Mass.: MIT Press, pp. 197–216.

Chodorow, N. 1978. *The Reproduction of Mothering.* Berkeley: University of California Press.

Epstein, Cynthia Fuchs. 1988. *Deceptive Distinctions: Sex, Gender, and the Social Order.* New Haven and London: Yale University Press & Russell Sage Foundation.

Flanagan, O. 1991. *Varieties of Moral Personality.* Cambridge, Mass.: Harvard University Press.

Friedman, Marilyn. 1987. "Beyond Caring: The De-moralization of Gender." *Canadian Journal of Philosophy (Supplementary Volume 13: Science, Morality and Feminist Theory):* 87–110, reprinted in Larrabee.

Gilligan, C. 1982. *In a Different Voice: Psychological Theory and Women's Development.* Cambridge: Harvard University Press.

1988. *Mapping the Moral Domain,* ed. C. Gilligan, J. Taylor, and J. Ward. Cambridge, Mass.: Harvard University Press.

1990. "Joining the Resistance: Psychology, Politics, Girls and Women." *Michigan Quarterly Review* 29 (4, Fall).

Grimshaw, J. 1986. *Philosophy and Feminist Thinking.* Minneapolis: University of Minnesota Press.

Harding, Sandra. 1987. "The Curious Coincidence of Feminine and African Moralities: Challenges for Feminist Theory." In *Women and Moral Theory,* ed. Diana T. Meyers and Eva Feder Kittay, Totowa, N.J.: Rowman & Littlefield.

Houston, Barbara. 1987. "Rescuing Womanly Virtues: Some Dangers of Moral Reclamation." In *Canadian Journal of Philosophy,* ed. Kai Nielsen and Marsha Hamen. 13 Supplemental. Calgary, Alberta: University of Calgary, pp. 237–62.

Hume, David. [1752] 1957. *An Inquiry Concerning the Principles of Morals.* New York: Liberal Arts Press.

Kerber, L. 1986. "Some Cautionary Words for Historians." *Signs 11:* 304–10.

Kohlberg, L. 1981. "Essays on Moral Development." *The Philosophy of Moral Development* 1. New York: Harper & Row.

1984. "Essays on Moral Development." *The Philosophy of Moral Development* 2. New York: Harper & Row.

Kymlicka, Will. 1990. *Contemporary Political Philosophy: An Introduction.* Oxford: Clarendon Press.

Larrabee, Mary Jeanne (ed.). 1993. *An Ethic of Care: Feminist and Interdisciplinary Perspectives,* New York: Routledge.

Maio, Kathi. 1988. *Feminist in the Dark: Reviewing the Movies.* Freedom, Calif.: The Crossing Press.

Miller, Jean Baker. 1976. *Toward a New Psychology of Women.* Boston: Beacon.

Murdoch, Iris. 1972. *A Fairly Honourable Defeat.* New York: Penguin.

266

Nagel, Thomas. 1986. *The View from Nowhere*. New York: Oxford University Press.

Nodding, N. 1984. *Caring: A Feminine Approach to Ethics and Moral Education*. Berkeley: University of California Press.

Okin, Susan. 1989. *Justice, Gender, and the Family*. New York: Basic Books.

Puka, B. 1990. "The Liberation of Caring." *Hypatia* 5: 58–82. Reprinted in Larrabee.

Railton, Peter. 1984. "Alienation, Consequentialism, and the Demands of Morality." *Philosophy and Public Affairs* 13 (2): 134–71.

Rollins, Judith. 1985. *Between Women: Domestics and Their Employers*. Philadelphia: Temple University Press.

Rosenblum, Nancy L. 1989. *Liberalism and the Moral Life*. Cambridge, Mass.: Harvard University Press.

Sandel, Michael J. 1982. *Liberalism and the Limits of Justice*. Cambridge: Cambridge University Press.

Sarton, May. 1976 (1961). *The Small Room*. New York and London: W. W. Norton.

Scheffler, Samuel. 1982. *The Rejection of Consequentialism: A Philosophical Investigation of the Considerations Underlying Rival Moral Conceptions*. Oxford: Clarendon Press.

Schopenhauer, Arthur. [1841] 1965. *On the Basis of Morality*. Trans. E. F. J. Payne. New York: Bobbs-Merrill.

Selznick, Philip. 1987. "The Idea of a Communitarian Morality." 75, No. 1. *California Law Review*.

1992. *The Moral Commonwealth: Social Theory and the Promise of Community*. Berkeley: University of California.

Smith, Adam. [1759] 1970. *The Theory of Moral Sentiments*. In H. Schneider, ed., *Adam Smith's Moral and Political Philosophy*. New York: Harper and Row.

Spelman, Elizabeth V. 1988. *Inessential Woman: Problems of Exclusion in Feminist Thought*. Boston: Beacon Press.

1991. "The Virtue of Feeling and the Feeling of Virtue." In *Feminist Ethics*, ed. Claudia Card. Lawrence: University Press of Kansas.

Stocker, Michael. 1981. "Values and Purposes: The Limits of Teleology and the Ends of Friendship." *Journal of Philosophy* 78: 747–65.

1990. *Plural and Conflicting Values*. Oxford: Clarendon Press.

Taylor, Charles. 1989. *Sources of the Self: The Making of the Modern Identity*. Cambridge, Mass.: Harvard University Press.

Tocqueville, Alexis de. 1945. *Democracy in America*, ed. Phillips Bradley. New York: Vintage Books.

Tronto, J. 1987. "Beyond Gender Difference to a Theory of Care." *Signs* 12: 644–61, Reprinted in Larrabee.

Wong, David. 1988. "On Flourishing and Finding One's Identity in Community." In *Midwest Studies in Philosophy*, vol. 13, *Ethical Theory: Character and Virtue*, Notre Dame, Ind.: University of Notre Dame Press.

267

Index

269